WELCOMING THE STRANGER

Welcoming the Stranger

Abrahamic Hospitality and Its Contemporary Implications

ORI Z SOLTES AND RACHEL STERN, EDITORS

With a Foreword by Endy Moraes

Distributed by Fordham University Press
NEW YORK 2024

Copyright © 2024 The Institute on Religion, Law & Lawyer's Work and the Fritz Ascher Society for Persecuted, Ostracized, and Banned Art

Fordham University Press has no responsibility for the persistence or accuracy of URLs for external or third-party Internet websites referred to in this publication and does not guarantee that any content on such websites is, or will remain, accurate or appropriate.

Fordham University Press also publishes its books in a variety of electronic formats. Some content that appears in print may not be available in electronic books.

Visit us online at www.fordhampress.com.

Library of Congress Cataloging-in-Publication Data available online at https://catalog.loc.gov.

Printed in the United States of America

26 25 24   5 4 3 2 1

First edition

Contents

	Image List	vii
	Foreword	xi
	ENDY MORAES	
	Preface	xv
	ORI Z SOLTES AND RACHEL STERN	
	Introduction	1
	Section One. Building on the Past: Theology, History, and Their Practical Implications	9
1	Welcoming the Stranger in the Jewish Tradition	11
	ORI Z SOLTES	
2	Hospitality in Christian Traditions: A Key Virtue and its Applications	27
	THOMAS MASSARO	
3	A Migrant 4 Life Journeys to the New Tower of Babel: Christianity and Immigration	43
	CRAIG MOUSIN	
4	Welcoming the Stranger in Islam: Abrahamic Hospitality and Contemporary Implications	72
	ZEKI SARITOPRAK	

5	Epilogue: India and the Dharmic Traditions of Hospitality	82
	ORI Z SOLTES	

Section Two. Building the Present and Future: Programmatic Ideas and Realizations — 95

6	Fritz Ascher: A Jewish Artist in Germany	97
	RACHEL STERN	
7	Welcoming Beyond Offering Safe Heaven: Aspiring to Partner with Refugees	125
	CAROL PRENDERGAST	
8	De-story to Destroy, Re-Story to Restore	137
	MOHSIN MOHI-UD-DIN	
9	Immigration Courts in Need of an Article I Overhaul	155
	MIMI TSANKOV	
10	Epilogue: Future Strangers: Digital Life and Hospitality To-Come	159
	LINDSAY ANNE BALFOUR	
	Conclusions: An Unfinished Epilogue	177
	ORI Z SOLTES	
	Bibliography	181
	Author Biographies	189
	Index	193

Image list

COVER	David Stern, *Snow Crash (Lost Agency)*, 2018–19. Acrylics and pigments on paper, 27 × 35 inches © David Stern / Artists Rights Society (ARS), New York	
FIG 1	Rembrandt van Rijn, *Abraham Serving the Angels*, 1646. Oil on panel, 6.3 × 8.3 inches. Private collection, USA. Public domain, via Wikimedia Commons	10
FIG 2	*Abraham Meets the Three Strangers*, 11th century. Fresco. Saint Sophia Cathedral, Kyiv. Public domain, via Wikimedia Commons	26
FIG 3	*Immigrant 4 Life*, Querty Project, April 16, 2018	42
FIG 4	*MAGA Jesus*, January 6, 2020. Photographer Tyler Merbler. https://flic.kr/p/2kro7Tv (https://uncivilreligion.org/home/media/maga-jesus)	48
FIG 5	David Stern, *Snow Crash (Lost Agency)*, 2018–19. Acrylics and pigments on paper, 27 × 35 inches © David Stern / Artists Rights Society (ARS), New York	71
FIG 6	Siona Benjamin, *Tikkun Ha-Olam* (Fixing the World), 2000. #46 in the series, *Finding Home*. Gouache and 22K gold leaf on paper, 11.5 × 9" inches. Private Collection	81

FIG 7	Fritz Ascher, *Male Portrait in Red*, ca.1915. White gouache over graphite, watercolor and black ink on paper, 10.5 × 8.7 inches © Bianca Stock	96
FIG 8	Unknown Photographer, *Fritz Ascher*, 1939. © Bianca Stock	99
FIG 9	Unknown Photographer, *Ascher Family: Wedding Charlotte Ascher*, 1918. © Bianca Stock	100
FIG 10	Fritz Ascher, "*The Intriguer*," c. 1913. Black ink over graphite on paper, 8.9 × 5.6 inches. Nicole Trau Collection © Bianca Stock	101
FIG 11	Fritz Ascher, *Loner (Der Vereinsamte)* c. 1914. Oil on canvas, 47.2 × 37.4 inches © Bianca Stock	103
FIG 12	Fritz Ascher, "*What is paradox!!!??*," 1913. Black ink and graphite on paper, 15 × 11.6 inches © Bianca Stock	104
FIG 13	Fritz Ascher, *Burial*, c. 1919. White gouache over black ink on paper, 8.7 × 10.6 inches © Bianca Stock	105
FIG 14	Fritz Ascher, *Golgotha*, 1915. Oil on canvas, 53.4 × 69 inches © Bianca Stock	106
FIG 15	Fritz Ascher, *Der Golem [The Golem]*, 1916. Oil on canvas, 71.9 × 55.3 inches Photo Jens Ziehe. Jüdisches Museum Berlin GEM 93/2/0 © Bianca Stock	107
FIG 16	Fritz Ascher, *Pagliaccio (The Clown)*, 1916. White gouache over graphite, watercolor and black ink on paper, 17.25 × 12.3 inches © Bianca Stock	108
FIG 17	Fritz Ascher, *Bajazzo*, 1924/1945. Oil on canvas, 47.6 × 39 inches © Bianca Stock	109
FIG 18	Fritz Ascher, *Figural Scene*, c. 1918. Black ink over watercolor and graphite on paper, 14.8 × 18.5 inches © Bianca Stock	111
FIG 19	Fritz Ascher, *The Tortured (Der Gequälte)*, 1920s. Oil on canvas, 59 × 79.4 inches © Bianca Stock	112
FIG 20	Fritz Ascher, *Beethoven*, 1924/1945. Oil on canvas, 38.5 × 47 inches © Bianca Stock	115
FIG 21	Fritz Ascher, *Female Head in Three Quarter View*, 1954. Grey gouache and black ink over watercolor on paper, 17.8 × 12.2 inches © Bianca Stock	117

FIG 22	Fritz Ascher, *Sunset (Untergehende Sonne)*, c. 1960. Oil on canvas, 49.2 × 50 inches © Bianca Stock	118
FIG 23	Fritz Ascher, *Two Sunflowers*, c. 1959. White gouache and black ink over watercolor on paper, 24.5 × 17.6 inches © Bianca Stock	119
FIG 24	Fritz Ascher, *Trees*, late 1950s. Oil on canvas, 31.5 × 27 inches © Bianca Stock	120
FIG 25	Fritz Ascher, *Two Trees*, 1952. White gouache over black ink and watercolor on paper, 24.5 × 17.75 inches © Bianca Stock	121
FIG 26	Fritz Ascher, *Trees in Hilly Landscape*, 1968. Oil on canvas, 27.6 × 31.5 inches © Bianca Stock	122
FIG 27	Refugees, 2020. Photographer Wyatt Winborne © #MeWeIntl and #MeWeSyria	124
FIG 28	Refugee, 2020. Photographer Wyatt Winborne © #MeWeIntl and #MeWeSyria	136
FIG 29	Refugee learning a new language, 2020. Photographer Wyatt Winborne © #MeWeIntl and #MeWeSyria	154
FIG 30	Unknown Photographer: *Digital Portal* visually connecting Vilnius, Lithuania with Lublin, Poland. Designed by Joe Courtney, et al, UWE, Bristol, 2021	158

Foreword

ENDY MORAES

The concept of *welcoming the stranger* is present in all three Abrahamic religions. Often the phrase is understood as an expression recalling the immigrant arriving in a foreign land. But who is the stranger? If historical texts have anything to add, there is a layer of complexity about how the phrase should be understood. For instance, an ancient letter, written in the second century after Christ's crucifixion, affirms that "we are all 'strangers and pilgrims' before God."[1] In other words, an unknown person arriving at my doorstep, a person from another community, a person who practices another religion, a person who is part of another race, or another culture—these can all be strangers. Our attitude toward them is optional—while it ought to be an attitude of embrace, dialogue, and openness, our chosen attitude can just as easily be one of distrust and fear.

The Institute on Religion, Law, and Lawyer's Work has worked over the last twenty years to create spaces for open, positive, and constructive dialogue on issues relating to religion and law, including how values might impact a lawyer's work. In fostering spaces for genuine conversation, we have aimed to define "welcoming the stranger" broadly. Within that large breadth, when the Fritz Ascher Society approached us to host a conference that led us to this book on the intersection of "welcoming the stranger," Abrahamic (and Dharmic) hospitality, and immigration, it

---

1. Spadaro, A. (2017). "Welcoming the Stranger," *Journal of Catholic Education*, 21 (1). http://dx.doi.org/ 10.15365/joce.2101012017

seemed a natural fit for our work at the Institute. It also naturally aligned with the timeless mission of Fordham University at large.

Indeed, from its first seed, Fordham was established to provide immigrants with higher education opportunities. On June 24, 1841, Bishop John Hughes, an Irish immigrant, opened St. John's College in the village of Fordham, considering education to be the indispensable mean for immigrants to break loose from the cycle of poverty that trapped and prevented them from participating in what today we would call the American dream. Five years after the founding of St. John's, the college passed on to Jesuit leadership. In 1907, it achieved university status and officially changed its name to Fordham University. As a Jesuit and Catholic university, Fordham has not only welcomed immigrants as part of its student body but also has journeyed to offer a welcoming experience to all of its community throughout its history. Despite the University's historical approach to hospitality, the work of building a caring and welcoming community toward "the stranger" is never done.

That is because Abrahamic hospitality has not been developed by chance, but by conscious choice. It offers us examples of how strangers might be a gift to the communities into which they arrive. From the biblical story of Abraham's reception of three strangers to the Quranic injunctions to treat immigrants and travelers respectfully, the Abrahamic faiths encourage their followers to welcome newcomers warmly. Within the narratives that carry from Genesis to Revelation, almost every major biblical character was an immigrant or displaced person, a "stranger." For instance, Abraham left Ur to go to a land where he was a stranger. Joseph, son of Jacob, having been sold by his brothers, was an immigrant, a "stranger" in Egypt. Moses was saved by the pharaoh's daughter and a stranger at the pharaoh's palace, and then later a stranger in the land of Midian. Ruth was a Moabite immigrant in the land of Israel. Jesus was a refugee in the land of Egypt. His parents left on a dangerous trip trying to save his life, escaping a law that would kill baby boys in their homeland. Could similar stories be shared with us today by migrants arriving into different countries?

While the Bible constantly describes immigrants as among the most vulnerable, paired with a commandment to care for them ("The stranger who sojourns with you shall be to you as the native among you, and you shall love him as yourself; for you were strangers in the land of Egypt" Lev 19:34), the question is whether those biblical stories connect to us today. If so, how do we implement the guidelines that they provide amidst a large influx of migrants? According to the International Organization for Migration, approximately 3.6% of the global population, or

281 million people, were international immigrants in 2020.[2] As we witness the displacement of millions of people due to war, persecution, and economic hardship, exploring the contemporary implications of the age-old concept, "welcoming the stranger" regains thrust and can become as relevant as ever.

However, sometimes religious texts and concepts can be seen as merely abstract, and not as a practice, as if a religious or moral guideline has no contact with real life. My personal experience as an immigrant has been to the contrary. My religious community, the Focolare Movement, a Catholic ecclesial movement, and Fordham University, warmly welcomed a Brazilian arriving in New York. I can attest to the fact that it makes an enormous difference when people around you value your gifts and believe in your ability to contribute to the community. It makes me remember Catholic theologian Chiara Lubich's reflection on Mathew's gospel about the presence of God in each person, calling for a love without distinction. In a conversation with Muslim friends of the Focolare, she said, "we need to love everyone without exception, like God who sends sun and rain on the just and the unjust alike."[3] She stressed that "we cannot choose between people who are pleasant or nasty, beautiful or ugly, a fellow citizen or a foreigner, between those who are white, black or yellow, European or American, African or Asian, Christian or Jew, Muslim or Hindu. Love does not allow any discrimination."[4]

Abrahamic hospitality calls for a warm welcome of strangers. But how can we put it into practice? How do we balance, on the one hand, the concept of "welcoming the stranger," valuing each person as a gift, and, on the other hand, public policies that benefit everyone? These questions, coupled with a migrant crisis of great magnitude not seen since the Second World War, provide the perfect backdrop for the book *Welcoming the Stranger: Abrahamic Hospitality and Its Contemporary Implications.*

At its core, the book contributes to the ongoing dialogue around immigration and displacement, and challenges us to reflect on our attitudes toward newcomers. It is difficult to overcome the initial fear of "welcoming the stranger." Let us recall Pope Francis's words to the United States

---

2. International Organization for Migration. (2022). *World Migration Report, 2022.* World migration report. Retrieved May 2, 2023, from https://worldmigrationreport.iom.int/wmr-2022-interactive/#:~:text=The%20current%20global%20estimate%20is,over%20the%20past%20five%20decades

3. See Matt 5:45.

4. Love of Neighbor. (2002). Chiara Lubich to the meeting of Muslim Friends of the Focolare, November 1st, 2002. Retrieved May 12, 2023, from https://www.youtube.com/watch?v=C_GfgCLrZlY

Congress in 2015, when he said, that "building a nation calls us to recognize that we must constantly relate to others, rejecting a mindset of hostility to adopt one of reciprocal subsidiarity, in a constant effort to do our best."[5]

On that note, this book will take the reader on a journey through personal narratives, scholarly analysis, and theological and practical insights, where the authors recognize the challenges of navigating cultural differences, language barriers, and legal frameworks while offering valuable considerations on how to overcome such obstacles and promote inclusion and integration in our communities. I encourage all readers to engage with this book's insights and to join the vital conversation it seeks to inspire.

---

5. VISIT TO THE JOINT SESSION OF THE UNITED STATES CONGRESS. ADDRESS OF THE HOLY FATHER. United States Capitol, Washington, D.C., September 24th, 2015. Retrieved May 10, 2023, from https://www.vatican.va/content/francesco/en/speeches/2015/september/documents/papa-francesco_20150924_usa-us-congress.html

Preface

ORI Z SOLTES AND RACHEL STERN

The seeds for this volume were planted in a conversation between its two editors in the spring of 2019. The context was not only the increasingly stringent restrictions on immigration to the United States under the Trump administration, particularly as it applied to groups desperate to come over the border from Mexico in the face of drug-cartel violence and its siblings and refugees from the torn-apart Middle East (most obviously, Syria) fleeing for their lives and hoping to find safe places for themselves and their children in Europe or America. It was also the profoundly hostile view of refugees and immigrants that was being promoted by the administration and applauded by its base.

That attitude seemed to us—one of us the grandchild of immigrants and the other an immigrant to these shores a mere three decades ago—to contradict the best of what America has been as a refuge and an embracer of immigrants who have shaped the United States and its neighbors over the past several centuries. Moreover, it seemed to contradict central principles lodged in the diverse Abrahamic traditions from which so many of those most vocal in their anti-immigrant, anti-stranger, anti-refugee stance claim to derive spiritually.

It occurred to us that we might organize a conference on the subject, that would consider it first from a theological perspective, given that in all of the Abrahamic traditions, which together make up an estimated 67% of the US population, there are such powerful injunctions regarding hospitality to the stranger. Since one of us lives in Washington, DC and teaches at Georgetown University, it made sense to begin by shaping a conference to take place on that campus. Under the umbrella of the Center for Jewish Civilization in Georgetown's School for Foreign Service—with sponsorship assistance from The Fritz Ascher Society for Persecuted, Ostracized, and Banned Art; Georgetown's Theology Department; Georgetown Center for Jewish Life; and Georgetown's Prince Alwaleed Bin Talal Center for Muslim-Christian Understanding—the first iteration of the conference, "Welcoming the Stranger: Abrahamic Hospitality and Its Contemporary Implications took place on October 28 of that same year.

Since the second of us lives in New York and because New York is the home of the Fritz Ascher Society for Persecuted, Ostracized and Banned Art, it made equal sense to offer the conference in its second iteration there. Fordham Law School's Institute on Religion, Law, and Lawyer's Work presented itself as a perfect partner.

Thanks to the unexpected intervention of Covid, the Fordham version of the conference was delayed until November 14, 2022. One of the outcomes of that delay was the need to switch some of the speakers. Thus it became necessary for Ori Z Soltes to discuss at Fordham and write about the Jewish perspective on our subject, whereas Rabbi Rachel Gartner spoke at Georgetown. Soltes' paper is included in this volume. Reverend Craig Moussin spoke at Georgetown and Thomas Massaro, SJ, spoke at Fordham, but each contributed a paper to our narrative. Zeki Saritoprak, Rachel Stern, and Carol Prendergast all spoke at both conferences and contributed chapters to this volume, and Lindsey Balfour presented at Georgetown, and a significantly modified version of her paper is also presented here. Conversely, both Mohsin Mohi ud-Din and Mimi E. Tsankov spoke in New York and have contributed to our written narrative.

We also decided that it might be useful to add a chapter on the dharmic religions—most specifically, Hinduism—as a kind of epilogue to the first section of the book, in order to further flesh out the diverse conceptual articulations of welcoming strangers into one's community. It should be noted, moreover, that not only is a range of topics presented in our text, but that the speakers did not follow a single pattern of presentations and accordingly the chapters that follow also offer a degree of formal and stylistic diversity rather than being enslaved to a particular mode of consistency.

It is a pleasure to acknowledge Brittany Fried, Jocelyn Flores, and Bethania Michael for their help in realizing the Georgetown conference; and Endy Moraes—who has also contributed the foreword to this volume—as well as Cristina Outeirinho and Kathleen Horton for facilitating the organization of the Fordham conference. We are also grateful to the Allianz of America Corporation for generously sponsoring the conference at Fordham.

One of the unanticipated positive consequences of the Covid-pushed delay in presenting the New York conference was that it provided time for us to decide to put the contents of the papers being presented into a book and were happily able to engage Fordham University Press as our publisher in the aftermath of the second conference. We are grateful to Richard Morrison, Kem Crimmins, and Mark Lerner at Fordham University Press for the skillful manner with which they turned this narrative into a handsome book, which underscores the subject's continued relevance in an increasingly complicated and troubled world. Special thanks also go to Harrison Hunt and Anna Perlman, two outstanding Georgetown students who proofread the text and suggested many small but important changes in syntax and style.

We are deeply grateful for the generous support of a donor who made this publication possible and wishes to remain anonymous. Additional funding was provided by the Fritz Ascher Stiftung at Stadtmuseum Berlin [Fritz Ascher Foundation at the Museum of the City of Berlin] and Reinwald GmbH in Leipzig.

We live at a time when there are far more refugees across the globe than at any time in human history, including during the most war-torn parts of the last century. This volume falls between the obligation to think and speak about the issues and that of acting on them.

Welcoming the Stranger: Introduction

ORI Z SOLTES

One of the signal moments in the narrative of the biblical Abraham is his insistent and enthusiastic reception of three strangers (Gen 18). He is a man who is preoccupied at that moment, together with his wife, Sarah, by the pain of their situation: a long, loving, and yet complex marriage, the most significant complication of which is that they have not shared the joy of producing a child together. There is, however, no hint of pain or hesitation when the patriarch looks up and sees the three strangers approaching his dwelling. He immediately gets up from his place and, rather than waiting to see whether or not they will even actually approach his tent, he hurries to meet them on the road and invites them to pause on their journey and refresh themselves by enjoying the hospitality that he can offer.

He chooses the best from among his flocks and asks Sarah to prepare it effectively . . . He provides his guests—no longer *strangers*—with drink. He asks after their well-being. As a keeper of flocks, Abraham himself relocated with some frequency as his animals followed the available grazing land. His designation in the Hebrew language as a *Hebrew*—'*eevree*—indicates precisely that: someone who passes ('-v-r is the root of the Hebrew word) from place to place. He owns no land himself—until, later, well after this extended moment of hospitality, when he seeks to purchase the Cave of Makhpelah as a burial site for Sarah (Gen 23). The landowner from which he purchases it, Ephron the Hittite, requests that Abraham buy the entire field in which the cave is located. In a condition of mourning for his wife, the patriarch neither argues that point nor negotiates at all on the price.

But this was—to repeat—well after he welcomed those strangers to whom he extended hospitality. As a wanderer he understood what it meant to be far from home and how comforting it could be to be invited into someone's home to rest, and to eat and drink safely. As it turns out, these strangers were not everyday individuals; like all travelers, they brought news from afar, but their extraordinary news came from an inconceivable—divine—distance. It was less a piece of news than an announcement to Abraham and Sarah: that, at their advanced ages, she would finally become successfully pregnant and bear Abraham a son.

For the purposes of this discussion, while there are other significant elements within the larger story of Abraham and Sarah and those who derive spiritually from them, we note how that moment of hospitality is a beginning point of inspiration for all three Abrahamic traditions as they evolve and develop the details of their respective teachings. Nor is this the only moment during the Hebrew period when a noteworthy act of hospitality to strangers occurs, reinforcing the Abraham's lesson.

On the one hand, in the very next chapter of Genesis, the nephew of Abraham, Lot, comes to dwell in the nearby city of Sodom—Gen 19:19 observes that he "came there as a stranger—a *ger*." On the other hand, in the same chapter in which he entertains the three strangers, Abraham experiences his first moral test, as God decides to confide in him—"Shall I hide from Abraham my plan?" (Gen 18:17)—the divine intention of destroying Sodom and Gomorrah, due to their prevailing evil behavior. Abraham doesn't simply cheer on their punishment. These are people who, among other specific things that the reader will see, sought to deal dangerously with the strangers whom Lot, emulating Abraham, had invited into his home and now protects from the Sodomites—even to the point of offering them his own daughters in lieu of giving up the outsiders who, it turns out, are also divinely-appointed messengers, who in the end protect *him* and inform him of the imminent destruction of the city. (They have arrived, in fact, to facilitate that destruction.)

Abraham's response to that divine plan is to be concerned that there might be some righteous people among the Sodomites, for the sake of whom the city should be spared. He negotiates with God—gradually down from the possibility of 50 to that of 10 righteous individuals—but it turns out that not even a minyan who are not active practitioners of evil can be found in the entire city.[1] The point is that Abraham offers such an out-of-the-ordinary response. The further point is that only Lot and

---

1. In the Jewish tradition, the uttering of a large range of key prayers requires a minimum of 10 adult male participants, which is called a *minyan*. Forgive the pun.

his family are rescued—after we have seen them exercising the hospitality that becomes a synecdoche for their moral propriety.[2]

As for Abraham, the most severe test—not of his moral convictions as much as of his faith in God's absolute righteousness as a model for his convictions—arrives in Genesis 22, when God demands that he take that very long-hoped-for son, Isaac, and offer him as a sacrifice to God on Mount Moriah. Abraham—the very Abraham who negotiated at length regarding the Sodomites—might surely have demurred. He might have paused and asked God about the promise of generations of descendants as myriad as the stars in the sky and the sands of the shore. He might even have gone so far—particularly given how uniquely intimate his relationship with God had been for so long—as to beg for his son's life, shed a tear or two. But the laconic text offers a more than laconic Abraham, whose response to the command is simply to act, getting up at dawn and taking Isaac to the place designated by God.

On the one hand, we recognize the spiritually heroic uniqueness of the patriarch whose faith in God is so perfect at that moment that he can respond as he does. But one of the glories of the narrative is that it offers Abraham—as it does every biblical hero—as also simply and merely *human*. A careful read to the end of the chapter and the one that follows yields a small and very important datum: Isaac (it had worked out; not Isaac, but a divinely-sent ram, caught in a thicket, was offered for sacrifice, in the end) eventually made his way back to Hebron where his mother Sarah still dwelled, but Abraham went instead to Beersheva. Tragically, he never saw the love of his life again while she was still alive—for the text reads that he "came up to Hebron to mourn for his wife." It is easy to understand this: as a mere human, a spouse and parent like you and me, he was no doubt terrified to tell Sarah what he had almost done with their only son! So Abraham was both the consummate moral hero and also a man simply scared of his wife.

And this is the chapter in which Abraham the wanderer and welcomer of strangers purchases his one and only piece of real estate, as a burial site for Sarah. It is the combination of his graciousness as a host and his simple humanity that underscore how we can and *must* emulate him—we cannot excuse ourselves by asserting that we are not spiritual supermen, because Abraham wasn't always one either, even if at most times he

---

2. It is noteworthy that Abraham's concern leads later to rabbinic distress over the destruction of these cities. This is reflected in the discussion of how Lot's wife, who turned around to look as the family fled, was transformed by God into a pillar of salt: they infer that she took some satisfaction in the destruction and should not have done so.

was one. The news that strangers bring into the home, in exchange for food, drink, and shelter, can be as entertaining as stories of where they have come from, or as profound as yielding hints of the future of one's family or of one's community or communities beyond one's own.

The text—the Torah or Pentateuch, in which the stories of Abraham and Sarah, and those of Lot and his wife and daughters, are told—is understood by traditional Judaism, Christianity, and Islam to be part of a revelation accorded to Moses many generations later, when the myriad descendants of Abraham, now called Israelites, were once again wanderers. Two important things had changed, however, aside from the manifold increase in their numbers—and one had not. The first change was that the term "Israelite" carried with it not only a connotation, up to a point, of common ethnic heritage (from Abraham, Sarah, and their son Isaac and his wife, Rebecca, and their son, Jacob and his wives, Leah and Rachel, as well as those wives' handmaids, and their many sons). More importantly the term bore the connotation of having embraced a covenant with God adumbrated by way of a varied narrative and diverse commandments (613 of them) in the Torah. The second change was that they were now wandering—for 40 years through the wilderness—but on a path *back to home*, from Egypt to the Promised Land, rather than wandering aimlessly or following grazing flocks.

What hadn't changed was the imperative to welcome the stranger, particularly since they had been strangers, in the end, in the Egypt from which they had just departed in seeking a return to Canaan. Among the subtle and oblique reminders of this imperative is that, embedded in what had now become the story of the Israelites, two particular features of the story of Moses the eventual Law-giver stand out. One is when, in his own flight from Egypt as a young man, he found hospitality among the Midianites. The priest, Jethro, who welcomed the stranger into his home, in the end gave Moses his daughter, Tzipporah, as a wife (Ex 3). This led to Moses' role as a keeper of his father-in-law's flocks, which led him out into the wilderness where he encountered the Burning Bush and with it, the divine imperative to return to Egypt to lead the Israelites out of bondage. It also led to a series of miraculous events that so impressed Jethro that he embraced the God of Israel (Ex 18:9–12). So the spiritual stranger was welcomed into the House of Israel, and the idea that the term "Israel" has spiritual rather than simply ethnic connotations was underscored.

We may understand several issues provoked by the sweep of this story. One is that the revealed text is often obscure and always requires interpretation in order to understand the import of its narrative elements and to comply with its commanding aspects. A second is how, within the expanding storylines of the Hebrew Bible, the *dicta* of the Torah are often repeated and amplified in the prophetic and other books that follow the Torah. On the one hand, *welcoming* the stranger by remembering that "you were strangers in the land of Egypt" is enjoined upon the ancient Israelites (Ex 23:9, Lev 10:33–34), but further, on the other hand, *oppressing* the stranger is condemned by their prophets throughout the Hebrew Bible. Beyond Exodus 23:9, we are enjoined in Jeremiah 7:6 and 22:3, as well as in Ezekiel 22:7, and in Zechariah 7:10, for example.

These sentiments will be repeated in the New Testament and the Qur'an and elaborated in the interpretive literatures of Judaism, Christianity, and Islam, but each of these traditions will focus on the same idea in its own unique ways. Indeed, among the important differences of interpretation within the Abrahamic spiritual family is that, whereas Judaism and Christianity accept Gen 22 at face value Islam does not. So not only is Isaac the son who climbs up the mountain with Abraham, but Ishmael, Abraham's older son by Sarah's Egyptian handmaiden, Hagar, had previously been sent away with his mother. If he and Isaac are depicted as coming *together* again later, to bury Abraham (Gen 25) *as sons and brothers*, yet the Torah narrative continues mainly through Isaac. By contrast, the Qur'an is ambiguous as to which son Abraham offered and the interpretive traditions of Islam spent several centuries debating as to which son it actually was. Ishmael, however, is the son through which the primary thread of Abraham's spiritual lineage passes—all the way to the Prophet Muhammad.

Among the unequivocal ideas in which the three traditions concur—in moving from the Torah through the Hebrew Bible to the New Testament and the Qur'an and beyond those texts to a vast sea of rabbinic, patristic-scholastic, and hadith-*shar'ia madhab* interpretive literature—is that of welcoming the stranger not just as an abstract, theoretical idea but one that requires constant active enactment.

Such notions have nonetheless been seriously challenged on many occasions throughout history—at no time more profoundly than in the 20th and 21st centuries. Among the most stunning negations of the imperative to welcome the stranger, the era of the Holocaust certainly stands out. The larger, murderously-proportioned calamity began by the decision of the German National Socialist government in the mid-1930s to turn specific groups of German citizens into strangers was a process that expanded over the following decade to overrun much of Europe. While there was a series of procedures that marginalized a range of groups based on their political affiliation, religious sensibilities, or physical and mental shortcoming, the 1935 Nuremberg Laws offered the first distinct encapsulation of the idea of redefining "strangers" in order to disenfranchise them on a formal government level—denying Jews, specifically, a range of rights the possession of which was part of being a citizen of Germany.

One of the places where many refugees sought a welcome was the United States—and many more were left in Europe under conditions that made survival profoundly challenging, to say the least. Our own American immigration history raises obvious and rather disturbing questions as to what we are as heirs to the Abrahamic tradition. The US has had a long history of tension between its inclinations to welcome the stranger to expand what we are as a nation of immigrants and a more selfish attitude yielding not only inhospitality but even hostility to would-be immigrants. Barely half a century after American independence, by the 1840s, a group had already been formed that called itself—without irony—"nativists." That is, they asserted of themselves that they were native to these shores (regardless of the obvious fact that their parents or grandparents or great-grandparents had come from elsewhere) and declared their concerted opposition to allowing more people—or at least certain kinds of people—access to American citizenship and all that that concept implied.

Whereas some welcomed immigrants as bringing important and colorful threads to the American tapestry, others pushed to diminish the range of hues. The latter sentiment ultimately prevailed over the former even as an era of massive immigration dominated the period between 1881 and 1924. If on the one hand the Chinese Exclusion Act in 1882 sought to limit severely the influx of immigrants from Asia—and when it expired a decade later it was replaced by more stringent restrictive legislation—on the other, southern and eastern Europeans also found the door into America gradually closing. While in the course of a more than four-decade-long period some 4 million immigrants arrived on these shores, as the strictures narrowed gradually regarding who might enter from where, that tightening culminated with the Johnson-Reed act in 1924 that all but slammed the door shut.

We were thus positioned to refuse admission to countless potential victims of the fascism spreading from Nazi Germany across much of Europe beginning barely a decade later. Beyond the Holocaust, deliberate marginalization and disenfranchisement leading to genocide is all too apparent in the ninety years that follow from the Nazi period to our own time, from Bosnia and Cambodia to Rwanda. In the aftermath of September 11, 2001, the United States—still wrestling with the question of welcoming the stranger that began in the mid-19th century—began an emphatic twist toward closing the door on those seeking refuge on these shores, expanding the process that began by the early 20th century. We arrived once again at an unprecedented slamming of that door within virtually moments of the inauguration of Donald Trump—and proceeded during the four years that followed to expand our articulation of the imperative to marginalize particular religious and ethnic groups. The repercussions may be felt not only across the country but across the globe.

As we approach the centenary of the Johnson-Reed Act, we might—we *should*—find ourselves re-asking vehemently the question of how we are succeeding or failing to live up to the biblical-qur'anic injunctions regarding welcoming the stranger. The volume that follows this brief discussion is derived from a twice-held conference—once at Georgetown University in Washington, DC, and once at Fordham University in New York City—organized for the purposes of considering this very issue. Both the double conference and the papers that are now the chapters of this book consider the matter from a theoretical and theological perspective on the one hand and also from the perspective of concrete historical instances within the past 85 years in which aspects of this multi-valent narrative have played out.

The first section of our volume offers five chapters that offer four theological perspectives. The first chapter, by Ori Z Soltes, discusses the notion of welcoming the stranger as it is discussed in Judaism. The second chapter and third chapters, written by Thomas Massaro, S.J., and Reverend Craig Mousin respectively, offer two different overlapping but differently-angled discussions that apply the tenets of Christian thought regarding hospitality to the world of today with its myriad refugees and would-be immigrants—and to the United States in particular, whose majority population has historically been comprised of Christians of diversely Protestant and Roman Catholic denominations.

The fourth chapter focuses on welcoming the stranger within Islam. Its careful and detailed analysis is authored by Zeki Saritoprak. The fifth chapter, written by Soltes after the Fordham conference, diverges from the Abrahamic traditions to offer a somewhat contrastive perspective as articulated in the dharmic traditions, with particular focus on what is understood by practitioners of the Kraishnite form of Hinduism. As a kind of epilogue to the first section of the overall narrative, the chapter teases out the paradoxic relationship between pure Hindu theology as it pertains to social action in general and the history of Hindu-dominated India with regard to hospitality to the stranger.

The second section of the book turns from theology to its practical application in history, the present, and with regard, prescriptively, to the future. Chapter six turns to a specific historical instance in which, against the backdrop of government inhospitality, the courageous hospitality of individuals made possible the survival of someone who might well otherwise have perished. Authored by Rachel Stern, it shares the story of Fritz Ascher, a Jewish painter in Germany who survived the Holocaust in the heart of Berlin thanks in particular to the bravely-offered, regime-defying hospitality of Martha Graßmann.

Chapter seven was written by Carol Prendergast, and reports on the organizations with which she has worked in the past many years that have hosted refugees and asylum-seekers, not merely providing refuge but helping to facilitate their success at weaving themselves into the tapestry of America.

Chapter eight was authored by Mohsin Mohi-ud-Din, writing, as he points out, neither as an academic nor as a mental health clinician, but as a survivor of violence from war and abuse and as an artist and activist who for over 15 years has led community-building solutions for advancing the health and human rights of the world's most vulnerable and dismissed groups and individuals. His narrative—based on his experience along the frontlines of community fragmentation exacerbated by forced displacement, war, and inequality—offers a plea to readers to recognize that "I am also more than the pain and injustice I, and millions more like me, endure."

Chapter nine was authored by Honorable Mimi Tsankov, President of the National Association of Immigration Judges (NAIJ), who discusses the need for an overhaul of the immigrant court system as it currently functions in the United States.

The last chapter might be said to function as a kind of epilogue to this volume's second section, in addressing the issue of encountering the stranger in the digital reality that dominates our world. Lindsay Balfour, who teaches Communication Studies and authored *Hospitality in a Time of Terror: Strangers at the Gate*, turns the idea of border-crossing and engaging the other in a different and very contemporarily relevant—transhuman, cybernetic—direction.

The overall arc of this volume's narrative leads from layered pasts in their engagement with theory and actuality toward the present and the condition, across the world and in particular across the United States, of strangers, refugees, and would-be immigrants, leading ultimately to questions of future. Indeed, the underlying question that these diverse discussions address in compendium is: how do we engage our multiple pasts and how do we construct our present and shape our future—and the future of our children and their children?

Section One

Building on the Past: Theology, History, and Their Practical Implications

FIG 1 Rembrandt van Rijn, *Abraham Serving the Angels*, 1646. Oil on panel, 6.3 × 8.3 inches. Private collection, USA. Public domain, via Wikimedia Commons

1 / Welcoming the Stranger in the Jewish Tradition
ORI Z SOLTES

I Beginnings: Abraham and others within the Torah

Abraham the Hebrew engaged in a heavy discussion in order to acquire the Cave of Machpelah as a burial site for his beloved wife, Sarah (Gen 23). He offered to purchase the cave from the "children of Het"—more specifically, Ephron the Hittite—presenting himself as "a stranger (*ger*) and a dweller (*toshav*) among you." At two points in the negotiations, the patriarch—no doubt immersed in grief—did not offer a scintilla of counter-negotiation to Ephron's offer: that Abraham purchases the entire field on which the cave was located, and not just the cave; and that he pay 400 shekels for it. If the lack of a back-and-forth may be ascribed to Abraham's mournful condition, the fact that he had to buy a burial site in the first place underscores that he was a man who owned no land. He was apparently wealthy enough—he had a large enough retinue of retainers and shepherds and the like that he could raise a small army of 318 men (Gen 14:14) to rescue his nephew, Lot, and possibly other Sodomites and Gomorrans from Chedorlaomer the Elamite king and his allies—but that wealth (explicitly adumbrated in Gen 13:2) as counted in cattle, silver, and gold—did not include real estate.

Indeed, the reference to him as a Hebrew also underscores that reality: the root of the term, '-v'r, signifies someone who moves from place to place: a migrant, a refugee, or, in his case, a keeper of extensive flocks. Thus wherever he came to dwell for whatever period of time, he remained, in some sense, an outsider. The terms he uses to identify himself to Ephron and his associates are significant, particularly the first. *Ger* is a term with the implication of being a guest and comes, in the subsequent Israelite view, to be understood to refer to any non-Israelite who abides by the seven Noahide Laws.

It is a more positive term than the more neutral term, *zar*—with its implications of being a stranger, a foreigner—and both of these terms are different from the term *nokhri*, which has a more dangerous connotation. *Nokhri* offers the implication of undermining the host community. In the Israelite-Judaean case, with its unique religion—its worship of a single, invisible God is distinct from the idea of many different, visible gods and goddesses, which characterized the religions of all of their neighbors—is rather explicit with regard to worshipping foreign gods, and therefore potentially or even actually undermining Israelite-Judaean faith. By far the most commonly used term in the Hebrew text is *ger*, with its positive implications. This is the term used in Exodus and Deuteronomy and in Jeremiah.[1]

Interestingly, neither term is used to refer to the three individuals whom Abraham had hastened to welcome to his tent by the terebinth trees of Mamre, in Gen 18. They are evidently strangers, come from elsewhere, but the text merely refers to them as "men" (*anasheem*). One might understand that the point of this—because for traditionalists, no word in the Torah, which is comprised of God's words, can be accidental or incidental—is to underscore with some subtlety that the stranger to whom one ought to extend hospitality should not be viewed as a stranger, but as a human being as you, the host, are. Abraham's demonstration of

---

1. The most obvious exception is in the Book of Ezra (10:3) in which the priest-scribe enjoins the Judaeans to "send away their foreign wives." The term used in Ezra (in a verbal form) is *nakhar*. Desperate to pull together the Judaean community that has spiritually and culturally unraveled in the century since the return from exile and the rebuilding of the Temple in Jerusalem refers to pushing out those—family members, no less—whom he sees as undermining Judaean spirituality. It is not their foreignness in the ethnic or political sense that threatens the community, but those promoting idol worship, who are thus intensely detrimental to the community. That prescription by Ezra is delivered in the context of his having redacted the text of the Torah designed to outline a covenant between the Judaeans and their God in detail. And the biblical book that bears his name represents him as reading out the entirety of the Torah before the Gate of Water of Jerusalem at the time of the harvest festival when so many Judaeans were gathered there—and that the people wept in hearing the divine words and realizing how far they had fallen from keeping the covenant. The previous verse (10:2) refers to one individual (Shekhaniah, son of Yehiel) proclaiming that "we have trespassed against our God and taken pagan wives"—where the term that I am here translating as "pagan" is the same term, *nokhri* (in the grammatically feminine plural form: *nokhriyot*).

universalist humanism, over and against a particularistic or sectarian perspective of "us" and "them" stands out.

For Abraham can well understand the condition of those who wander, rather than being land-held. Not only because he is a Hebrew, but because the text had specified earlier—in Gen 14:13—that the Mamre to whom the terebinths belong was an Amorite, (in other words: Mamre is not a place but a person) underscoring that the site of Abraham's tent is on another man's property of a tribe presumably different from that of Abraham. But Abraham's hospitable nature is part of his generally broad view and generous view of people.

Indeed, the narrative of Gen 18 not only moves swiftly from his invitation to hospitality to the description of the food that he serves them to the announcement that Sarah will bear a child within the year to the explicit reminder that God can do anything. This sequence is immediately followed by an altogether different—and yet clearly connected—sequence pertaining to the very Sodom (and Gomorrah) whose inhabitants Abraham had rescued some time earlier. In the dialogue regarding the divine decision to destroy these cities as paradigms of evil—including their stunning acts of inhospitality toward the strangers (in this case the text explicitly refers to them as angels!) whom Lot has welcomed (Gen 19:1ff), Abraham is once again an exemplar of this principle of thinking of all humans as important and worthy of survival: he "begs" God that the cities be spared if there can be found 50—then 40, then 30, then 20, and finally only 10—righteous ones (*tzadeekeem*) within them.

Abraham sets a very high bar with regard to many things, but his level of concern for his fellow human beings without asking particularities of their beliefs or ethnicity, expressed in these passages, stands out. They also form narrative preludes to the consummate test of the patriarch's uniqueness: the test of faith that shapes Gen 22. For what could be more inconceivable than that after the extraordinary divinely-assisted birth of Isaac—when both Sarah and Abraham were at such advanced ages—the same God would demand the sacrifice of that son (Gen 22)? Famously, Abraham did not hesitate for a moment—did not, in fact, even respond to God verbally, but acted, taking Isaac on a dawn journey to Mount Moriah to fulfill God's command. Abraham has been referred to as the Knight of Faith for his seamless certainty that God's will, fulfilled, will yield a positive outcome: a faith beyond all reason and beyond ordinary faith.[2]

---

2. Kierkegaard coins the phrase in a number of works, most noteworthily in *Fear and Trembling* and in the *Concluding Unscientific Postscript*.

The problem with the height of the precipice of faith upon which Abraham stands is that it could induce us to believe that, since we, ordinary people, cannot climb to such spiritual heights, then perhaps we have no obligation to go where he does in other matters—less egregious than that of slaughtering a beloved child—such as that of welcoming the stranger. The text of Genesis does not allow us that luxury, however. Because when we juxtapose the end of Gen 22 and the beginning of Gen 23 we are struck by a thunderbolt: Abraham never saw Sarah again alive after the adventure on Mt Moriah! Isaac may have gone back to dwell with his mother, in Hebron, but Abraham went to Beersheba (Gen22: 19) from which he "came to mourn for the death of Sarah." The explanation is obvious: he was afraid to face her after what he had nearly done! One might imagine Sarah's fiercely angry response. Surely she who giggled at the thought that she and Abraham would have such pleasure, presumably both of sex and of having a child together at their advanced ages, when she overheard that announcement from the strangers—and who named Isaac *Yitzhak* ("laughter") to commemorate her spontaneous disbelieving and also joyous reaction—would surely have lambasted her husband for his knife-wielding craziness.

So Abraham—fled—to Beersheva. Put otherwise: he was at that moment just an ordinary man caught in a moment of fear of his wife's extraordinary fury at him. So Abraham the hero is also merely Abraham the everyman. The consequence of this is that we cannot look at him as a model who is *too great for us to emulate*, but rather one whom we can and *need* to emulate, always aspiring to transcend our ordinary inclinations as he did. Thus his acts of welcoming the stranger are injunctions for us to act similarly. Indeed, we are perhaps enjoined to exceed Abraham's action if we juxtapose this story, as the rabbinic tradition is wont to do, with the interpretation of the passage instructing us to "build a fence around the roof" (Deut 22:8) to mean to build a fence around the Torah. The rabbinic tradition further interprets this idea to mean that we should carry out divine commandments well beyond the limits of where and how they are explicit—this is called a *khumrah* in Hebrew—lest we inadvertently fall short of fulfilling them.

We can see a version of this in the text of Genesis itself, when Abraham's hospitable act is first emphatically emulated by Lot—who invites the two angelic strangers whom he encounters at the gate of the city, (where he is sitting, apparently, waiting for an opportunity to welcome some stranger) not merely to dine, but to spend the night in his home. He urged them greatly (Gen 19:3)—no doubt aware of how dangerous a place Sodom is for strangers—and made a feast for them, and sought to protect them when his neighbors came knocking at his door demanding that he hand over the strangers. He goes so far as to offer his two young daughters to the Sodomites rather than giving up the strangers. As with Abraham and Isaac three chapters later, God intervenes in the end and Lot's faith and his goodness are rewarded: not only are the wicked neighbors blinded but Lot is warned to take his entire family away from Sodom so that he and they will be saved from the destruction of the city that will follow shortly from God's hand.

The eventual outcome of this handful of faith-based events is the fulfillment of God's promise to Abraham of many descendants—through Isaac and Rebecca and then Jacob-Israel, Leah, Rachel, and their handmaidens, and then Jacob's sons and the tribes that derive from them—who end up dwelling in Egypt, thanks to Joseph, and are led out of Egypt many generations later by Moses. The crucial turning point in the fortunes of Abraham's biblical descendants arrives when they receive the Ten Commandments at the foot of Mt Sinai. What had evolved from a small group of Hebrews—*wanderers*, with no necessary identifiable spiritual or ethnic connectedness (Abraham's God is *Abraham*'s God and becomes *Isaac*'s God on Mt Moriah when he also demonstrated extraordinary steadfastness of faith, and in turn becomes *Jacob*'s God after his extraordinary dream, out in the wilderness between Canaan and Haran, of a ladder connecting heaven and earth)—emerges as a people defined both to a certain extent by their common blood and to a more profound extent by their embrace of a spiritual covenant.[3]

Among the myriad other issues embedded within the commandments—that ultimately come, within the Jewish tradition, to be understood to number 613, as one reads beyond the Sinai moment through the rest of the book of Exodus and the following books of the Torah—is the injunction not to oppress the stranger (*ger*); "you know the heart of the stranger (*ger*), for you were strangers (*gereem*) in the land of Egypt." Nowhere could that straightforward instruction to empathize with the condition of those who are far from their native land be more explicit.

One of the more interesting issues regarding the organizing of the text of the Torah is that much of the legislative material that one finds in Exodus (and continuing in Leviticus and Numbers) is reiterated in

---

3. The primacy of spiritual covenant over ethnicity is signified by the statement that Jethro-Reuel, the Midianite priest who became the father-on-law of Moses, embraced the God of Israel when he witnessed all of the miracles accomplished by God on behalf of the Israelites (Ex 18:9–12). While an ethnic Midianite, he was a spiritual Israelite.

Deuteronomy. For our present purposes the more and less traditional ideas regarding how that organization came about is not important.[4] What we must note is that there are often slight shifts in nuance between the commandments as they appear in Exodus and again in Deuteronomy. Regarding the stranger, Deut 10:19 expands the imperative found in Ex 23:9: we are commanded to "*love* the stranger (vi-*ahavtem* et haGer), for you were strangers in the Land of Egypt"—offering an interesting manifestation within the Torah itself of the imperative to build a fence around the Torah by exceeding the bounds of its precepts: a *khumra*.

It might be instructive to note, more than incidentally, that in both Exodus and Deuteronomy, the fifth commandment—regarding one's parents—commands us to "honor thy father and thy mother." We are not commanded to love them, perhaps because in God's all-knowledge and understanding of humans, it is understood that one cannot *command* someone to *love*. One's parents may act in ways toward one that makes it impossible to love them, but one is commanded to honor and respect them because they are one's parents, regardless of whether or not one actually loves them. Yet in Deuteronomy we are commanded to love the stranger, making the notion of welcoming hospitality emphatic to the point of suggesting going beyond, even, how one might treat one's own parents.

II Carrying the Torah into the Prophetic Tradition

The Israelite descendants of those generations led by Moses beyond Sinai to the Promised Land in a 40-year journey through the wilderness eventuated as a Kingdom led by Saul, David, and Solomon, in turn. Five years after Solomon's death, a civil war led to a bifurcation into two kingdoms: that in the north, led by Jeroboam, which continued to be called "Israel," and that in the south, with Jerusalem as its capital, led by Solomon's son, Rehoboam, and called "Judah" after the tribe of Judah from which David and Solomon had come. Two centuries later (ca 722–21 BCE) the Assyrian Empire swallowed up the Northern Israelite kingdom, and its inhabitants were lost to history. That is: those "Lost Ten Tribes" ceased

---

4. These views, briefly put, range from the most traditional (that the entirety was received at Sinai) to the least traditional (that there were several authorial strands created at different times and places that were all compiled by Ezra a century after the return from Babylonian exile—of which the most extremely non-traditional view is that the entirety is man-made. This multiple-author concept is called the Documentary Hypothesis, and while it evolved gradually by the seventeenth century its classic formulation is associated with the 19th-century German academic theologian, Gerhard Wellhausen. Further refinements of that hypothesis continued into the 20th century.

to guide their lives by an awareness of the Covenant and its prescriptions. By 612 BCE the Assyrian Empire had been swallowed by the Chaldean/Babylonian Empire, and by 586 BCE Judah had been conquered, Jerusalem had been taken and destroyed—including the Temple built for/by Solomon three and a half centuries earlier—and every Judaean of threat or use to the Babylonians was taken into exile.

The Judaeans did not disappear. They eschewed the norms of their era—which would have been to assume that their God had been weak and was thus defeated, as they had been, by the Babylonian gods—and instead embraced the idea that God was universal and all-powerful: that God had meted out destruction and exile to the Israelites and Judaeans for their myriad failures to live up to the Covenant. In turning back to the Covenant with gusto, the Judaeans found that God had returned to favoring them, bringing the Achaemenid Medo-Persian Shah Cyrus II ("the Great") to the throne, who swallowed up the Babylonian Empire by 540 BCE and facilitated the Judaean return to Jerusalem two years later, to rebuild their Temple.

By tradition, the Torah is understood to have achieved its definitive textual form through the efforts of Ezra the Scribe nearly a century after the return from exile—the traditional date is 444 BCE. The ideas articulated in the Torah are often expounded and expanded in the books that follow: the Prophets and the Sacred Writings, which will complete what achieves a canonical form as the Hebrew Bible nearly 600 years later, in 140 CE. Among those post-Mosaic prophets particularly important to our discussion is Jeremiah—who prophesied to the Judaeans before and perhaps into the time of the destruction of the Temple and the exile. It was his words, perhaps, which the Judaeans in Babylon most directly reviewed in their minds: his repeated warnings regarding their covenantal failures and also his promises that, if they turned back to God, God would turn back to them.

Among the many utterances associated with Jeremiah is that which promises the Judaeans divine support, if they mend their ways, and they "do not oppress the stranger (*ger*), the fatherless (*yetom*) and the widow (*almanah*)" (Jer 7:6)—in other words, all of those typically at risk by virtue of being disenfranchised as law-protected members of the community—which is placed in the same verse with the words not to shed innocent blood or follow other gods. So not protecting those at risk is as deleterious an act as not believing in God or committing acts of murder. Moreover, it is important to note that the order of the three groups that symbolize all of the disenfranchised, "the stranger" is the first to be mentioned.

The prophet repeats this injunction as a straightforward commandment—as opposed to connecting it to a conditional context (if you do as I, God, say, I will remain covenantally and thus protectively connected to you)—and offers it not only to the people but to the King of Judah, speaking spiritual truth to political power. The broader context is the divine command to "execute just judgment (*mishpat*) and righteousness (*tzedakah*), and rescue the despoiled out of the hand of the oppressor [as Abraham had once done with regard to Lot and the others]; and do no wrong, no violence, to the stranger (*ger*), the fatherless (*yetom*), and the widow (*almanah*), nor shed innocent blood in this place" Jer 22:3). Again we note that the stranger is first-mentioned, and that the issue of spilling innocent blood completes the verse. And we might note further that the following two verses remind the hearer that if these words are obeyed, God will continue to elevate the House of David, but if they are ignored "The house will become a desolation" (Jer 22:5).

The Judaeans themselves would come to look at themselves as having abrogated these and other declarations and warnings by Jeremiah, and as having returned to uphold them in the course of the exile and in the aftermath of the return and reconstruction. Both the rebuilding and its aftermath were not easy, however: the community was fractured, for reasons beyond this discussion. One should note, however, as evidence of the complications, that it took 23 years for the Temple to be rebuilt, with the assistance of the most extensive empire the world had known at that point (and compared with seven years to build the First Temple), that Ezra's arrival into Judah from Babylonia and his Torah redaction, read out before the Gate of Water (about which events we have an account in the Book of Ezra itself) were a response to the chaotic spiritual slippage.

In any case, the simple Jeremiahan formula—live up to the Covenant and be rewarded by God, fail to do so and be punished—proved to be overly simplistic. The later Book of Job took on that moral complication directly: specifically, why it can be that the innocent suffer.[5] This proves

---

5. Job is presented as an outstandingly pious man who nonetheless loses everything and does not understand why—the reader, sitting God-like outside the text, understands that he is being tested so that God can prove a point to the Opposer/Questioner: the *satan*—but Job has no way of knowing that. His insistence on his moral innocence and the truth of that assertion is finally rewarded by an answer from God Itself out of the whirlwind from which God appears at the end of chapter 37. But God's answer, beginning in chapter 38, is a functional non-answer: listing so many of the extraordinary aspects of the Creation about which humans have no clue as to how they came into being, God's ultimate point to Job is: who are you to ask why the innocent suffer? Do you think that humans can know everything? There are things

to be an unanswerable question, but on the way to seeking that answer Job, in insistently proclaiming his innocence of any moral wrong doing, includes (at Job 31:32) the assertion that "no stranger (*ger*) had to spend the night in the street; my house was always open to the traveler/guest (*oreah*)." Indeed, the stranger is equated with the guest, since the connotation of *oreah* is more "guest" than merely "traveler."

My comment regarding the meaning of key words within this Jobian verse is interpretative, as is every comment that has preceded in the pages leading to this point. I have provided what may be construed as a Jewish interpretation of words and phrases that pertain in particular to the obligation to welcome the stranger. There is, however, no word or phrase in the Hebrew Bible—or for Christians, the Old and New Testaments and the Intertestamental texts; and for Muslims, the Qur'an—that does not require interpretation. The edifice of every religious tradition with a revealed text as its foundation is built by means of interpretation. Whereas the revealed texts themselves are understood to have a direct divine source, it is the human mind and sensibility that interprets.

There are certain truisms for this process. One is that God often speaks in terms less than obvious to the human mind, and at best, when there are still prophets who provide the revelations, they may be able to turn back to God for clarification. Thus after the initial conversation before the Burning Bush (Ex 3), Moses explicitly asks about God's Name, and God first replies "I am/will be that I am/will be"—hardly an answer that is easily understood even by Moses himself—and then God simplifies by saying that It is the God of Abraham, Isaac, and Jacob, so that Moses and the Israelites to whom Moses has just been dispatched will understand Who has sent Moses by God's past relationships and actions if not by way of an essence-bearing Name.

On the other hand, neither Moses nor his constituents asked God what it meant "not [to] seethe a kid in its mother's milk"—perhaps because at that time they all understood that this sort of gastronomic delicacy was considered objectionably cruel to God. It is rabbinic interpretation that, by way of a *khumrah* evolving over the centuries, interprets this to mean that a traditional Jew cannot mix meat and milk at the same meal—in fact, in true "fence-building" *khumrah* fashion not even milk and meat

---

that you are not designed to understand. The truth of Job's innocence is at least confirmed when, having abased himself before God and acknowledged human limitations, Job is rewarded with having everything returned to him, usually doubled—including his life span.

products (so cheeseburgers, and steak followed immediately by ice cream), are consumable in close conjunction.

A second truism is that, once the prophet(s) is/are gone, there is nobody to turn to who can turn directly to God, so the interpretive process will necessarily ramp up. A third truism pertains to the history of Second Temple Judaea (as we tend, gradually, to call it, following the pronunciational lead of the Greeks and Romans) as that history relates to the first two truisms regarding interpreting the revelation. This last is that, among the other schismatic aspects of the five centuries or so following Ezra— to put it simply—two groups eventually emerged. They were separated, by about the end of the first century CE, by their respective convictions regarding whether Jesus of Nazareth was someone special—Davidic, prophetic, even divine (but this was much later)—or nobody particularly different from other individuals in the previous few centuries who had followers who considered them anointed (*mashiah* in Hebrew; *khristos* in Greek).[6] Together with that difference there emerged a difference regarding whether prophecy had or had not ended after the time of Ezra and therefore regarding what texts actually constitute the revelation—the Bible.[7] So it is not only how shared texts *are* interpreted, but which texts *should* be interpreted.

III From Judaeanism to Judaism: The Rabbinic Tradition

Whereas Abraham was a Hebrew; and Moses and David were Israelites; and Ezra was a Judaean—as was Jesus; individuals like Rabbis Akiva and Shimeon bar Yokhai were Jews.[8] What emerges as the edifice of Jewish

---

6. The English-language equivalents of these two words are "messiah" and "Christ," respectively. The discussion of the nature of Jesus within the evolving Christian community culminated with the assertion that he was divine at the Council of Nicaea in 325 CE. That even at that time this perspective was not a given for everyone who called him/herself a Christian is evidenced, among other things, by the re-assertion of that point at the Council of Chalcedon in 451 CE.

7. That split will become more complicated with the Great Schism between the Eastern and Western Churches in 1054 and the Protestant Reformation beginning in 1517. Texts that Protestants consider outside the canon and apocryphal (eg, the first two Books of Maccabees or the Book of Judith) are part of the canon of both Catholics and Eastern Orthodox denominations; among the Eastern denominations, the Ethiopian and Eritrean Churches are alone in embracing the Book of Enoch as canonical.

8. By the time of Jesus, the term "Judaean" could have a religious connotation (I worship the God whose primary shrine is the Temple in Jerusalem); ethnic (I am from the lineage of the tribe of Judah—or at least one of the Israelite tribes); or political (I am a pagan, but I reside in the polity of Judaea). One cannot distinguish "Judaean" from

tradition are several floors of rabbinic discussion already begun orally during the last few pre-Christian, Judaean centuries—sometimes with issues and potential problems as the starting point and sometimes by way of direct attempts to understand words and phrases in the Torah and the other revelatory biblical books. These attempts engender varied levels of intensity of interpretive discussion. Both sorts of rabbinic discussion add floors and rooms that include those focused on the importance of welcoming the stranger.

The Talmudic tractate *Baba Metzia* 59b12–13 begins a process of furthering and perhaps refining the discussion of terminology. The first layer—the *Mishnah* (derived from that Judaean period of discussion)—comments that one who oppresses a *ger* violates three prohibitions and one who oppresses him in other ways violates two. The next layer, *gemara* (the written commentary on the *Mishnah* from the third-fifth centuries CE) elaborates by referencing three passages in the Torah: "You shall not mistreat the *ger*" (Ex 22:20); and "When a *ger* lives in your land, you shall not mistreat him" (Lev 19:33); and, interestingly, "You shall not mistreat a colleague" (Lev 25:17)—the last category of which, the discussion then notes, includes the *ger*. In turn the text continues by noting that three distinct Torah passages reference oppressing a *ger*: repeating Ex 22:20 but continuing the quote from the verse to include "nor oppress him"; referencing Ex 23:9 (quoted above); and adding (from Ex 22:34) that "you should not treat him like a usurer."[9]

Interestingly, it appears that by this time, *ger* is used to refer to a convert into the Jewish community. Given that by this time Jews are an archipelago of dispersed islands across the Roman (and non-Roman) worlds, and that both Jews and Christians are contending with each other theologically (and also for accepted status by the pagan Roman authorities that had granted that status to Judaeans back in 63 BCE)—until after 380 BCE, when the Emperor Theodosius made Christianity the official religion of the empire—there is a logic to this change in nuance. In the biblical context any stranger is almost certain to be of a different ethnicity and spirituality. By the Jewish-Christian period, given that Jews would be

---

"Jew/ish" in Hebrew (Yehoodee), Aramaic (Yehoodae), Greek (Iudaios), Latin (Iudaeus), and other languages in play at that time, which adds another layer of interpretational complication to the enterprise of understanding that era and the eventual distinction between Judaism and Christianity. Dispersion and a definitive Hebrew Bible are two obvious elements of Judaism that are not part of the world of Jesus.

9. The term *noseyh* is also translated as creditor. Both English terms suggest complications pertaining to financial relations.

living apart from their neighbors for the most part, in order to fulfill rabbinic prescriptions (such as not being spiritually polluted by proximity to pagan festivals, which would have been in abundance), a "stranger" who comes to dwell within the Jewish community is likely to be someone who, formerly a spiritual outsider, has joined the faith. And in the following paragraph (14), Rabbi Eliezer notes that causing discomfort to a *ger*—a convert—might induce him to return to his non-Jewish (Christian or pagan) way of life.

In any case, the exposition continues with reference to a comment by Rabbi Natan regarding Ex 22:20 ("... because you were strangers in the land of Egypt") that if you have a defect you do not point out that defect in another. As former *gereem*, Jews should not remind a convert in their community that he is a convert, which demeans him by reminding him of his defect. So within the competitive context for the first four-five centuries CE—competing for souls—the nuance of *ger* changes but the emphasis on empathy does not. As further layers are added to the rabbinic commentary, the distinction between a *ger toshav*, who dwells among you, and a *ger tzedek*, who exhibits specifically righteous behavior, is added to the conversation.

The first major medieval commentator whose words are added to the expanding page of Talmud is the Northern French—he also spent part of his life in Germany—Rabbi Shlomo Yitzhak, better known by his acronym, Rashi (1040–1105). By way of analyzing the passages in Exodus and Deuteronomy regarding the treatment of *gereem*, he observes that we all have our faults; we must remember this when dealing with others—and he broadens the connotation of *ger* to mean any kind of outsider, returning to a more biblical sort of nuance than characterizes the thinking of the earlier rabbis.

The concern for and interest in this topic continues as time moves on. Rabbi Avraham Ben HaRambam (1186–1237)—the son of the pre-eminent medieval thinker, Maimonides—also in the context of examining the Israelite experience in Egypt and the specific reference in Ex 23:9, asserts—clearly taking up and taking on the earlier rabbinical discussion in the *gemara*—in an era when forced conversions were not uncommonly imposed upon Jews in various parts of Christian Europe—that a *ger* does not refer merely to a convert to Judaism, but to any stranger who has come from a foreign land: that all strangers, universally, must be accorded a welcome, in emulation of Abraham and Lot.[10]

---

10. Avraham b ben HaRambam, *Perush HaTorah* (*Commentary on the Torah*), Ex 23. (in Hebrew).

Among the outstanding thinkers of the Jewish medieval period is Nachmanides (1194–1270), best known for his famous 1263 Barcelona Disputation. That term in the Christian-Jewish (as opposed to Christian-Christian) context emerged to refer to a debate forced upon a Jewish leader with a Christian opponent regarding the issues that had been separating the faiths for a millennium.[11] In Nachmanides' case the disputation focused on whether or not Jesus was the messiah. It was imposed by the Dominican order, politically powerful enough that Jaime I, King of Aragon, had to allow it. Jaime stipulated that full freedom of speech be permitted, and pronounced Nachmanides the winner ("never have I heard such an eloquent argument for a false faith" he commented), awarding him with a large financial prize and allowing him to publish his arguments, even visiting the synagogue on the Shabbat after the debate—but when, in the aftermath, the Dominicans insisted nonetheless that Nachmanides be exiled, the king could not prevent it.[12]

It is not surprising, perhaps, that someone whose three-year exile was extended by Pope Urban IV to a life-long separation from his home should have examined Exodus 23:9 carefully. He discussed how being a *ger* implies a position of powerlessness, but also, more importantly, of psychological vulnerability, so that the *ger* is enveloped in loneliness.[13] He surely wrote from practical experience, and not just as a theoretical theologian.

One might note that, as one follows from antiquity through the medieval period, the discussion begins to take for granted the importance of welcoming the stranger, and focus shifts instead to analyze who constitutes a *ger* and what that means. The anonymously authored thirteenth-century Book of Instruction/Education (*Sepher HaHeenukh*), focusing on Deut 10:19's injunction to *love* the stranger, that one must "have mercy on an individual in a city not of his birth . . . one should not pass by on the road one who is helpless, without family, friends, and protectors." The text adds that it is a universal idea to care for *anyone* who is a stranger, asserting that it developed as an idea from the Israelite experience in Egypt and evolved through the Jewish diasporic experience.[14]

---

11. In the Christian-Christian context a disputation is a discussion—most frequently regarding how, precisely, the miracle of transubstantiation occurs. (This is the subject of Raphael's famous 1508 fresco, *La Disputa*.

12. For more detail on the disputation, see Soltes, *Jews on Trial*, 102–112.

13. Nachmanides (Ramban), *Commentary on the Torah*, Vol 2, Ex 23, Rabbi Charles B. Chavel, transl.

14. *Sefer HaHeenuch*—also referred to as the *Book of Mitzvot*—is a comprehensive discussion of the 613 *mitzvot* (commandments) found, according to Jewish tradition, within the Torah. See *Sefer HaHeenukh, Parshat Ekev*, 431. (in Hebrew).

IV Remembering the Past to Shape the Present and the Future

Arguably the primary imperative within the Jewish tradition is to remember. This is the implication of the First Commandment (Ex 20 and Deut 5) that is on its surface simply a statement: "I am the Lord your God who brought you out of the Land of Egypt and out of the House Bondage." The real meaning of the revealed words, however, does not require an overly onerous interpretive effort to be understood, when placed within the larger context of the other nine—and, more broadly, the other 612—commandments in the Torah that form the foundation of the Jewish tradition. We are enjoined to *remember* that divine act, and every celebration—most emphatically and obviously the three pilgrimage festivals, Passover, Shavuot, and Sukkot, are marked by features that underscore that imperative.

The Passover Seder revolves around a series of reminders, both verbal and gastronomic, of the Israelite experience in and coming out of Egypt, repeatedly expressing an intention of feeling the experience as if, in every generation and every year, we were there and are not merely telling the story of our ancestors' experiences. Shavuot relives the moment at Sinai of embracing the Covenant—emphasizing Israelite eagerness by repeating the rabbinically-evolved dictum associated with their response to the offer of that contract: "we will do it and we will hear it" (*na'aseh viNishma'*)—that reverses the norm, which would be to hear the commandments first, before agreeing to fulfill them. The booth (*sukkah*) in which traditional Jews spend the week-long Sukkot festival—emulating both their wandering Israelite ancestors and farmers in the land gathering in the fall harvest—is understood by tradition to welcome *ushpizin* into its exposed-to-the-heavens interior. That Aramaic term,[15] meaning "guests" refers specifically to the seven "supernal guests"—founding fathers of the Jewish people: Abraham, Isaac, Jacob, Moses, Aaron, Joseph, and David—who are invited to visit the Sukkah.[16] They are intended to connect the biblical past of which they were part to the post-biblical world of which we are part. Each of these, moreover, visiting on one day of the week-long celebration, corresponds to a particular positive attribute, reminding us of the importance of exhibiting these attributes in

---

15. Ironically, the term is actually derived from the Latin word *hospes*, (from which we get the English words, "host," hospitality, and other similar terms).

16. Note that they are not in chronological order: Joseph precedes Moses and Aaron in the Torah. This is presumably because of the attributes or qualities to which each is understood to correspond. See the following fn.

our own lives, while as a compendium underscoring the importance of welcoming strangers as guests into our homes.[17]

The issue of remembering the past and breathing it in as if it were the present, while it pertains, in the context of the First Commandment, to remembering all that God did for the Israelites (and how the Egyptians suffered as the Israelites were pulled into freedom), broadens out both within the Torah and the Hebrew Bible and throughout evolving Jewish thought to encompass both the myriad other moments of divine intervention in Hebrew-Israelite-Judaean-Jewish—and human—affairs and also the myriad other explicit commandments and how over time they have been specifically interpreted.

That imperative, to *remember*, has been explored from Rashi's discussion of the First Commandment to the aftermath of the Holocaust in the contemporary Jewish world. The implications carry from multiple pasts to the present and future. It decisively encompasses remembering Abraham and Lot and the model of hospitality that they offer to us. Wherever Jews find ourselves as hosts we are enjoined to remember them and to remember our experiences as both hosts and strangers, wanderers and settlers, and to extend hospitality, welcome, and love to the stranger as an honored guest.

---

17. Thus, the first day corresponds to benevolence/love, the second to restraint/discipline, the third to beauty/harmony/truth, the fourth to endurance/victory, the fifth to splendor/humility, the sixth to foundation/connection, and the seventh to sovereignty/leadership. These are all part of the Tree of the *Sephirot* in kabbalistic thought—but that is another story for another time.

FIG 2 *Abraham Meets the Three Strangers*, 11th century. Fresco. Saint Sophia Cathedral, Kyiv. Public domain, via Wikimedia Commons

2 / Hospitality in Christian Traditions: A Key Virtue and its Applications

THOMAS MASSARO

The task of uttering a unified "Christian message" about almost any topic might at first appear to be a fool's errand. No doctrinal authority can claim to speak for all 2.5 billion Christians around the world in all their astonishing variety—Roman Catholics, Mainline Protestants, Evangelicals and members of the great variety of Orthodox Churches as well. On most pivotal ethical issues of our day, Christians of these many traditions and denominations employ markedly different methodologies and reach divergent conclusions regarding recommendations for both personal behavior and public policy.

Yet on the important theme of hospitality, we may indeed posit a common recognition on the part of all who call themselves Christians, of a moral obligation to "welcome the stranger." Though the details will vary from place to place and ecclesial community to community, it is fair to speak of a common commitment on the part of all sincere Christians to practice hospitality and to pursue an agenda of providing a warm welcome to all in need. As we shall see, hospitality emerges as an authentic Christian value, an aspiration rooted in sacred sources, and above all as a genuine virtue that guides compassionate behavior. The first part of this essay will describe foundations in scripture and Christian theology for the claim that hospitality is an essential virtue for Christians. The second part will explore some well-trod paths for applying this Christian vision of hospitality to challenging situations in the contemporary world, especially to the current crisis of refugees and global migration. Although the perspective of this essay arises from the Roman Catholic community (the single largest of the Christian churches across the globe), the sturdy generalizations provided below are common to practically all Christian communities.

Foundations in Scripture and Christian Theology

At the ethical core of Christianity is the love commandment—a universal obligation of benevolence and compassion towards all, including strangers and even enemies. The person whom all Christians recognize as Savior, teacher and moral exemplar is Jesus Christ, who calls his disciples to a way of the highest ethical goodness, despite our sinful tendencies that invariably prompt us to come up far short of moral perfection in the course of our earthly existence. One of the distinguishing marks of this goodness is hospitality. Throughout his own earthly lifetime, Jesus urged us to care for all our neighbors, especially those in need. In such powerful parables as the Good Samaritan (Luke 10: 30–37), the Prodigal Son (Luke 15: 11–32) and the Last Judgment (Matthew 25: 31–46), Jesus enjoins his followers to practice a generous love for all—including the stranger and alien, whose needs impose a true obligation upon us all. Jesus shows us the way to be practitioners of hospitality.

Anyone hiking the landscape of Christianity's endorsement of hospitality will soon stumble upon an apparent paradox. On the one hand, hospitality appears to be a noble *option* that each of us may choose to exercise at our own discretion. You cannot force someone to be a gracious and generous host, after all. In its essence, hospitality emerges as a voluntary response to the needs of some concrete person we encounter, upon whom we opt to bestow compassion and mercy. The human warmth and face-to-face character of any given display of hospitality accords it with honor and nobility. But on the other hand, when Christians reflect more deeply on the moral duties and systematic ethical obligations we are called upon to fulfill, the practice of hospitality takes on the cast of a solemn moral *requirement*. There is nothing optional or discretionary about satisfying our obligations to practice this absolute duty of social justice. While some people may excel in this virtue in heroic ways—think of Dorothy Day and her determined colleagues and successors in the Catholic Worker movement who operate remarkable houses of hospitality for the unsheltered and hungry—it seems that no one can claim the name Christian while shirking entirely the practice of social responsibility that includes care for those in dire need of hospitality.

These observations break no new ground in Christian ethical theory, but merely apply the age-old observation that Christian social ethics moves along two tracks or orientations. Christians recognize duties of *charity* and duties of *justice*. Both involve acts of a good will, but each proceeds with a distinctive style and set of concerns. Is your act of assisting the homeless or the traveler or the migrant a benevolent response best characterized as compassionate or altruistic in nature, geared to meeting the immediate needs of someone in distress? If so, such acts reflect the "charity orientation," which Roman Catholics associate with the corporal works of mercy—actions springing from the heart and directed to alleviating physical suffering and bodily needs. Or does your response arise rather from hard-headed calculations, geared to long-term solutions and systemic changes that will address social problems at their causal roots? Do your efforts display a methodical determination that is patient for "long-haul solutions," such as by advocating for public policies that, when fully enacted, will prevent poverty, disadvantage and social dislocation in the first place? If so, your acts reflect the "justice orientation" which displays the advantage of addressing inequities "upstream," so that the needs of the homeless or the refugee or the seeker of political asylum will be anticipated before social problems blossom and find their way to your doorstep.

To cut to the ethical chase, Christian theologians (such as the authors of official documents of Catholic social teaching) have long adopted a "both-and," or "charity-and-justice-combined" orientation, which looks to both short-term needs *and* long-range social planning. As its best, the dual approach sidesteps the moral perils associated with both extremes: neither applying mere band-aids when radical social surgery is required, nor indulging in a heartless preoccupation with political postures and theoretical abstractions at the highest levels when people are literally dying on our streets for lack of compassionate hospitality at the grassroots level.

Admittedly, those who follow either path live with continual tension, even unease, in evaluating the ethical status of their own efforts. If I volunteer my free hours at a homeless shelter, I may wonder (as did Dorothy Day herself on occasion[1]) whether the presence of so many "repeat customers" represents a failure to address the causal roots of the problem of homelessness. Conversely, if I channel my efforts at hospitality through the justice-oriented functions of a large bureaucratized nonprofit organization,

---

1. See Dorothy Day, *The Long Loneliness: The Autobiography of Dorothy Day* (San Francisco: Harper & Row, Publishers, 1981 [1952]). See especially Part Three ("Love Is the Measure," pp. 167–286) which records Day's occasional ruminations on the accusation that her work was ultimately futile, given the realities of the cycle of poverty that no exclusively charitable response would be capable of changing.

I may at times wonder whether routinized programs (however well-intentioned and however effective in the aggregate) excessively sacrifice the "warm touch" of spontaneous neighbor-to-neighbor compassion on the altar of efficiency. Do large-scale efforts somehow distort the virtue of hospitality by turning families in need into so many clients, who are "processed" within, in a system that is intent on accumulating evidence of quantifiable positive outcomes for social service interventions? Organized charitable agencies do sometimes seem to wander quite far off the path of compassion that Jesus described in his parables.

Bracketing for now the ethical perils associated with these "helping conundrums" and "Good Samaritan dilemmas" regarding extending hospitality to strangers, it will prove helpful to step back and consider how Christians have long framed the entire discourse on hospitality. Because proponents of both Christian charity and the social justice orientation are comfortable speaking of a *virtue* of hospitality, that convention will be adopted in what follows. Reflecting its roots in classical Greek and Roman thought, Christian theology recognizes virtues as habitual dispositions that shape character and make commendable behavior flow more readily from the well-formed actor. Hospitality is a virtuous practice endorsed in the scriptures recognized by Christians as normative for the faith life of their communities.[2] The biblical basis of this affirmation will be developed in the remainder of this section.

Further, sincere Christians are never satisfied until that *inward* virtue issues forth in *outward* practical measures to assist those in need. Eliciting commendable interior attitudes like hospitality is the stuff of theological treatises or exhortative sermons that Christians might hear on any given Sunday. Putting these commendable attitudes and motivations into practice is the stuff of parish outreach and community service, such as when eager volunteers run a St. Vincent de Paul community center out of their church basement, or when congregants support the Catholic Charities agencies of a given diocese, or through the methodical advocacy efforts of such parachurch organizations as Network, Bread for the World, Catholic Relief Services or the Jesuit Refugee Service. To coin a phrase, "it takes a large village indeed" to tackle deep social inequities, and religious communities of all stripes respond in myriad stirring ways—

---

2. A brief but highly insightful treatment of how hospitality (and the related notion of solidarity) came to be framed as a Christian virtue in the course of church history appears in James F. Keenan, S.J., *A History of Catholic Theological Ethics* (New York: Paulist Press, 2022). Drawing from both scripture and moral theology, pages 42–48 address this topic under the subheading "The Virtues of Hospitality and Solidarity."

ways that are inspired by a vision of hospitality and that proceed to make a substantial positive difference in the social landscape.

The endpoint of the most forward-thinking Christian responses to human need is of course always more than just charitable giving to keep people alive and breathing. Once we complete the frontline efforts to secure the physical safety and basic wellbeing of our brothers and sisters in need, we naturally seek to make these gains sustainable and replicable for the long term. The best models are never satisfied merely to engage in warehousing people, but rather are geared towards empowering members of under-resourced communities to succeed in shaping their own lives as they choose. In short, a "hand-out" is necessary and useful at times, but a "hand-up" is ethically far superior. Our commitment to universal human wellbeing includes the desire to see all people thrive and flourish, to develop their full potential, to build their skills so that they can truly be protagonists in human society—indeed to be agents of their own history. The practice of hospitality thus opens up into creative social projects supporting integral human development and even liberation that overcomes all forces of oppression.

It is in the scriptures that we discover the normative basis for these obligations as Christian communities recognize them. As ever when conducting scriptural exegesis, it is prudent to recall at the outset that the Bible is more interested in relating the overall narrative of salvation history than in providing abstractions and conceptual constructs relating to any particular topic, such as justifying the virtue and practice of hospitality. Rather, in the Hebrew Bible (whether we are considering the five books of the Torah or the more extensive text of the Tanakh) and in the Christian scriptures known as the New Testament, we find vivid accounts of hosts taking in travelers and feeding people when they are hungry, as well as repeated injunctions to ensure that sojourners and newcomers receive what they need to survive and even to feel welcome in the land. The hospitable person, starting with the portrayal of the generous actions of Abraham and Sarah at Mamre (in the account appearing in Genesis 18) and extending to the first-century communities addressed by the apostle Paul, is praised for striving to create conditions that allow everybody to benefit from experiencing an inviting atmosphere.

The Hebrew Scriptures contain especially rich resources establishing a moral obligation to practice hospitality and compassion to the visitor and the stranger. In the Torah and beyond, we encounter numerous stories of exemplary displays of hospitality and we hear such admonitions about care for the stranger as this in Deuteronomy 10: 18–19: "The Lord executes justice for the orphan and the widow and befriends the alien, feeding and clothing him. So you too must befriend the alien, for you were once aliens yourselves in the land of Egypt."[3] And of course the instructions on hospitality that appear in the texts of Christian scriptures contain strong echoes of these divine commands in the Tanakh, with similar normative effect.

The New Testament depicts many vivid incidents in which various characters give and receive a warm reception when encountering travelers, strangers or familiar parties, but on a dozen occasions in its 27 books it uses the abstract noun for hospitality, *philoxenia* in koine Greek—literally love of the stranger. Most of these 12 occurrences consist of moral exhortations to practice this virtue by extending generosity to others, though occasionally also to be a gracious *recipient* of hospitality. Notably, Jesus urges the disciples he sends out on mission to be gracious beneficiaries of hospitality (in Luke 10:7 and Matthew 10:10). Also emblematic is Romans 12:13 where Saint Paul includes hospitality in his list of Christian duties and among the varieties of works of mercy and fraternal charity. "Be generous in offering hospitality," writes Paul, who also adds the adjective "hospitable" to his list of qualities of a worthy presbyter in his Letter to Titus (1:8). The First Epistle of Peter (4:9) is beautifully vivid in describing meritorious behavior: "Offer hospitality to one another without grumbling. Cheerfully share your home with those who need a meal or a place to stay." Finally, although not specifically addressing the host-guest relationship, the words of Paul in 2 Corinthians 9: 6–7 echo the directive to manifest the qualities of magnanimity and generous welcoming, and may be described as "hospitality-adjacent": "He who sows bountifully will reap bountifully . . . for God loves a cheerful giver."[4]

Christians who are mindful of this rich heritage of scriptural texts and subsequent theological reflection over two millennia will absolutely prioritize not only the ethical stance of benevolence in general, but also the virtue of hospitality more specifically. To know the stories and theologies that support treating all our neighbors with compassion and mercy is to recognize hospitality as a key virtue and an exemplary practice, indeed

---

3. Quotations of scripture appearing throughout this essay are from the New American Bible (the standard translation for the Roman Catholic community in the U.S.).

4. These and other passages depicting displays of hospitality and exhortations to such practices from throughout the New Testament are treated in considerable detail in an influential and well-received account from esteemed American Protestant ethicist Christine Pohl. See her groundbreaking volume *Making Room: Recovering Hospitality as a Christian Tradition* (Grand Rapids, Mich.: William B. Eerdmans Publishing Co., 1999).

as an entire way of life, one that is fundamental to Christian identity. In extending warm hospitality to others and in graciously receiving the care of others, the Christian senses and discerns the presence of God in ordinary human interchanges. Indeed, to invoke an appealing eschatological dimension of this virtue, the sharing of food and communal space among hosts and guests characterizes Christian celebrations of the Eucharist or Holy Communion, and prefigures the heavenly banquet at the end of time.[5]

Providing insight into the spiritual wellsprings of this Christian virtue of hospitality is an implicit comparison that might occur to any contemporary observer of these texts that come to us from antiquity. Note the stark contrast between the practice of Christian hospitality and what routinely transpires in the modern "hospitality industry," which is part of the lucrative global tourist trade. The Christian understanding of the practice of generous welcoming is decidedly *not* based on one's ability to pay for lodging or food. No credit cards are necessary for the beneficiary of the Christian virtue of hospitality, which is never a profit-seeking transaction, but rather part of a deeper relationship, one grounded in altruism and the kind of self-giving love that Jesus preached. In its fullness, this human bond of trust and mutuality references our communal covenant with God, not our bank accounts. True Christian hospitality is definitely not about seeking to receive—to gain rewards, such as monetary compensation or status advantages—but about seeking opportunities to give.

Ultimately, what is at stake for Christians in the practice of hospitality is a prefiguring of the Kingdom of God, an opportunity to experience more profoundly the presence of God in the world, as is hinted at in the account of Abraham and Sarah hosting three unexpected and mysterious heavenly guests in Genesis 18. A fascinating verse of the New Testament (from the late first-century Epistle to the Hebrews) reflects back on this episode, distilling the lesson in this moral exhortation: "Do not neglect to show hospitality to strangers, for thereby some have entertained angels unawares" (Hebrews 13: 2).

---

5. This eschatological dimension may be described as part of the "surplus of religious meaning" associated with hospitality. This phrase is employed to good effect in a revealing treatment of the many dimensions of Christian hospitality, including the eschatological, in William O'Neill, S.J., "Christian Hospitality and Solidarity with the Stranger," in Donald Kerwin and Jill Marie Gerschutz, eds., *And You Welcomed Me: Migration and Catholic Social Teaching* (New York: Lexington Books of Rowman & Littlefield Publishers, 2009), 149–55 at 150.

The second part of this essay will apply these scriptural teachings to the contemporary refugee crisis. Related as it is to a larger global surge in migration, the plight of tens of millions of refugees and asylum seekers is surely the most urgent social issue upon which Christian reflection on hospitality may shed helpful light. This present section closes now by pointing to some further theological resources and insights that might motivate people of faith to apply the virtue of hospitality in constructive ways, and perhaps to commit themselves to a productive agenda that will benefit these tens of millions of increasingly desperate "people on the move," whatever the reasons behind their displacement. Since we have already been mining the narratives of holy scripture for insights into hospitality, we might consider one further gospel episode.

Although it appears in only one of the four canonical gospels, in chapter 2 of Matthew—the account of the struggle of the Holy Family (that is, Jesus and his earthly parents, Joseph and Mary) in their own time of exile in Egypt—is important for Christians in their appreciation of hospitality. The new parents fled clandestinely to Egypt to escape the murderous jealousy of King Herod who was hunting down potential rivals, including their newborn son Jesus. Of course, this is an episode that thematically recapitulates the earlier captivity of the people of Israel in Egypt as well as foreshadowing its subsequent and recurring diaspora status.

Though Christians do not consistently remember this story as such, based on this account Jesus was indeed himself an endangered émigré, a temporary refugee very early in his life. This renders the Holy Family as an archetype of displaced people and naturally generates empathy among Christians for others who suffer the perils and uncertainties of all "people on the move."[6] For this reason the "flight into Egypt" may be considered a "dangerous memory" that demands more from Christian communities than is often recognized. Surely, Mary, Joseph and Jesus owed their very lives to hospitable people in and near Egypt as they made their way to that unfamiliar land. How could sincere followers of Jesus, even at a distance of 2000 years, turn their backs in good conscience on migrants, refugees and asylum seekers in their own moments of profound precariousness?

Sadly, self-proclaimed "Christian nationalists" fail to connect the dots here, as do many others who support highly restrictive policies to exclude

---

6. For this reason, Pope Pius XII titled his 1952 apostolic constitution urging greater support and pastoral care for migrants *Exsul Familia*, or "The Holy Family in Exile." The full text appears at: https://www.vatican.va/content/pius-xii/la/apost_constitutions/documents/hf_p-xii_apc_19520801_exsul-familia.html

migrants and refugees from any hope of finding a safe haven on other shores. Such a distorted nationalism is in the end revealed as lacking in any authentic religious inspiration, but emerges rather as a face of ethnic hatred and a desperate ideological attempt to bolster majority privilege against perceived threats to narrow identity interests. A worse distortion of the Christian message of inclusion and universal neighbor-love is hard to imagine. Further analysis of such counter-signs to Christian hospitality is offered in the final section of this essay.

The gospels also portray Jesus as the recipient of gracious hospitality during the years of his itinerant public ministry when he frequented the homes of many who hosted him. Like a well-known character from the world of classic American cinema, Jesus "always depended on the kindness of strangers."[7] On several occasions, including episodes depicted in Luke 10: 38–42 and John 11: 1–44, he appears to have relied on the repeated kindness of a particular household in Bethany consisting of three siblings: Martha, Mary and Lazarus (whom Jesus would miraculously resuscitate from the dead). We don't witness Jesus actually practicing hospitality by opening his own home to others (a hard task for an itinerant preacher in any case), but he nevertheless practices a kind of prodigious hospitality in accepting, serving and welcoming (at least in a metaphorical sense) the sick, notorious sinners, tax collectors, children, lepers and others devalued and ostracized from the community, freely offering them his gracious presence, healing powers and easy acceptance as any generous host would. Further, in a chapter (14) of the Gospel of Luke replete with teachings on the value of humility, Jesus offers pointed instruction regarding how to be a generous host to all, including those who are poor and currently excluded (see vv.12–14). The clear moral lesson shared here is to avoid being the kind of host who is revealed in the end as a status-seeking social climber intent in parlaying his or her hosting duties into further social advantages. There is no room in true hospitality for selfish calculation or instrumental purposes, which is antithetical to the virtue itself.

Narratives like these, where Jesus gives and receives hospitality and even comments on the proper understanding of this virtue, have long shaped the Christian imagination, leading many to resolve to practice hospitality in their own personal lives—in the first instance, on the small scale of face-to-face encounters with those in need, perhaps by opening

---

7. The reference, of course, is to the final line spoken by the character Blanche DuBois (played by actress Vivien Leigh) in the 1951 film version of Tennessee Williams's *A Streetcar Named Desire*, directed by Elia Kazan.

their homes to travelers in need. Surely contributing to this commendable dynamic is the fine tradition of hospitality practiced in the monasteries of Benedictine religious communities, subscribing as they do to the Latin motto *"Hospes venit, Christus venit,"* or "Christ is present in every guest."[8] It is impossible to determine how much credit for motivating ordinary Christians to practice hospitality may be ascribed to this monastic tradition, but there is no more impressive model than the "open doors" of hundreds of monasteries for well over a millennium of Christian history.

Also relevant is the legal and ecclesiastical tradition of *sanctuary*, in which individuals who are fleeing persecution or who are being pursued by legal authorities may find temporary refuge and protection within the sacred spaces of church precincts. Church properties are recognized (at least in certain cultural contexts and legal jurisdictions) as a "free space" retaining a measure of immunity from the full sway of political officials and legal establishments, and they generously lend that protection to those in dire circumstances. While there is an impressive contemporary sanctuary movement in many jurisdictions within the United States that seeks to address the plight of refugees, it remains far from clear precisely how the promise of sanctuary applies to the political situation of people such as undocumented immigrants today. The safe haven promised by municipalities which have declared themselves "sanctuary cities" remains tenuous at best, and has not always prevented arrest and deportation by state and federal authorities. Nevertheless, this traditional notion continues to be a valuable Christian resource for reflection on the contemporary plight of "people on the move" and what we might owe them.

Applying the Christian Vision of Hospitality to the Contemporary Refugee Crisis

The foregoing section inventoried numerous religious and secular resources available to Christians as they form their consciences regarding responsibilities to enflesh the virtue of hospitality in their personal

---

8. The first words of chapter 53 of *The Rule of Saint Benedict* are generally translated along these lines: "All guests who present themselves are to be welcomed as Christ." Saint Benedict of Norcia was a sixth-century church reformer known as "the Father of Western Monasticism. On a related note, many Christian writers have reflected on the post-Resurrection appearance of Jesus to the two disciples on the road to Emmaus (in Luke 24: 13–35) to reach such conclusions as: "When you welcome others, you welcome Christ."

behavior. The further challenge, of course, is the social dimension, where people of faith committed to practicing the virtue of hospitality consider the contemporary implications of such religiously inspired mandates for public policies. Whatever moral convictions we might adopt for our own personal ethical behavior, we also need to discern a set of reasonable expectation for what should procced on the higher levels of social institutions and even the national communities we inhabit.

Weighty questions regarding the specifics of policy applications abound. What does it mean to live out the virtue of hospitality "on the macro scale"—that of pluralistic civic communities, even that of a large nation of over 330 million people, as tens of millions of refugees and asylum seekers clamor for the relative safety to be found within its borders? These applicants for refugee status arrive for a myriad of reasons, fleeing from wars, murderous gangs, drug cartels, political oppression and the effects of climate change, among other "push factors" accounting for the current upsurge in migration. The flow of refugees from Ukraine is the latest and most dramatic crisis we face, but sadly it is just one of many. Among the perplexing questions is whether and how enlightened migration policy should distinguish among the many motives that might drive the members of a given family of displaced persons out of their native country and bring them to our borders awaiting permission to enter. Do certain motivating factors automatically render a person worthy of admission, while other pretexts disqualify someone from any welcome at all, even if it is temporary in nature?

The stupendous complexity of immigration policy militates against assuming an easy resolution of conflicting goals. Refugee resettlement is a costly and complicated process; proposals for revised procedures at the border perennially raise objections on legal and economic counts. Will new arrivals steal jobs from established citizens or perhaps represent dire security threats? Will the costs of resettlement fall disproportionately on certain local populations and strain the budgets of border regions? The constraints are myriad, and even with the best of intentions, "the devil is in the details." Even Pope Francis, who over the past decade has emerged as the world's most prominent advocate of extending greater hospitality to refugees, has repeatedly recognized the serious burdens facing transit nations and destination nations as they ponder the best ways to be of assistance to the tens of millions of souls who find themselves in the current tide of refugees.[9]

9. See chapter 5 ("Tireless Advocacy for the World's Most Marginalized People: Migrants, Refugees and Victims of Human Trafficking"), pp. 119-148 in Thomas

No nation can take on all comers at its borders, it goes without saying. But one undeniable proposition is that the sincere Christian on a quest to be more Christ-like and to demonstrate a serious commitment to the wellbeing of all our neighbors will do better than what we routinely witness coming from American government and even from American Christianity and its leadership in recent decades. To reckon with our collective shortcomings, just recall the horrendous "family separation policy" that was enacted at the southern border during the Trump administration, with delayed and uneven responses to this human rights atrocity on the part of Christian leaders. Many questions arise: To what extent are Christians in our country willing to make serious sacrifices—whether measured in volunteer hours, political capital, charitable donations or even tax dollars—to practice the virtue of hospitality on a large scale? Will this particular religious community (and others who share such values) support the generous investment in resettlement initiatives required to enact gospel values and overcome exclusion? Will the tug of conscience and the knowledge of our religious tradition support an enhanced commitment to greater generosity as true hosts?

Instructive models of superior ethical responses do exist, if only American Christians seek them out. Two such commendable responses were endorsed within the span of a few months by the United States Conference of Catholic Bishops (USCCB). In December 2002, this body of Catholic leaders published a substantial document called "A Place at the Table: A Catholic Recommitment to Overcome Poverty and to Respect the Dignity of All God's Children." Approved the previous month by an overwhelming vote of well over 200 assembled bishops, this "pastoral reflection" employs the motif of table fellowship to inspire members of the Catholic community to address the problems of persistent poverty and hunger in the most affluent society in the history of the world.[10] As a statement of the social mission of the church, it invoked images associated with hospitality, though it did not specifically treat the plight of newcomers seeking

---

Massaro, S.J., *Mercy in Action: The Social Teachings of Pope Francis* (Lanham, MD: Rowman & Littlefield, 2018). Francis has repeatedly professed his awareness of the disproportionate (often frankly impossible) burden that falls on certain frontline nations (often called "transit nations") which receive millions of refugees because of their geographical proximity to "sending nations" (such as venues of ongoing civil wars, as in Syria and Yemen). His calls for greater global solidarity, for an end to tragic indifference and for a fair sharing of the burden of the current refugee crisis are heartening, but of course do not in themselves solve the root problems.

10. The full text is available on the website of the USCCB at: https://www.usccb.org/resources/place-table

a welcome at the border. But just weeks later, the U.S. Bishops extended the case for a generous response to people in peril by issuing a joint statement with the Mexican Bishops Conference.

The breakthrough migration policy document in question was published January 22, 2003 and bears the evocative title "Strangers No Longer: Together on the Journey of Hope: A Pastoral Letter Concerning Migration from the Catholic Bishops of Mexico and the United States."[11] While not pretending to resolve all the issues regarding migration policy mentioned above, the 108 paragraphs of this document recommend collaborative pastoral responses to the ongoing migration crisis and ventures to recommend long overdue policy reforms in both nations that, if enacted, hold the promise of advancing a wide range of human values. Sections of the joint statement address the need for addressing the root causes of migration (pars. 59–62), creating legal avenues for migration (63), legalization of the undocumented (68–71), encouraging rational employment-based migration (72–77), humane border enforcement policies and tactics (78–92), protecting the human rights of migrants (93–99), reform of the visa system, and respect for the principle of family reunification. The statement calls for enhanced coordination on both sides of the U.S.-Mexico border, both within the Catholic community and beyond it, on the level of national and regional policy.

Of course, no document, however eloquent and well researched, can improve the lives of so many people in need without organized outreach and follow-up. While by no means able to offer a cure-all, the U.S. Bishops do maintain a Department of Migration and Refugee Services geared to advancing this agenda of care for migrants and improvement of the conditions they face as they attempt to navigate the legal and logistical maze of migration. These national efforts mirror those of a Vatican office (part of the Roman Curia of the worldwide Catholic Church) called the Pontifical Council for the Pastoral Care of Migrants and Itinerant People.[12] Under the leadership of Pope Francis, this office has been upgraded and better resourced in recent rounds of Vatican reorganization. The enhanced migration secretariat is now part of an expanded Dicastery for Promoting Integral Human Development, which includes impressive outreach

---

11. The full text appears at: https://www.usccb.org/issues-and-action/human-life-and-dignity/immigration/strangers-no-longer-together-on-the-journey-of-hope

12. The website of this Vatican office (updated when it was promulgated in 2016) is located at: https://www.vatican.va/roman_curia/pontifical_councils/migrants/index.htm

to internally displaced persons besides those who cross borders in search of a better life.

As noted above, merely establishing an ambitious bureaucracy does not guarantee the accomplishment of an effective extension of hospitality to those in need, but such organized efforts certainly represent a genuine commitment to welcoming the stranger, even at the macro level. Within the Roman Catholic communities on the national and global scenes, these continued investments in social service programing and outreach amount to a necessary (if not sufficient) condition for putting the virtue of hospitality into action in concrete ways. U.S. Catholic leadership receives occasional criticism for its uneven and sometimes delayed response to migration-related injustices, including a perceived flagging of joint efforts since those two documents were published over 20 years ago, but even an unfinished agenda is at least a marker of a commendable corporate commitment.

These organizational efforts are supplemented by impressive scholarly contributions from the Catholic academic community as well. Prominent American Catholic ethicists such as David Hollenbach, S.J., and Dr. Kristin Heyer have conducted in-depth research and published a large number of highly insightful books and articles in recent years calling attention to the refugee crisis, marshaling existing intellectual resources from the tradition of Catholic scholarship and proposing constructive approaches that recommend enlisting new energies to alleviate the plight of refugees. Outstanding examples include the volumes *Kinship Beyond Borders: A Christian Ethic of Immigration*[13] (in which Heyer proposes a thorough re-visioning by which migrants may be more consistently recognized as truly members of a single human family) and *Humanity in Crisis: Ethical and Religious Response to Refugees*[14] (in which Hollenbach diagnoses the pathology of indifference to the plight of refugees and argues for broader recognition of their human rights as well as the duties of all members of the international community to assist and welcome them). While we are unlikely to "think our way to a perfect world," no solutions will likely be discovered without such efforts at creatively employing the available intellectual resources at our disposal.

---

13. Kristin E. Heyer, *Kinship Beyond Borders: A Christian Ethics of Immigration* (Washington, DC: Georgetown University Press, 2012).

14. David Hollenbach, S.J., *Humanity in Crisis: Ethical and Religious Response to Refugees* (Washington, DC: Georgetown University Press, 2019). See also the influential volume edited by the same author: *Driven from Home: Protecting the Rights of Forced Migrants* (Washington, DC: Georgetown University Press, 2010).

While this survey of organizational and scholarly contributions from the Catholic community is surely encouraging, by no means should it prompt us to ignore the deep-seated problems that remain. Practicing hospitality has never been easy—even on the small scale of throwing a dinner party when so much can go wrong: from kitchen disasters to clogged toilets just as the guests are arriving to other hosting imbroglios that we may all easily imagine. Being a warm host requires large doses of savvy and pluck besides generosity and good will. On the larger scale, if we wish to advance an agenda of welcoming the stranger and practicing hospitality in enhanced ways, we will surely need to counteract the perennial human temptation to yield to hostility and suspicion, not to mention outright hatred. It is certainly incumbent upon people of faith to reject those tragically still prevalent and thoroughly toxic attitudes of anti-Semitism, Islamophobia and all varieties of xenophobia, which is the direct opposite of hospitality.

In the United States alone, our national history shows how frequently such virulent hatreds surface and come to be institutionalized in policies and practices that perpetuate them, from Jim Crow and Chinese Exclusion laws to less official discriminatory practices such as "red-lining" and "sundown towns." A clear-eyed view of U.S. history reveals that for most of our national life people of color have been sent the decidedly inhospitable message that they were not welcome in large swaths of territory dominated by the white majority, which restricted their rights to free movement and much else. A survey of even quite recent social and policy history reveals the persistence of the vice of inhospitality—countersigns that work against the virtue of welcoming all equally. As individuals and as a nation of great wealth and privilege, we still have much work to do if we are to live up to the challenge issued by Jesus so long ago: "When much has been given . . . , much will be required . . . More will be asked of one to whom more has been entrusted" (Luke 12: 48).

For all these reasons, in our age of persistent distrust and suspicion of outsiders, hospitality turns out to be a virtue that is still quite countercultural, even subversive in many ways. Practicing hospitality in a consistent way is demanding because it calls us to move beyond our fears and insecurities to show love to our neighbors, even those about whom we might initially harbor suspicion. But hospitality is in the end a requirement of ethical consistency for all Christians, for whom it is a revered virtue, a great grace and a sure blessing for all time.

FIG 3 *Immigrant 4 Life*, Querty Project, April 16, 2018

3 / A Migrant 4 Life Journeys to the New Tower of Babel: Christianity and Immigration[1]

CRAIG MOUSIN

I Introduction

A street art painting of Jesus Christ, with a crown of thorns on his head and a placard hanging around his neck proclaiming "Migrant 4 Life" peers out from a wall in a street in Florence, Italy.[2] A poster-version of the famous Warner Sallman's *Head of Christ*,[3] now contemporized with a red Make America Great Again cap on his head, stood witness to many who stormed the capitol on January 6, 2021.[4] Religion can be a force that

---

1. This chapter is based upon a talk given at Georgetown University in 2019. Part of this talk was subsequently published as Craig B. Mousin, "Constantine's Legacy: Preserving Empire While Undermining International Law," in Slotte, P., & Haskell, J., eds., *Christianity and International Law: An Introduction (Law and Christianity)*. I have included part of the discussion here and developed additional themes in this chapter. I thank Maribeth Conley and Antonio Del Fiacco for their assistance with this chapter.

2. Qwerty street art photographed in Florence, Italy in 2018 by Emily Steinhert. Cited with permission of the Qwerty Project.

3. Warner Sallman, *Head of Christ*, https://www.warnersallman.com/collection/images/head-of-christ/

4. *MAGA Jesus*, Department of Religious Studies at the University of Alabama & The Smithsonian's National Museum of American History, (January 6, 2021): https://uncivilreligion.org/home/media/Trump%20Jesus.jpeg; *see also*, Yonat Shimron, "Poll: A third of Americans are Christian restrictionists and most are white evangelicals," Religion New Service, https://religionnews.com/2023/02/08/a-third-of-americans-are-christian-restrictionists-and-most-are-white-evangelicals/, February 8, 2023. I cite these two images for the purpose of contrasting Christian approaches to immigration.

brings followers together or becomes the force that excludes and makes those not within it—the other—the one who does not belong to the community.[5] Religion can generate great care and compassion or fuel racism and bigotry.[6] Ideology regarding immigration similarly can either reinvigorate communities to celebrate our nation's founding principles of equality and diversity or cause conflict that divides or excludes.[7] Christian responses to immigration in the United States have ranged from the extremes represented by those two portraits of Christ with dramatic consequences to those who seek asylum or immigrate into this nation. For purposes of this chapter, I will compare voices from the restrictionists who would follow MAGA Jesus or would prioritize the enforcement aspect of immigration law with those I identify as receptionists who emphasize welcoming the Migrant 4 Life and advocating for immigrants and refugees.[8]

No one interpretation can describe a Christian response to immigration over four centuries since Europeans commenced colonization of this land. Christianity's history in the United States has been marked by migration and change. Martin Marty recalls that the initial indigenous wayfarer to cross into the North American continent was only the first of many pilgrims who contributed to the cultures and religions in this land.[9]

As Jaroslav Pelikan notes, Christians have imagined many images of Jesus that reflected their faith. Jaroslav Pelikan, *Jesus Through the Centuries, His Place in the History of Culture.*

5. Jonathan Sacks, *The Dignity of Difference, How to Avoid the Clash of Civilizations*, 42, 46; *see also*, Martin E. Marty, "The Widening Gyres of Religion and Law," 45 DePaul L. Rev. 651, 661 (1996): (Nation's founders understood "religion's potential for defining and 'binding' a people, just as it had the potential for unsettling them and being disruptive of their civil life.")

6. Rachel Mikva, *Dangerous Religious Ideas, The Deep Roots of Self-Critical Faith in Judaism, Christianity, and Islam*, 194.

7. Abraham Lincoln welcomed immigrants as they often knew best the spirit of equality and democracy aspired to by our founders and critiqued those who wanted to exclude immigrants for losing the founders' hope for our democracy. Abraham Lincoln, "Lincoln's Reply to Judge Davis at Chicago on Popular Sovereignty, the Nebraska Bill, Etc, July 10, 1858," in *Speeches and Letters of Abraham Lincoln, 1832–1865*, Merwin Roe, ed., 225–26. Barbara F. Walter notes that immigration "is often a flashpoint for conflict" that can lead to civil wars. *How Civil Wars Start and How to Stop Them*, 76.

8. A current census finds that approximately 67% of the United States population identify as Christians. Within that group white evangelicals constitute about 14%, many of whom would identify with the MAGA Jesus. Those religiously unaffiliated approach 27% and 6% belong to other religions. "PRRI 2022 Census of American Religion: Religious Affiliation Updates and Trends," February, 24, 2023: https://www.prri.org/spotlight/prri-2022-american-values-atlas-religious-affiliation-updates-and-trends/.

9. Marty, Martin, *Pilgrims in Their Own Land, 500 Years of Religion in America*, 5.

Immigrants have constantly renewed this nation, but also, as important, the experience of internal migration offered opportunities for new Christian denominations and sects to grow, challenging any single belief as orthodoxy.[10] The first-generation Puritans soon learned that mobility, opportunity to dissent and move from homogenous cultures would soon upset even the most firmly held beliefs.[11] As Gordon Wood comments, "the basic fact of early American history was the growth and movement of people," leading to "phenomenal" unplanned growth of settlement.[12] Such growth not only tested the new political institutions such as town government and colonial government, but challenged established understandings of denominational authority and provided a rich soil in which to nurture new faiths, new interpretations of Scripture, and ultimately, scores of new faith traditions resulting in over 200 Denominations and over 1200 religions claiming recognition.[13] Change rarely slowed down, as Martin Marty concluded:

> Never have there been so many systems of spiritual striving existing so close together as in America. The neighbor or newcomer of a different faith or way has always represented a threat or an opportunity to those already here. The great difference between the modern pilgrims and their native American ancestors involves the pace of change. More kinds of strangers keep coming, and they disrupt established ways."[14]

Immigrants seeking to enter and asylum-seekers continue to disrupt the body politic today.

To address the multitude of ideas put forth since Christian ideas arrived, this chapter will describe three main themes percolating through United States history. First, I will look at Roman Catholic social thought. I name a second group restrictionists who at one end follow MAGA Jesus as their guide, but also include white nationalist Christians and others who seek to dramatically limit or end any immigration and call for a

---

10. Obviously, many factors have influenced religion in the United States. Martin Marty offers five considerations: *Pluralism, Experimentalism, Structuralism, Enlightenment, and Voluntarism*. Martin E. Marty, *Religion and Republic: The American Circumstance*, 31–50.

11. See, e.g., Mark Noll's description of both the power of the Puritan model, but also how quickly dissent arose in *A History of Christianity in the United States and Canada*, 40–41).

12. Gordon Wood, *The Radicalism of the American Revolution*, 125–6.

13. Marty, "Gyres," *supra* at 672.

14. Marty, *Pilgrims, supra*, 5

secure Border Wall and strict enforcement against newcomers. I categorize a third group as receptionists who seek to follow the biblical hospitality of welcoming the stranger—the Migrant 4 Life—and provide more immigration opportunities and convert enforcement into better legal processes to welcome immigrants and determine asylum eligibility.[15] Roman Catholic social teaching serves as a fulcrum between the opposite poles. Most American Christians who think about immigration fall into categories between these opposite ends of the spectrum. Readers may examine their own interpretation of Scripture as a guide to policy choices in light of the range of these views. The First Amendment to the Constitution prohibits the government from establishing a religion or enacting a particular faith into law.[16] Most of the individuals cited in this chapter would concur that their interpretation of Christian principles should guide the person of faith to discern appropriate policies influenced by faith, but not enact, for example, biblical laws as laws of the land.[17] Christians remain divided over how to respond to immigration, yet alone, what has been characterized as illegal immigration. In using these three perspectives, however, I acknowledge that there are many other voices.[18]

---

15. This debate is not new. Others use different terms to describe the alternative positions. For example, Elizabeth Collier poses restrictionists versus non-restrictionists in "Arguing About Immigration: The Claims of Restrictionists and Non-Restrictionists," in Elizabeth W. Collier and Charles R. Strain, eds., *Religious and Ethical Perspectives on Global Migration*, 229; Jennifer Lee Koh poses a pro-immigrant Christian view versus an enforcement-minded Christian view in Jennifer Lee Koh, "Agape Grace, and Immigration Law: An Evangelical Perspective," in *Agape, Justice and Law, How Might Christian Love Shape Law,* Robert F. Cochran, Jr. and Zachary R. Calo, eds..

16. First Amendment, United States Constitution, "Congress shall not establish a religion...."

17. A few still argue, however, that federal law permits greater leeway and still yearn to establish a Christian America. See, e.g., Dr. Robert Jeffress, "America is a Christian Nation," (Founders "designed our brilliant system of government not on enlightenment principles but upon precepts gleaned from the Bible."): https://firstdallas.org/america-is-a-christian-nation/

18. See, e.g.: Brett C. Hoover, *Immigration and Faith, Cultural, Biblical, and Theological Narratives*, (Paulist Press, NY, 2021); Alberto Ares Mateos, *Sons and Daughter of a Pilgrim, Towards a Theology of Migration*, (CRISTIANISME I JUSTÍCIA, Barcelona, 2018); "Strangers No Longer Together on the Journey of Hope," January 22, 2003: https://www.usccb.org/issues-and-action/human-life-and-dignity/immigration/strangers-no-longer-together-on-the-journey-of-hope e.g.; Jennifer Lee Koh, *supra* ; Rev. Mark D. Roberts, "Illegal Immigration: Seeking a Christian Perspective," (2010): https://www.patheos.com/blogs/markdroberts/series/illegal-immigration-seeking-a-christian-perspective/ Victor C. Romero, "Christian Realism and Immigration Reform," 7 U. ST. THOMAS L.J. 310 (2010): https://ir.stthomas.edu/ustlj/vol7/iss2/5.

I also acknowledge that one can hold very strong enforcement-oriented beliefs, yet offer hospitality to refugee resettlement or asylum-seekers who have entered our land.

All three have developed, to some extent, under a culture that often exudes a belief in American exceptionalism—that God has called us within this land, in Perry Miller's term of "errand into the wilderness" as a chosen people to establish a garden under God's realm.[19] In the beginning, however, they recognized that their human finitude could lead to failure. In what some call the first Mission Statement for his new community, John Winthrop presented a sermon to his community shortly before they arrived in Massachusetts in 1630.[20] Winthrop pointed to Deuteronomy 15 and accentuated the critical need for a liberal generosity to neighbor and other as the biblical verse encouraged them to "open their hand wide" to all as they engaged in a new covenant with God leaving behind the corruption of the British Empire.[21] Not only did this covenant define the new religion, but according to Perry Miller, it became "the theoretical foundation . . . for the state and church in New England."[22] This covenant theology which has dominated the first two and half centuries of our national life continues to play out in our contemporary responses to immigration with both our failings and successes. Despite the Puritan desire to be a united community, dissent and different interpretations of Scripture led to division. Mark Noll explains that "[e]arly New England dissent was often more Puritan than the colonial establishments themselves."[23] Just a few years later, the Puritans banished Roger Williams to Rhode Island for challenging the strong link between church and secular government. Through the new colony in Rhode Island, Williams planted the seeds of our First Amendment protections for religious liberty by urging opposition to an established church.[24] He founded the first Baptist Church with its belief in the separation of church and state. But forces of commerce and land speculation as well as continued development of scriptural

---

19. Perry Miller, *Errand, supra*.

20. Daniel T. Rodgers, *As a City on a Hill, The Story of America's Most Famous Lay Sermon*,17.

21. Marilynne Robinson, *When I Was a Child I Read Books*, 79–81.

22. Perry Miller, *supra*, 59.

23. *Ibid*, 55.

24. Baptist Joint Committee, "Baptist Freedom Fighters,": https://bjconline.org/mission-history-baptist-heritage/; see also Walter P. Shurden, "How We Got That Way: Baptists on Religious Liberty and the Separation of Church and State,"(1996) https://bjconline.org/how-we-got-that-way-2-2/.

FIG 4 *MAGA Jesus*, January 6, 2020. Photographer Tyler Merbler. https://flic.kr/p/2kro7Tv (https://uncivilreligion.org/home/media/maga-jesus)

interpretation, even in his new colony, resulted in a failure to live up to the most basic principles.[25]

The inability to reconcile biblical principles with those who were the other haunts Puritan history, both for members within and also for the indigenous and enslaved persons in the colonies. Failure has also marked it from its inception as genocide against Native Americans and institutional slavery revealed both sides of immigration as the colonists devastated the Native Americans and also failed to welcome enslaved human beings made in God's image. Both continue to haunt our public lives today. Indeed, from a Christian perspective, our failure to live up to the covenant today may be in part responsible for our failures to welcome and protect the stranger. Yet, the covenant has also led us in exceptional ways as diversity, pluralism, and internal migration have continued to add to scriptural interpretations, especially regarding the newcomer and the other.

II Roman Catholic Responses to Immigration

Understanding Roman Catholic responses to immigration provides a fulcrum to compare the two poles represented by MAGA Jesus and

---

25. Mark Noll, *History, supra* at 60; see also, Alan Simpson, "How Democratic Was Roger Williams," *The William and Mary Quarterly, Jan.*, 1956, Vol. 13, No. 1 (Jan. 1956), 53, 66–67.

the Migrant 4 Life, not because it was the first faith response to immigration in the United States, but because its Roman Catholic polity and its social thought have had the most definitive expressions of responses to immigration.[26] Roman Catholics have also experienced the negative and positive consequences of immigration in America. The Puritans, arriving as Europe was starting to negotiate solutions to the religious wars spawned, in part, by the Reformation, still feared the power of the Roman Catholic Church and saw themselves offering a new city on a hill in opposition to Rome. In the years after the Civil War, Catholic immigrants were often maligned, threatened, and persecuted. They were seen as a threat to American values, undemocratic and often influenced by alcohol and poor work habits. The metaphor of immigrants invading our promised land led Know Nothing Party nativists and the Ku Klux Klan as well as public officials to threaten and discriminate against Catholics.[27] Catholic immigrants found themselves on the victim side of discrimination and persecution occurred until greater cultural acceptance occurred subsequent to the election of President John F. Kennedy and Vatican II.[28]

Roman Catholic social thought commenced with its central belief in human dignity as central to its moral theology. Elizabeth Collier cites the critical significance of the Bible's earliest words that all human beings are created in God's image and likeness which stands before any division into nations or other human constructs (Gen. 1:27).[29] In addition, the Roman Catholic understanding of stewardship arises out of God's call to care for the earth, recognizing that all things within the earth are gifts of God, not simply possessions for humans.[30] Collier concludes that the church emphasizes the idea that the "dignity and flourishing of the human person must be the primary category of concern.... Most laws governing migration focus almost exclusively on the needs of the nation-state. The social teaching asserts that the needs of the individual (the stranger, alien,

---

26. For a more detailed description of Roman Catholic responses, see Chapter Two in this volume. This brief summary serves as context to compare the two other poles of biblical perspectives. See also, "Strangers No Longer Together on the Journey of Hope," January 22, 2003: https://www.usccb.org/issues-and-action/human-life-and-dignity/immigration/strangers-no-longer-together-on-the-journey-of-hope e.g.

27. Mark Noll *History, supra*, 209–210

28. *Ibid*, 537–39.

29. Elizabeth W. Collier, "And They Fled into Egypt, Migration in the Light of Scripture and Catholic Social Teaching," in Collier and Strain, eds., *Perspectives, supra*, 151.

30. *Ibid*, 155.

migrant) must be considered as well and hold a primary place in the discussion."[31]

Rev. Thomas Bretz summarizes three main elements of the Roman Catholic approach to immigration. First, "people have the right to migrate to sustain their lives and their families." This idea finds resonance in international law establishing that individuals are not serfs tied to the land, but when circumstances call for it, they may leave. Second, "a country has the right to control its borders and control immigration." Here, the church again recognizes the right and duty of the nation-state to defend its borders and determine who may be permitted entrance. Thus, the individual's right to leave a country finds no reciprocal right to enter another nation, again a principle recognized under international law. Finally, the church attempts to balance these first two principles by stating, "a country must regulate its borders with justice and mercy."[32]

Pope Francis has emphasized welcoming the stranger as a critical witness to the refugees seeking safe haven. In his writings and personal commitments, he has modeled hospitality. He cites the Parable of the Good Samaritan to inspire welcome:

> So this encounter of mercy between a Samaritan and a Jew is highly provocative; it leaves no room for ideological manipulation and challenges us to expand our frontiers. It gives a universal dimension to our call to love, one that transcends all prejudices, all historical and cultural barriers, all petty interests.[33]

A challenge he posed to educational institutions can also call all Christians to build "a place of welcome, protection or accompaniment, promotion and integration for all, to the exclusion of none.[34]

---

31. *Ibid*, 157.

32. Fr. Thomas Betz, OFC, "Catholic Social Teaching on Immigration and the Movement of Peoples," https://www.usccb.org/issues-and-action/human-life-and-dignity/immigration/catholic-teaching-on-immigration-and-the-movement-of-peoples

33. Francis, "Fratelli Tutti." The Holy See, 3 Oct. 2020, www.vatican.va/content/francesco/en/encyclicals/documents/papa-francesco_20201003_enciclica-fratelli-tutti.htm, 83.

34. Pope Francis, "Address of His Holiness Pope Francis to Participants in the Meeting on Refugees Promoted by the Pontifical Gregorian University," September 29, 2022: https://www.vatican.va/content/francesco/en/speeches/2022/september/documents/20220929-incontro-rifugiati.html

III MAGA Jesus: Restrictionist Interpretations of Scripture

A. THE NEED FOR A STRONG NATION-STATE TO PROTECT BORDERS.

Those who claim the Bible as articulating God's principles as including limit-to-immigration policies concentrate on three key issues symbolized in the Tower of Babel Story (Gen.11:1–9). The people decided to build a tower that would reach to the heavens. God disagreed and scattered the people. Ralph Drollinger, who has led Cabinet-level Bible Studies and has advised political leaders throughout the world[35] asserts that "'so the Lord scattered' is a passage one must count as fundamental to the immigration debate" because it serves as "the basis for multiple, independent nations, the existence of which is so fundamental to a proper Christian world view and understanding."[36] For Drollinger, Babel teaches that God destroyed the Tower of Babel because God saw a united humanity under one government as a threat to Divine sovereignty. Pursuant to this fundamental belief, the scattering indicates that God requires many independent nation-states as critical to human flourishing. Each nation contains a particular people in a particular location with a particular culture and history with established and recognized borders. James Edwards concludes that Scriptures pose a "special obligation we all have toward those closest to us and to the specific communities wherein we reside."[37] There is a "biblical obligation that civil authorities have to protect people and the communities entrusted to their care."[38] To protect that particularity, nations need to protect the inhabitants of each nation, requiring strong borders, defenses against foreign invaders, and impenetrable border walls. By this logic, fulfilling that goal calls for an effective detention and deportation regime.

To buttress Dollinger's fundamental finding from Genesis, enforcement-minded defenders argue that Christians must obey the leaders of

---

35. Mattathias Schwartz, "How the Trump Cabinet's Bible Teacher Became a Shadow Diplomat," October 29, 2019: https://www.nytimes.com/2019/10/29/magazine/ralph-drollinger-white-house-evangelical.html?searchResultPosition=4.

36. Ralph Drollinger, "What the Bible Says About Our Illegal Immigration Problem": https://capmin.org/wp-content/uploads/2016/09/What-The-Bible-Says-About-our-Immigration-Problem-by-Ralph-Drollinger-2019.pdf (emphasis in original).

37. James Edwards, "A Biblical Perspective on Immigration Policy" in *Debating Immigration*, Carol Swain, ed., 56.

38. *Ibid.*

the nation-state and its laws. Based on those principles, anyone defiling the national boundaries or breaking the laws that protect them may be punished, and if necessary, detained and deported. Relying primarily on Romans 13: 1–7, they assert that God has ordained the magistrates and governors of the nation-states to defend the sovereignty and protect the people. Thus, civil law shall not be broken. To maintain the sovereignty of the nation-state, its borders must be defended, and immigration regulated. For Edwards, the Bible leaves no doubt that "civic boundaries have meaning and, in fact, have God's ordination."[39]

Christian restrictionists point to that commitment to the law as part of their response to immigration. United States immigration law establishes a presumption of immigrant status if one cannot prove that one is a citizen or has been inspected and admitted at a federal point of entry, and is subject to deportation unless otherwise granted status by the law.[40] The law designates those not citizens as aliens.[41] Therefore, they conclude, if not lawfully present, one is an illegal alien and should be excluded or deported.

B. WELCOME THE *GERIM*, BUT NOT THE *ZAR*.

By responding to illegal aliens rather than simply human beings in need—vulnerable strangers—restrictionists rebut those who cite Scripture as God's command to welcome the stranger. Israel recognized different categories of persons residing with Israel. The Bible characterized those who resided in Israel and followed Israel's law as *ger* [sing.] or the *gerim* [plur.] whom God commands the Israelites to welcome and treat as the native (Lev. 19:33–34). James Hoffmeier stresses, however, that the Bible distinguishes between the *gerim* as lawful resident and the *zar*, the foreigner as illegal alien.[42] The foreigner or the enemy are given a different name, *nokhri* or *zar*, and must be treated differently. Thus, restrictionists can accept that certain strangers may fit within the biblical call to welcome the stranger, but they situate the illegal aliens within the group that the Bible called *nokhri* or *zar*—foreigners or enemies who must not

---

39. James Edwards, "The Return of the Pharisees," *Center for Immigration Studies*, February 28, 2012: https://cis.org/Edwards/Return-Pharisees

40. 8 U.S.C. § 1184 (b).

41. 8 USC §1101(c).

42. James K. Hoffmeier "The Use and Abuse of the Bible in the Immigration Debate," (2011): https://cis.org/Report/Use-and-Abuse-Bible-Immigration-Debate

be welcomed with open arms.[43] Restrictionists conclude that as an enemy, illegal aliens should be deported.

C. STEWARDSHIP OF NATIONAL RESOURCES.

By naming them illegal, restrictionists also define stewardship differently. Stewardship is a duty of the state to protect its citizens from the purported crime of illegal aliens who, they allege, steal the resources of the citizen by both entry and by residing within the land. As Edwards argues: "the government has the duty to defend the nation against foreign invaders" and "it safeguards the public good for a particular group of people, in a particular geographic location, who belong to a particular body politic."[44] By naming them illegal before they have even had a day in court to adjudge the validity of the term, the restrictionists make the migrant and asylum-seeker the other who brings nothing but ruin to the nation. They allege that illegals steal jobs, rob the nation of social service benefits, spread disease, commit crime, and undermine the rule of law. The governor has the duty to preserve those resources by good stewardship through deportation and building walls to keep the alien out.[45] Currently the world counts over eighty million refugees or displaced persons. The restrictionists believe that if we have open borders many will seek to come to this nation, thus robbing us of our resources. [Former] Attorney General Sessions defended the decision to build a border wall based, in part, on Nehemiah's return to Jerusalem "to build a wall" sarcastically adding, "it wasn't to keep the people in."[46] He saw his duty as Attorney General to implement federal statutes and policies as well as construct the physical defense of a border wall.

IV Welcoming the Migrant 4 Life to Our Land

Those at the other end of the theological divide of Christian responses to immigration include some who come from the radical side of the Protestant Reformation, some who claim the liberation side of Catholicism, and

---

43. For more detail on these terms, see Chapter One in this volume.
44. James Edwards, "A Biblical Perspective on Immigration Policy," *supra*.
45. Carol Swain, *Be the People, A Call to Reclaim America's Faith and Promise*, 156.
46. Penny Starr, "Sessions on Border Security: Nehemiah Build a Wall in Jerusalem and 'It Wasn't To Keep People In,'" CNN News (June 13, 2016, 8:22 PM). https://web.archive.org/web/20190320125202/https://www.cnsnews.com/news/article/penny-starr/sessions-border-security-nehemiah-built-wall-jerusalem-and-it-wasnt-keep (archived version from the Internet Archive).

others who seek to exemplify living justly in the most powerful nation in the world. Some have roots in the Sanctuary movement of the 1980s, most recently rejuvenated in the crackdown against immigrants in the last two decades. The deaths on the border and the inhuman detention of asylum seekers and other immigrants for civil violations has inspired others. Others simply respond to the biblical call to welcome the stranger.

Surprisingly, those who promote greater welcome to the immigrant and asylum-seeker rarely cite the Tower of Babel story found to be so fundamental to Drollinger's understanding of immigration. Certainly, proponents across the wide divide agree that the Genesis story sent a message contesting the arrogance of building a structure to the heavens and the scattering of the people. Biblical scholars, however, debate whether the scattering was a curse or a blessing.[47] Babel did represent the misuse of power, but the lessons derived support claims from both sides. Babel represents a perfect symbol of the immigration debate within this chapter. Drollinger names the story "fundamental" as he interprets God scattering the people and establishing nation-states.[48] In contrast, Bernhard Anderson writes that the creative freedom that sparked the idea of such a tower "is both the grandeur and the misery of humanity. On the one hand, it enables human beings to rise above the limitations of their environment and . . . build a city that affords unity and protection. . . .On the other hand the 'will to greatness,' which also reflects anxiety, prompts an assertion of power that stands under the judgment of God whose created purpose includes richness, variety, and proliferation."[49] These distinct interpretations, however, lead followers in opposite directions. The Tower of Babel, therefore, again serves as a starting point from which to examine the three same elements so critical to the restrictionist perspective: the power of the nation-state, Israel's welcome to the *gerim,* and the stewardship of resources.

The seeds of the story reflect the debate within ancient Israel of the people moving from a migrating, nomadic culture to a more sedentary, urban environment that continues today in the distinction between MAGA Jesus and the Migrant 4 Life.[50] Growing urban centers could exercise military and political power over God's people. Thus, according to Rabbi Rachel Mikva, God destroyed the tower because "a unified purpose

---

47. Walter Brueggemann, *Theology of the Old Testament, Testimony, Dispute, Advocacy,* 494, n. 4.
48. "What the Bible Says," ibid.
49. Bernhard W. Anderson, *From Creation to New Creation,* 178.
50. Claus Westermann, *Genesis 1–11,* 543-4.

leads only to totalitarian pursuit of power."[51] Rabbi Jonathan Sacks concurs that "Babel is a critique of imperialism."[52]

In contrast to Edwards and Drollinger, for those who welcome the Migrant 4 Life, Babel teaches at least two lessons. First, for those who advocate "Build the Wall" as the source of security, the border wall becomes an idol of national defense to protect the dream of a nation of one tribe, one race, denying God's sovereignty. The people in Genesis said, "let us build a wall to the highest heavens. Compare the language of former President Trump, "We will build a wall;" "This wall can't be climbed" and "It's a very powerful—very powerful wall."[53] Daniel Smith-Christopher claims that "[t]his particular border has become a shrine to false national pride" and "this border has become an idol."[54] Dorothee Soelle reminds us that when the ancient Israelites succumbed to worshipping a golden calf, "it was a symbol of security and welfare."[55] Although Soelle was describing the nation-state's reliance on nuclear weapons for security, her words ring true about the adoration of those who seek to "build the wall." Her conclusion applies to the defenders of the Border Wall:

> If the 'window of vulnerability,' as it is called in military language, is finally closed up and walled up, the supposedly secure people inside the fortress will die for a lack of light and air. Only life that opens

---

51. Rachel Mikva, *Dangerous, supra,* 115.

52. Rabbi Jonathan Sacks, *Not in God's Name, Confronting Religious Violence,* 192. Sacks also disagrees with Drollinger's conclusion that the scattering gave God's imprimatur to the nation-state, pointing out that God had already divided the world into nations in Genesis 10.

53. Alex Pappas, "Trump visits border barriers near San Diego: 'The wall can't be climbed,'" September 18, 2019: https://www.foxnews.com/politics/trump-border-wall-near-san-diego-climb-barriers

54. Daniel L. Smith-Christopher, *Jonah, Jesus, and Other Good Coyotes, Speaking Peace to Power in the Bible,* xi. Our language has even seen a new addition in the term the "Babel Syndrome." Pope Francis described a plague he called the "Babel Syndrome" when opposite sides of a theological debate argue and fail to listen to one another. See Junno Arocho Esteves, Catholic New Service, "Pope Francis: Theology begins with sincere dialogue, not 'conquering' spirit" June 21, 2019: https://thedialogorg/vatican-news/pope-francis-theology-begins-with -sincere-dialogue-not-conquering-spirit/. José Luis Fiori describes the contemporary United States intent to continue its world power influence through expanding military spending as the "Babel Syndrome": "Babel Syndrome and the New Security Doctrine of the United States," *Journal of Humanitarian Affairs* Volume 1, No 1 920190, 42–45.

55. Dorothee Soelle, *The Window of Vulnerability, A Political* Spirituality, Linda M. Maloney, transl., 8.

itself to the other, life that risks being wounded or killed, contains promise.[56]

Those who receive the Migrant 4 Life with hospitality argue that the Border Wall will stifle our communities by not welcoming the stranger. Soelle asks, "what god is worshiped and adored in a particular society?"[57] MAGA Jesus followers proclaim, "Build the Wall." Those who follow the Migrant 4 Life seek the diversity of humanity and welcome the sojourner in our midst.

This idea of welcoming diversity and the gift of the stranger highlights the second lesson receptionists take from Babel. The story of the Tower reminds humans that, as Israel found its own identity in exile, we are all strangers and exiles on earth relying on God's protection (Heb. 11:13). For Anderson, Abraham and Sarah "represent a new people who, in contrast to the builders of Babel do not strive to make a great name but whose name is 'made great' by God's blessing (Gen. 12:1–3)."[58] Much of the Hebrew Bible involves the Israelites wrestling with the covenant and the promise of land and the impact of exile. When reviewing the entire Hebrew and Christian Scriptures, Walter Brueggemann argues that for both Jews and Christians, "the core of faith . . . is situated in the matrix of exile."[59] Exile and protecting a land are constant historical realities that require response and scriptural explanation. He adds:

> The very land that promised to create space for human joy and freedom became the very source of dehumanizing exploitation and oppression. Land was indeed a problem in Israel. Time after time, Israel saw the land of promise become the land of problem. The very land that contained the sources of life drove kings to become agents of death. Society became the frantic effort of the landed to hold onto the turf, no matter what the cost.[60]

Mark Hamilton observes that, because biblical Israel lived both as a migrating people and a host to migrants, the people understood both the perils of exile and the perils of securing the land.[61] Abraham and Sarah were both

---

56. *Ibid.* at 7.
57. *Ibid.*
58. Anderson, *Creation, supra* at 178.
59. Walter Brueggemann, *Theology,* supra, 77.
60. Walter Brueggemann, *The Land: Place as Gift, Promise and Challenge in Biblical Faith,* 10.
61. Mark W. Hamilton, *Jesus, King of Strangers: What the Bible Really Says About Immigration,* 15.

migrants and hosts for the stranger who came to their door. They taught Israel that even when they thought they were home in Israel, they still were not permanent residents. Rabbi Jonathan Sacks calls this sense of being an exile even in one's own land, "the central, haunting irony of the Pentateuch."[62] One of God's requirements for possession of the land without succumbing to a new form of slavery necessitated securing the land without violating the rights of others. Instead, Yahweh required justice for the most vulnerable: the widow, the orphan, and the migrant. Robert Heimburger concludes, "A reading of Deuteronomy 10:12–22 demonstrates that right judgment for widows and orphans stands at the heart of divine justice. It also revealed that in Deuteronomy, reflecting Yahweh's love for migrants is at the center of what it means to be attuned to the God of the universe."[63] Key to the disagreement between the followers of MAGA Jesus and the Migrant 4 Life, Heimburger concludes, is that "[i]t appears that not only justice for the vulnerable but also justice and love for migrants remain requirements for every nation. If a nation is to continue possessing its land it cannot practice injustice toward migrants."[64] Babel forces each to answer Soelle's question where one primarily finds security: within the nation-state that fails to practice justice and mercy to the stranger or within God's embrace?

A. THE NATION-STATE MUST WELCOME THE MIGRANT 4 LIFE WITH JUSTICE AND MERCY.

In contrast to the restrictionist view, those who find biblical precepts inspiring greater hospitality and welcome to migrants and refugees point to the inclusion of the stranger, alien, or sojourner, within those vulnerable populations God wants humans to protect—the widow, the orphan, and the stranger. Those who follow the Migrant 4 Life do not accept the preeminence of the nation-state or read Romans 13:1–7 in the same light held by the restrictionists. First, prioritizing obedience misses Mark Hamilton's observation that Israel was unique in incorporating dissent because "[m]any biblical texts operate on the assumption that the ruled may critique the ruler in the light of transcendental ideals couched as divine revelation."[65] Smith-Christopher finds in Jesus' ministry the duty to oppose

---

62. Sacks, *God's Name, supra*, 186
63. Robert W. Heimburger, *God and the Illegal Alien, United States Immigration Law and a Theology of Politics*, 121.
64. *Ibid.*
65. Mark W. Hamilton, "Critiquing the Sovereign: Perspectives from Deuteronomy and Job 47," *Restoration Quarterly*, (2005), 237

positions that lead to violence against the other in the name of protecting our borders.[66]

The alternative Babel story that critiques unified power, should give pause to too literal a reading of Paul's language. Rarely do restrictionists read those seven verses in light of all of Paul's writings. Theodore Jennings points out that "a fragment of Paul's discourse has been isolated from the context of his argument as a whole in order to render the entire discourse harmless so far as world is concerned."[67] This short passage, written by a man imprisoned more than once by the Roman Empire and finally executed by the Empire, suggests that Paul's life provides a poor model for a reading that calls for submission and obedience. Significantly, most who cite this passage in Romans, typically only cite the first seven verses, leaving out verses 8–10. If one reads beyond verse 7, however, Paul tells us to "owe no one anything except to love one another; for the one who loves another has fulfilled the law." (Rom. 13:8). He concludes with "Love does not wrong to a neighbor; therefore, love is the fulfilling of the law." (Gen. 13:12).

Moreover, the New Testament provides little support for such a narrow reading of Romans 13:1–7. As Michael Budde comments, Christians are "members of a community broader than the largest nation-state."[68] He argues not that we disregard our family or proximate members of community—those for whom James Edwards argues we have a particular responsibility—but that "being a Christian, one's primary and formative loyalty, the one that contextualizes and defines the legitimacy of other claimants on allegiance and conscience—[are] those of class, nationality, and state. . . ."[69] Surprisingly, he echoes a voice from America's earliest days, that of Jonathan Edwards, who exhorted his parishioners that if any among them were poor, they should open their hand to their neighbor, specifically adding that the Levitical command refers not "only [to] those of their own nation, but even strangers and sojourners."[70] The Deuteronomist exhorted Israel to take care of those most vulnerable—the widow, the orphan, and the stranger—because Israel had known exile in Egypt. For Budde and Edwards, Christians should do likewise.

---

66. Smith-Christopher, *Jonah, supra,* xiii.

67. Theodore W. Jennings, Jr., *Outlaw Justice, The Messianic Politics of Paul,* 192.

68. Michael Budde, *Foolishness to Gentile: Essays on Empire, Nationalism and Discipleship,* 194.

69. *Ibid,* 193.

70. Jonathan Edwards, "Christian Charity or the Duty of Charity to the Poor, Explained and Enforced," (1732), https://biblebb.com/files/edwards/charity.htm

The biblical emphasis on exile undermines the conclusion that nationalism is the only response to Romans 13 as constitutive of the Christian experience.[71]

This debate between the relative prioritization of the realm of God and the nation-state coincides with the earliest debates within Christianity. Christianity has never fully resolved the distinction between the early Church of the first three centuries and its evolution after Constantine's legalization of Christianity in 313 (with the Edict of Milan) and Theodosius' adoption of Christianity around 380 as the religion of the Empire.[72] That debate continues to divide responses on immigration. Emperor Constantine's effort to unify the Roman Empire, in part, by embracing the Christian Church as a valid, non-subversive form of faith, transformed the Church significantly. That transformation expanded emphatically seven decades later.[73] What had been scattered local communities debating the meaning of the life of Jesus and the resulting Gospels, relying on voluntary contributions, grew into a religion with clergy paid by the Empire and basilicas and temples built by the Emperor, with a new unified Canon.[74]

Although scholars still argue regarding the extent of the change from multiple voices to a more unified one after establishment, the structural changes and the historical link of Christianity to the worldly Sovereign continues to influence voices engaged in interpreting that relationship to this day.[75] A. James Reimer observes the destructive consequence when politics and religion are fused in the nation-state: "true theology loses its own ground; it no longer witnesses to transcendent, revelatory norms by

---

71. Christopher L. Smith-Christopher, provides additional biblical critique of loyalty to the government in *A Biblical Theology of Exile*, 25–26

72. Christianity had been treated by the pagan Roman authorities for most of the first three centuries of its history as politically subversive (as a *superstitio*), enduring occasional active persecutions particularly under the emperors Septimius Severus, Decius, and, most notoriously, Diocletian. Constantine saw that Christianity was not only not politically subversive but could be the glue that helped hold the far-flung empire together. He involved himself in certain internal Church matters (such as the debate, at the Council of Nicaea in 325, regarding the nature of Jesus). By the time of Theodosius, the Church had achieved political hegemony across the Empire. [ed.]

73. For an expanded explanation of the effects of Constantine's edict, see Craig B. Mousin, "Constantine's Legacy: Preserving Empire While Undermining International Law", Slotte, P., & Haskell, J. eds., *Christianity and International Law: An Introduction*, 367–370, https://ssrn.com/abstract=3960335

74. David Dugan, *Constantine's Bible: Politics and the Making of the New Testament*, 115.

75. Rachel Mikva, *Dangerous, supra*, 131

which critically to evaluate political society and thereby sanctify finite, historical empires, nations, parties, movement, groups, and figures."[76] Those who follow the Migrant 4 Life continue to engage the multiple voices and challenge barriers that exclude the sojourner otherwise established by the nation-state.[77]

B. WELCOME THE STRANGER

Despite those restrictionists who distinguish between the stranger and the foreigner, receptionists who welcome the Migrant 4 Life stress the importance of hospitality for the stranger over the sovereignty of the nation-state. Both ends of the immigration debate recognize that God called Israel to care for the vulnerable. Again, they diverge in their conclusions of who comes within the mantle of the sojourner. Recall the distinction between the stranger and the foreigner raised by Hoffmeier.[78] In contrast, André LaCocque clarifies that the Bible situates the sojourner on par with widows and orphans: "Not only are they not to be oppressed (Ex. 22, 20; 23, 9), they are actually . . . to be treated with charity and love (Lev. 19, 33–34). They enjoy considerable privileges (Lev. 19, 10; 23, 22; Num. 9, 14; 15, 14f; 35, 15)."[79] In over 36 places, the Bible informs Israel to treat the stranger as the native or assure the safety of the widows, orphans and strangers.[80] Hoffmeier's distinction between the vulnerable stranger and the foreign enemy may sound appropriate in a twenty-first century nation-state, but the biblical emphasis on protection applies to both the *ger* and the *zar*. Perhaps the primary biblical example can be found in the Book of Ruth. André LaCocque points out that "Ruth the Moabite, metaphorically, excellently represents 'the other.'"[81] One can acknowledge that Hoffmeier accurately describes categories in ancient Israel, but Ruth demonstrates that the categories are less critical in the

---

76. A. James Reimer, "Trinitarian Orthodoxy, Constantinianism, and Theology from a Radical Protestant Perspective," in S. Mark Heim, ed., *Faith to Creed, Ecumenical Perspective on the Affirmation of the Apostolic Faith in the Fourth Century*, 158.

77. Daniel Smith-Christopher, *Jonah*, ("Jesus invites us to cross borders—often violating, for the sake of the gospel, the loyalties we humans have built to separate us from one another."), xviii.

78. See Hoffmeier, "Use and Abuse," *supra*.

79. André LaCocque, "The Stranger in the Old Testament" *Migration Today* 15 (1970) 56.

80. Jonathan Sacks, *The Dignity of Difference, How to Avoid the Clash of Civilizations*, 58.

81. André LaCocque, *Ruth: A Continental Commentary*, 3

response we owe the vulnerable. LaCocque adds that not only was Ruth, herself "a foreigner and also an enemy,"[82] but "the book of Ruth has something to say on the subject of judicial systems, and it certainly has something to say on the subject of the presence of foreigners among us. It recalls that God himself is on the side of immigrants, widows, orphans, the poor, and the marginal."[83]

Indeed, Patrick Miller states "the stranger no less than the sister/brother or neighbor, is a *moral category*, one whose very existence in the midst of a community requires certain modes of response."[84] Significantly, the response goes beyond mere kindness to another. Rabbi Jonathan Sacks acknowledges such response to the other is not easy or instinctual, but he argues this may be that "*We encounter God in the face of a stranger.* That, I believe, is the Hebrew Bible's single greatest and most counterintuitive contribution to ethics. God creates difference; therefore, it is in one-who-is-different that we meet God."[85] We may live in particular communities and have responsibilities to members of those communities, but the stranger offers an opportunity distinctly different.

Too often, those who name the alien in the United States as an illegal alien invent modern categories that do not fit within the biblical narrative. In some ways the argument stems from disagreement about facts as much as about biblical interpretation. Of the almost 10 million persons assumed to be undocumented immigrants residing in the United States, over two-thirds have lived here for more than ten years.[86] Some studies of those young people eligible for DACA protection and their families found significant numbers eligible for other immigration remedies. Those folks, paying taxes, attending our schools, working in our communities, worshipping with us seem more comparable to the *gerim* than the unproven appellation of illegal alien. Mark Hamilton undermines the significance of calling those residing here illegal aliens: "The migrant does not appear in law as a problem, but as a welcome guest that, if anything, gives the redeemed people opportunity to demonstrate their gratitude to Yahweh for the exodus and to each other their commitment to generous, ethical lives."[87]

---

82. *Ibid.*
83. *Ibid.* 154.
84. Patrick Miller "Israel As Host to Strangers, 549
85. Sacks, *Dignity, supra*, 59.
86. Jens Manuel Krogstad, Jeffrey S. Passel and D'Vera Cohbn, "5 facts about illegal immigration in the U.S." (2016): https://www.pewresearch.org/short-reads/2019/06/12/5-facts-about-illegal-immigration-in-the-u-s/
87. Mark Hamilton, *Jesus*, 97.

Seeing God in the face of the stranger underscores our shared humanity. In the New Testament, Jesus' parable of the Good Samaritan underscores the power of love over law, mercy over regulation, and the call to be a neighbor to all, even one's enemies (Luke 10:29–37).[88] Modeling how a biblical dialogue leads to new truths, a lawyer questions Jesus to define one's neighbor. In response, Jesus shares a story. The road from Jerusalem to Jericho found three persons walking away from Jerusalem. Each saw a stranger who had been beaten and left to die. Jesus gives no identification of the man's nationality or ethnicity. The Priest and the Levite walk by without offering any aid. Under the Torah, the written law prohibited either to offer immediate assistance.[89] For Brad Young, those that followed the law abandoned the wounded person, just as the robbers had abandoned him.[90] In contrast, the Samaritan stops and seeks a way to heal. Given the cultural assumptions held by many who heard Jesus tell this story, many believed Samaritans did not follow the written law, and it would be likely, the Samaritan would be the least likely to stop and offer aid.[91] Steven Notley and Jeffrey P. García stress the critical significance of naming a Samaritan as the one who heals: "For a community that is routinely regarded as not observing the commandments with exactness, the Samaritan's mercy on behalf of one who is likely an ethnic foreigner to him is intended to be particularly acute in a Jewish setting."[92] Young adds that the law may have even put the Samaritan at greater risk as many would have assumed he had attacked the wounded man.[93]

The Parable of the Good Samaritan rebuts the legal distinction offered by the those refusing to welcome the sojourner in contemporary society. The restrictionists seek to rebut this fundamental biblical ethic of welcome by distinguishing the immigrants and asylum-seekers they wish to deport as illegal aliens, and thus, not analogous to the *gerim* whom the Bible bids us welcome. National boundaries or legal status, however, did not influence the Samaritan's response. For LaCocque, Jesus' response

---

88. This section builds on an earlier discussion of the import of the Good Samaritan story with regard to our duty to the immigrant or asylum-seeker, in Mousin, "Constantine's Legacy," *supra* 390–91.

89. Brad H. Young, *The Parables, Jewish Tradition and Christian Interpretation*, 107, 110.

90. *Ibid.*

91. *Ibid* at 103.

92. Steven Notley and Jeffrey P. García, "'But a Samaritan . . . Had Compassion': Jesus, Early Christianity, and the Samaritans" in *The Samaritans A Biblical People*.

93. Young, *Parables*, supra, 117.

"transcends all legal definitions"[94] as "even one's enemy can become one's neighbor"[95] Young notes, "In order to understand or define the meaning of neighbor . . . one must first become a neighbor. One discovers a strong reciprocity in the sense that to define neighbor one must first become a neighbor."[96]

C. STEWARDSHIP OF NATIONAL RESOURCES.

In the restrictionist's view that the state has a responsibility to protect, they underscore the need to uphold the rule of law and to defend against a purported invasion of national borders and addressing undocumented persons subsequently living within the land. Those who welcome the Migrant 4 Life emphasize that protecting the rule of law has led to consequences where the nation breaks its own laws as well as commitments it has covenanted with under international law. Billions of dollars are expended for detention and deportation, but much less to ensuring that the rule of law as implemented by immigration courts, asylum offices or the first contact at ports of entry are implemented properly. Due process of law and fundamental fairness wilt in the shadow of intense enforcement tactics.[97] The restrictionists call for stewardship to protect the family, but ignore that the human family suffers under strict enforcement and law enforcement impunity when laws are violated in the name of national security.[98]

Carol Swain argues, "illegal aliens who have entered our country without our consent have broken our law and diminished respect for the rule of law."[99] Indeed, these individuals lose almost their human status, let alone dignity, when they get reduced to simply being called illegals.[100] Certainly,

---

94. André LaCocque, "Jesus's Hermeneutics of the Law: Reading the Parable of the Good Samaritan," in *Creation, Life, and Hope: Essays in Honor of Jacques Doukhan*, Jiri Moskala, ed., 267–68. *See also*, Northley, *supra* at 69: The Good Samaritan parable teaches, "in instances of human need and acts of mercy, ethnic/national distinctions are of little importance."

95. André LaCocque, *Jesus, the Central Jew,* 121, *See also*, Smith-Christopher, Exile, 9.

96. Young, *supra*, 117. *See also*, Francis, "*Fratelli Tutti.*" *supra*, 56–86.

97. Reece Jones, *Nobody is Protected, How the Border Patrol Became the Most Dangerous Police Force in the United States*, 234.

98. Craig B. Mousin, "Episode One, Portland, What Border are We Defending," *Lawful Assembly*," March 29, 2021: https://lawfulassembly.buzzsprout.com/1744949/8231859-episode-1-portland-what-border-are-we-defending

99. Carol Swain, *Be the People, A Call to Reclaim America's Faith and Promise*, 16."

100. Ralph Drollinger, Letter to the Cabinet, Senate, and House Bible Studies, January 26, 2019, (Accordingly, in God's eyes, our President has every biblical right to

Christians will vary in interpretations of Scripture, but the restrictionists put their thumb on the scale tilting the debate against illegal aliens. Their reliance on the term illegal alien undermines their reliance on Scripture by commodifying human beings as illegals rather than as persons created in God's image. Moreover, such a claim misunderstands United States law. Our nation prides itself that as a nation under law, every person is innocent until proven guilty. Although immigration is a civil proceeding, one cannot be deported or removed absent an adjudication by an immigration judge that one has violated the law. Significantly, immigration and refugee law remain quite complex with many grounds for removal—conditions or actions by one seeking admission that make them ineligible for admission or remaining in the United States.[101]

Restrictionists, moreover, misread a fundamental reality of the biblical story. I previously engaged in a thought experiment, asking what would have happened if United States immigration law were in effect at the time of the Bible. Surprisingly, almost every major biblical protagonist from Abraham and Sarah to Saint Paul would have been excluded or deported for an immigration law violation. Many, such as Moses, had committed crimes such as murder. St. Paul persecuted early Christians. Others such as Noah and Ruth had life events that would make them excludable or deportable under United States law.[102] Jesus may have violated more provisions of immigration law than anyone else—any single one would have been enough to remove him from the story, but cumulatively, would have made him what the restrictionists call an illegal alien. I asked whom are we keeping out today by a strict enforcement of our immigration law?

In the current day, moreover, the law also contains numerous remedies that may lead to citizenship, even if one entered without authorization. Most importantly, the Refugee Act of 1980, which brought the United States into compliance with the Convention for Refugees, explicitly states that the Attorney General will provide a process for discerning eligibility for asylum to one seeking asylum "irrespective of status."[103] The nation-states of

---

construct a wall in order to keep out illegals." (emphasis in original). https://capmin.org/wp-content/uploads/2019/01/The-Bible-and-The-Wall-by-Ralph-Drollinger-2019.pdf

101. For a summary of United States immigration law, see Craig B. Mousin, "Immigration Reform: What Can Religious Voices Require of the State," in Collier and Strain, *Perspectives, supra,* 331–33.

102. Craig B. Mousin, "You Were Told to Love the Immigrant, But What if the Story Never Happened? Hospitality and United States Immigration Law," *Vincentian Heritage Journal*: Vol. 33: Iss. 1, Article 8 (2016).

103. 8 U.S.C.§ 1185 (a)(1).

the world that adopted the Convention and Protocol, recalled the horrors of the Holocaust where refugees were trapped and unable to cross borders, only to be thrown back to the persecutor's punishment. Asylum-seekers fleeing persecution who are forced to cross borders without inspection would seem to meet Swain's definition of illegal alien, but not the definition set out by United States immigration law. The law provides them with a legal process to ascertain their eligibility even if they evaded inspection in crossing the border precisely to protect them from future persecution.

In addition, immigration laws provided additional remedies beyond asylum. One study demonstrated that when young undocumented persons applied for DACA status, an Obama administration process that permitted eligible minors who had been brought to this nation by their parents without lawful authorization to apply for a temporary status, over 14% had other immigration remedies, but had been unable to access appropriate legal services to allow them to gain lawful resident status prior to DACA.[104] These minor children brought to this nation by family members have lived almost their entire lives as members of communities. They have attended our schools, graduated and served communities as nurses, doctors, lawyers, teachers, and in many areas of commerce. Their very presence and interaction with others provide a contemporary living example of the biblical *gerim*—vulnerable sojourners in our midst who continue to contribute to the common good.

In the name of enforcement and the goal of full border security, we have built a massive Border Wall—a Tower of Babel—that mimics the arrogance of the original story. This Babel Border wall also fulfills the imperialism that Rabbi Sacks found so telling in the Genesis story. Our nation's historical military and economic intervention in Central and South American nations includes exploitation of human labor and natural resources. It continues today. The United States has funded authoritarian governments that have violated human rights during civil wars, taught torture, and forced many communities from their native land.[105] Should we be surprised that many flee violence and seek asylum elsewhere only to face a Border Wall or legal policies that establish a secondary barrier that undermines our lawful commitments to refugees?

---

104. Donald Kerwin, Roberto Surao, Tess Thorman, and Daniela Alulema, "The DACA Era and the Continuous Legalization Work of the US Immigrant-Serving Community," February 8, 2017: https://cmsny.org/wp-content/uploads/2017/02/CMS-Legalization-Report-FINAL.pdf

105. For additional information on United States policy, see Mousin, *Hospitality*, *supra* n at text between n. 162 and 166.

In addition, the planet faces an existential crisis as climate change threatens long standing agricultural production, desertification of the formerly fertile soil, and displacement from land by floods and landslides caused by the ever-changing weather.[106] The nations in the northern half of the globe bear responsibility for much of the carbon in the atmosphere now accelerating climate change.[107] Yet when we build a wall to prohibit those seeking safety, we fail to acknowledge our responsibility for the breakdown of civil society and the rule of law in those nations that leads to asylum-seekers fleeing for safety. Stewardship extends beyond seeking to protect one's family or town. Receptionists believe stewardship for the entire human family and the earth itself will meet both the goals of protecting one's family and lead to a flourishing of the entire human family and the renewal of the earth as well.

V A Return to the Covenant: From Debate to Dialogue

One conclusion almost all involved in the immigration debate can agree on is that current immigration law is broken. When Christians who follow MAGA Jesus and Migrant 4 Life find themselves as opposites in a debate culled from Scripture, they construct the logjam that has frustrated decades of attempts to reach immigration reform that fixes the problem. Mediator Kenneth Cloke proposes that to end political polarization and paralysis, participants must move from debate to dialogue.[108] In mediator's parlance, participants need to move from concretized positions that stake out opposing sides in a debate to shared interests.[109] Christians historically found new meaning through self-critical interpretation of Scripture.[110] Given our scriptural foundations, we can find our common elements to begin to shift the debate to dialogue. First we can try to reframe the debate.

---

106. Abrahm Lustgarten, "The Great Climate Migration," *New York Times Magazine*, July 23, 2020: https://www.nytimes.com/interactive/2020/07/23/magazine/climate-migration.html

107. Laura Cozzi, Olivia Chen, and Hyeji Kim, "The World's Top 1% of emitters produce over 1000 times more CO2 than the bottom 1%," (February 22, 2023), https://www.iea.org/commentaries/the-world-s-top-1-of-emitters-produce-over-1000-times-more-co2-than-the-bottom-1

108. Kenneth Cloke, *Dance of Opposites*, 238–246.

109. *See, e.g.,* Roger Fisher and William Ury with Bruce Patton, ed., *Getting to Yes, Negotiating Agreement Without Giving In*, 42–46.

110. Rachel Mikva, *Dangerous, supra* 196.

Restrictionists pose the debate as law and order versus those who propose open borders. Much of the contemporary thinking on immigration responds to their perception that those who favor immigration too often are simply open border cosmopolitans seeking a universal world, and therefore, undermine any immigration legislation. Receptionists protest that the enforcement priority undermines the rule of law, yet rarely pose the argument in terms of open borders. Restrictionists rarely cite any Christian receptionists who argue for open borders. Note the caution Michael Budde asserts when examining the role of Jesus, Mary, and Joseph in the biblical story: "Perhaps Christians should dare to raise the prospect of open immigration as something worth exploring."[111] Suggesting that receptionists only want open borders appears to be a debater's ploy rather than address the receptionist's plea to reduce the budgets that militarize the border and transfer funds to a humanitarian and more efficient regulation of the border in conjunction with a comprehensive immigration reform that meets society's contemporary needs.[112]

It is often unsaid or remains unclear at what point in United States history the MAGA Jesus claims America was great and needs to now be replicated. Perhaps it might be best to return to one of the nation's first Christian documents, John Winthrop's lay 1630 sermon. Like Scripture, its historiography of interpretation reveals substantial disagreements on his original meaning. Most recently, Ronald Reagan and his admirers adopted the "city on a hill" as a touchstone for the American greatness that the MAGA Jesus and his followers seek today. Yet Reagan's interpretation of Winthrop was only one more iteration of that sermon, and an incomplete one at best.[113] Perhaps it is best to return to Winthrop to gain a fuller context of his aspirations for what would make his new society succeed in living up to its covenant with God and provide a foundation for dialogue.

Winthrop knew that he and his band were immigrating to escape the corruption of the world's greatest military and cultural power of its day. He saw Israel's Exodus experience as a model to follow. The Puritans had mixed religious and secular motives, in leaving England, but central to

---

111. Budde, Michael L., "'Who is My Mother?' Family, Nation, Discipleship, and Debates on Immigration," The Journal of Scriptural Reasoning (2011). 8. http://jti.lib.virginia.edu/journals/ssr/branches/wordpress/issues/volume10/number1/ssr10_01_e03.html.

112. The National Immigrant Justice Center offers five ways a humanitarian approach to immigration could effectively address the current issues at the border: https://immigrantjustice.org/staff/blog/solutions-humane-border-policy

113. Rodgers, *Lay Sermon, supra*, 234.

those who agreed to the covenant, was to model a new life in covenant with God. Winthrop argued that they adopt the generous and liberal belief in a Christian's duty of living under charitable principles based on the Deuteronomy 15. Marilynne Robinson argues, our often crabbed and pejorative recall of Puritans as harsh, morose, and punitive people misreads how they anticipated responding to God's grace with generous liberality of the gifts God had bestowed on them.[114] Winthrop knew that human finitude, fatigue, and greed would tempt them to fail, especially in light of the difficulties a new land would bring, yet his sermon posed that challenge. His city on a hill language, far from boasting of a yet unachieved American exceptionalism, instead contemplated that the eyes of the world would be upon them as a congregation gathered, as of a city on a hill, to see if they could craft a more perfect community within God's vision or whether they would they fail.

His fear of failure inspired him to counsel, "for we must consider that we shall be as a City upon a Hill, the eyes of all people are upon us."[115] The phrase has resonated for three hundred years highlighting both our perceived belief that we were chosen as a new people to accomplish great things. Many forget, that in humility, Winthrop concluded, "if we deal falsely with our God in this work we have undertaken and so cause him to withdraw his present help from us, we shall shame the faces of many of God's worthy servants, and cause their prayers to be turned into Curses upon us till we be consumed out of the good land whither we are going."[116] Given how the city on the hill became a metaphor for American exceptionalism, many have forgotten or never learned that if we fail to do justice that we are undeserving of this land and should be forced out into exile. Much like the challenge Israel faced in living in the Promised Land but called to not harm the sojourner, Winthrop knew they had adopted a challenging goal. Winthrop, like his biblical predecessors, feared failure if they just took the land and did not offer an open hand of generosity. He concluded that should they fail to live up to the covenant's call to justice, then God would surely hurl them back into the sea.

The Migrant 4 Life followers ask those who claim the MAGA Jesus and other restrictionists if our response to new waves of immigrants and asylum-seekers have lived up to the generosity of that covenant. The Puritans knew the call of Deuteronomy 15 to ensure all those created in the

114. Robinson, *Books, supra* 78–79.
115. John Winthrop, "A Model of Christian Charity," quoted in Robert N. Bellah, *The Broken Covenant, American Civil Religion in Time of Trial,"* 2nded., 15.
116. *Ibid.*

image of God were cared for by the community. The Deuteronomist and the Puritan knew well that the vicissitudes of life would lead to differences in wealth and poverty, economic security and vulnerability. The call to welcome the stranger, to treat the stranger as the native, to ensure that the orphan, the widow, and the sojourner were cared for exists precisely because humans often fail to live lives of justice for all. Hence, Winthrop's call to charity—kindness and care.

Winthrop's charity did not mean, as many restrictionists claim, to simply open borders. He later penned a defense of immigration rules that would regulate admission to the colony. He was Governor when the colony exiled Roger Williams for contesting Puritan orthodoxy. But he also laid the seeds of a future refugee policy, noting immigration policy should include elements of mercy.[117]

VI Conclusion

Although the positions of the followers of Migrant 4 Life and MAGA Jesus fall on opposite ends of the immigration debate, one interest they share is a concern for the vulnerable. They disagree, however, on whom the vulnerable are and how we respond to their needs. Perhaps Constantine's decision to unify the Roman Empire through the legalization of an outlaw religion—Christianity—and bring its followers within the political body provides an example of bridging the divide in our nation. Offering legalization to the millions of undocumented within our nation and providing the DACA members a path to citizenship will not only reap benefits, but may also help secure our borders and enable more effective and just resolution of immigration and asylum applicants.

Roman Catholic Social Thought invites the debate between national security and welcoming the stranger. Some critique its emphasis on national security as going too far to stifle the breadth of the welcome. Yet, it provides a framework for Christian followers of MAGA Jesus and the Migrant 4 Life to balance national security with hospitality. Indeed, the structure of our current immigration law, if properly implemented and enforced, retains elements for applying Christian principles to immigration. A comprehensive immigration law would foster family reunification and economic growth through welcoming family and employment visas to meet the needs of our economy.

---

117. John Winthrop, "John Winthrop on Restriction on Immigration," *Puritan Political Ideas, 1558–1794*, Edmund S. Morgan, ed., 146

Providing a path to citizenship for the DACA applicants and their families as well as the many undocumented who have become the modern *gerim*, those living here for many years, paying taxes, contributing to our communities, would truly welcome the stranger and strengthen the common good. We could reduce pressures at our borders by shifting our funding priorities from deportation and detention to humanitarian reception of asylum-seekers with increasing emphasis on due process adjudication at the border. In so doing, we would live up to our commitments to refugees who seek our land due to climate change or military and economic exploitation, and adapting our refugee law to respond to twenty-first century challenges. Finally, could we join with Pope Francis in greeting those at our borders with "a place of welcome, protection or accompaniment, promotion and integration for all?"[118] Perhaps, then we can follow what Andre LaCocque calls the lesson of the book of Ruth: "the generous interpretation of the reality regarding a foreigner overflows the ethnic boundaries and transforms the view of the world."[119]

---

118. Francis, *supra*.
119. LaCocque, *supra*, Ruth, 5.

FIG 5 David Stern, *Snow Crash (Lost Agency)*, 2018-19. Acrylics and pigments on paper, 27 × 35 inches © David Stern / Artists Rights Society (ARS), New York

4 / Welcoming the Stranger in Islam: Abrahamic Hospitality and Contemporary Implications

ZEKI SARITOPRAK

In Islam, taking care of the needy and giving alms to those whose situation is worse than yours are fundamental aspects of the faith. Most people are aware that *zakat*, compulsory charity, is one of the five pillars of Islam. The Qur'an says: "*Zakat* is for the poor and needy, those who work to collect [it], those whose hearts are inclined to the truth [i.e. new converts to Islam], the freeing of slaves, those in debt, those who fight in God's way, and the traveler. God has ordained it. God is All-Knowing, All-Wise (9:60; see also 2:177). Indeed, many verses of the Qur'an remind people of the importance of taking care of those in need while showing the rewards for such charity. Beyond this, Islam gives paramount importance to social harmony and charity is one way of building bridges between those of means and those without. There is a well-known hadith in which the Prophet is asked: "Which act in Islam is the best?" He responded "To give food and to greet everyone with 'peace' whether you know them or you do not." (al-Bukhari, hadith no: 28)[1] On another occasion, the Prophet told his followers that they should "not disdain or trivialize any good deed no matter how small it might seem, even just smiling [is such

---

1. "*Hadith*" refers to a unique body of literature in Islam, of which there is not quite an equivalent in Jewish or Christian literature. It is not the revealed word of God, as the Qur'an is, but neither is it merely the interpretive man-made literature associated with a range of schools (*madhab*s) of jurisprudence that constitute *shar'ia*. Hadith typically records words of the Prophet Muhammad (in his own right, rather than as a conduit through which God is speaking) and/or features him as a key figure in a given narrative. Thus hadiths carry heavy weight in Muslim thought, offering expansions of ideas—and sometimes exfoliations of verses—offered in the Qur'an. [ed.]

a deed]." (Muslim, hadith no: 2626) So even the simple act of smiling at someone on the street is a positive act. These are universal principles that were valid at the time of the Prophet and are at least as important if not more important today in our society.

If we are to explore the importance of welcoming the stranger in Islam, we should start by addressing what the main source of Islam, the Holy Qur'an, says about the subject. In the Qur'an there are many instances of hospitality and taking care of the needy and strangers. Of these, perhaps one of the most important and succinct verses discussing the idea of welcoming strangers in Islam, is the following. "Worship God and associate nothing with Him, and do good to parents, and to relatives, orphans, the needy, the neighbor who is kin, the neighbor who is a stranger, the companion at your side, the traveler, and those whom your right hands possess. Indeed, God does not like those who are proud and boastful" (4:36; see also 2:215, 17:26) The term that is used here for traveler is *ibn al-sabil* and literally means the "son of the way," which is generally understood as a person who has traveled significantly, i.e. someone who has traveled outside of his or her own hometown or region. Commentators on the Qur'an describe this term in several ways. In his commentary on Qur'an chapter 9 verse 60 (see above), Ibn Kathir discusses *ibn al-sabil* by describing him or her as "travelers [sic] passing a city who have nothing which helps them to continue on their journey, even if they have property in their home city" (Ibn Kathir vol. 4, 169). Broadly speaking, then, someone who is an *ibn al-sabil* is a traveler who is not in his or her hometown being in need or not in need. God commands one to be kind and do what is beautiful to those travelers because they are in a situation of strangeness and need and they cannot find the things that they had in their home countries. Given its prominence in this verse, it is clear that care for the travelling stranger, no matter his or her circumstances, is an important element of Islamic faith.

Another word in the Islamic tradition for strangers is *gharib* (pl. *ghuraba*). The Prophet of Islam praised strangers; he personally took care of them when they arrived in his city. Several narrators recorded versions of the same story of the Prophet speaking of the *ghuraba*. In one version, the Prophet said: "'Blessed are the strangers.' The companions asked, 'Who are the strangers?' The Prophet responded: 'The strangers are the people who are stripped of their family and relatives'" (Ibn Majah, hadith no: 3388). Another hadith, narrated by the prominent companion Abu Huraira, expands on this idea and further explains why strangers are blessed in Islam. He reported that the Prophet said, "Islam began as something strange [i.e. as a small minority] and it will return to being strange, so blessed are the strangers." (Muslim, hadith no: 145. A similar hadith is found in Ibn Majah, hadith no: 3987)

In his book on the concept of *fitan* (trials, tribulations, turmoil, etc.), Nuaym bin Hammad (d. 843CE), an early Islamic scholar and hadith collector, records a valuable statement that Abdullah bin Umar narrated from the Prophet on the theological meaning of *ghuraba*. The Prophet said "Of the people, the most beloved to God are the strangers." The Prophet then was asked, who is a stranger? He responded: "Those who escape oppression because of their religion and get together around Jesus, the son of Mary" (Hammad, vol. 1, p 77). From the theological context, it is clear that the Prophet is describing a time of turmoil during which people will be forced to migrate due to oppression and leave their homes and property. The exact timing of this is only known to God, but it is near the end of time, when Muslims believe that Jesus will descend from Heaven to Earth to bring justice. These refugees will gather around Jesus. The exact meaning of this narration is elusive, but perhaps the gathering around Jesus is symbolic of the message of Jesus: love and mercy. Hence, people who embrace Jesus' message of love and mercy will be open to accepting these refugees. In my book *Islam's Jesus*, I prefer to interpret such a hadith allegorically and not literally, to mean that dialogue among Christians, Muslims, and Jews can bring a time of peace where strangers are welcome and oppression ends and the flow of refugees will be prevented.

In addition to this, we should briefly mention that in Islamic ethics, the guest is known as the guest of God. Some would say that this is because, religiously speaking, guests bring blessings with them. Additionally, there is a famous hadith that says: "Those who believe in God and the Day of Judgement let them honor their guests." In other words, if you believe in God and the Day of Judgement, you must honor your guests. This is therefore a central principle not just of Islamic theology, but of the Islamic ethical tradition as well.

Let us now turn to some examples of welcoming the stranger. The Islamic tradition has a well-developed literature on the proper care and welcoming of strangers. There are many examples from the Qur'an, hadith, and later Islamic history and I will not be able to mention them all. It is important to start with the Prophet of Islam's treatment of strangers and the destitute. Even in the earliest days of the Prophet's prophethood, there is ample evidence to easily conclude that most of the people who accepted his message were strangers, *al-ghuraba* in Mecca. Apparently, the elite group from Mecca were not happy with the Prophet's fondness and care for these social outcasts many of whom were from the lowest rungs of society in Mecca, the *al-Mawali*, the slaves and servants. The Meccan elite told him that they would accept him if he kept these strangers and poor people away from him. A Qur'anic verse came and rejected their request. The verse says: "Do not repel those who call upon their Lord in the morning and in the evening, seeking His countenance. You are not accountable for them and they are not accountable to you. If you do repel them, [then you will] be among the wrongdoers. (6:52) Muqatil bin Sulaiman's *tafsir* records that this verse about *al-ghuraba* among the companions of the Prophet was revealed when Abu Jahl, a stern opponent of the Prophet said, "Look at the those who are following Muhammad. They are our slaves and some Bedouins, and [other] humiliated people. If he accepted only the elite and the leaders of the tribes, we would have followed him." They asked the Prophet's uncle, Abu Talib, to tell him this and to repel them. He told the Prophet what they had said and then the Qur'anic verse came as a divinely-ordained response.[2] (Muqatil bin Sulaiman, v 1, p. 563)

Such sentiment was common among the elites of Mecca and those who know Islamic history will know that, due to persecution faced by the small Muslim community in Mecca, they were forced to flee to the city that would later become known as Medina. The Muslim migration (*hijra*, in Arabic; see below) to Medina illustrates many instances of care for strangers. It starts with the care the newly arriving Muslim refugees were shown by the citizens of Medina. The Qur'an says "But those who before them had homes (in Medina) and had adopted the Faith showed their affection to those who came to them for refuge, and entertained no desire in their hearts for things given to the (latter), but gave them preference over themselves, even though poverty was theirs [i.e. they were in poverty themselves]. And those saved from the covetousness of their own souls, they are the ones who achieve prosperity" (59:9). Despite the hard circumstances faced by both the newly arrived Muslims and the previous residents of Medina, because of their goodness and kindness to each other, they were taken care of and their needs were met. Abu Huraira again narrates that when they were in Medina the Prophet said: "The food for two persons is sufficient for three, and the food of three persons is sufficient for four." (al-Bukhari, hadith no: 5329)

The Prophet's care for the poor and strangers was a constant occurrence in Mecca and continued after his community's migration to Medina. In Medina, there was a place adjacent to the mosque of the Prophet that was available for strangers, the poor and destitute. This was famously known as the *Suffa*. It is believed that the number of people who took

2. *Tafsir* is exegesis; qur'anic *tafsir* offers elucidation, and explanation of the revealed text. It is somewhat analogous to rabbinic *midrash*.[ed.]

shelter there totaled more than 400. The Prophet would bring these people food and cook for them. In addition, some of the Prophet's companions who were financially stable would bring them to their homes to feed them.

The Qur'an is also replete with examples of proper care for strangers and travelers. The two most famous of these are the stories of the Prophets Joseph and Moses. Joseph and his story is found in chapter 12 of the Qur'an, which is named after him. Like most prophetic narratives, Joseph's story in the Qur'an is similar to what is found in the Bible, with subtle differences. Joseph was put into a well due to the jealousy of his brothers and he was found by a caravan. He was taken to Egypt where was sold in a market for a small amount of money. The Qur'an tells us that the king [pharaoh] of Egypt and his wife were the ones to purchase him. The Qur'an recounts their conversation: "And the Egyptian who bought him, said to his wife: 'Make his stay comfortable, perhaps he will profit us or we shall adopt him as a son.' Thus did We establish Joseph in the land, that We might teach him the interpretation of events. And God has full control over His affairs but most people do not know" (12:21).

To summarize, the Qur'anic narrative continues to relate how, eventually, Joseph proves his loyalty to the king and his expertise in affairs of state and he rises to be in the second highest position in Egypt. He is eventually reunited with his family and gives thanks to God saying: "My Lord, You have given me the kingdom and taught me the meaning of dreams. You are the Creator of the heavens and the earth. You are my Protector in this world and in the next. Make me die a *muslim* and unite me with the righteous ones" (12:101).[3] The story of Joseph shows how God made him a stranger and then a minister in Egypt who himself took care of strangers. This is important for showing the proper relationship between strangers and their hosts. For the host, being kind to those in need can bring great benefit to the host person or country. We see this same thing countless times in our own world today.

Perhaps the best-known of the prophetic stories is the account of Moses's migration from Egypt to Midian due to the oppression of Pharaoh.[4]

---

3. The term "*muslim*" means "one who submits/surrenders [to the will of God]" in Arabic. In English-language orthography one can distinguish that word with a miniscule "m," as referring to anyone who submits to God's will, from the word with a majuscule "M," which refers to one who adheres specifically to the principles of Islam as initiated by the Prophet Muhammad. [ed.]

4. In the Qur'anic language, Pharaoh is used as a proper name for the Egyptian ruler and not a title as it is often used in English, i.e. the Pharaoh Ramses. I am using Pharaoh here as a name and hence the omission of the definite article.

The outlines of Moses's story are well known from Exodus and the story in the Qur'an generally matches the Exodus story. In the Qur'an we find most of this story in chapter 28. The chapter begins by describing Pharaoh and his associates as criminals for dividing people. "We recite to you from the news of Moses and Pharaoh in truth for a people who believe. Indeed, Pharaoh exalted himself in the land and made its people into factions, oppressing a sector among them, slaughtering their [newborn] sons and keeping their females alive. Indeed, he was of the criminals. And We wanted to confer favor upon those who were oppressed in the land and make them leaders and make them inheritors and establish them in the land and show Pharaoh and Haman and their soldiers through them that which they had feared." (28:3–6)[5]

The chapter then gives us a description of Moses's mother and how Moses came to live in the court of Pharaoh. The Qur'an does not give details regarding his life at the court of Pharaoh, but skips to the moment when Moses, due to striking and accidentally killing one of Pharaoh's men who was arguing with a member of Moses's people (i.e. the Children of Israel), is forced to flee for his safety (28:15–20). The Qur'an recounts the prayer that Moses gave when he feared that he would be captured as he fled, "Lord protect me from the wrongdoing people" (28:21), and tells how he hopes for God's guidance "Perhaps my Lord will show me the right path" (28:22).

Now a refugee, he finds himself in the town of Midian where he meets two girls and helps them to water their sheep (28:23). This is followed by another prayer: "My Lord! Truly, I am in need of whatever good that You send down to me" (28:24). The shepherdesses take Moses to see their father, Suyab (Jethro), who says to Moses: "Fear not. You have escaped from the wrongdoing people" (28:25). Here in the Qur'an we have Moses as a refugee exemplifying the actions a refugee should take: to pray for God's assistance and to be of service to those a refugee meets along his way. It also outlines the response and responsibility of the host: to take in the refugee and give him or her shelter. Moses also exemplifies the condition of being a refugee and an immigrant (*muhajir*). *Muhajir* comes from the word *hijra*, which has been translated as both migration and emigration. In its verb form and as an active participle, the root h-j-r, from which *hijra* is derived, is mentioned several times in the Qur'an. This is

---

5. It is worthy of note that the Qur'an puts the pharaoh and Haman—the villain in the biblical Book of Esther, set in Persia nearly a millennium after the story of Moses in Egypt—in the same verse. For God, of course, time and space are not limited in the linear (past-present-future) manner in which they flow for humans. [ed.]

certainly in keeping with the idea found in Exodus 22:21 "Do not mistreat or oppress a stranger, for you were strangers in Egypt."

If we move from this to look more broadly at theological and legal issues related to the care of strangers and those in need, we find that an essential element of the Islamic faith is the protection of the life of innocent individuals. From a theological perspective, this includes strangers, migrants and refugees all of whom are considered innocent and hence must be protected. A further religious duty of those who are financially able to do so is to give shelter to those in need. Refugees, in turn, are bound by certain rules and laws. Classical Islamic jurists elaborated on some of these cases. For instance, al-Sarakhsi (d. 1090), a famous Hanafi jurist, said:

> [I]f a Muslim enters a foreign abode [*dar al-harb*], having been given asylum, and found a treasure, if they found this in the house of some of the people they will return it to them. What is in the house belongs to the owner of the house. By accepting the asylum contract, they have guaranteed that they will not betray the trust. Therefore, they are obliged to fulfill what they promised. (al-Sarakhsi vol. 2, 215)

Similarly, Akmal al-Din al-Babarti (d. 1384) said: "When Muslims enter a foreign abode, as traders, it is not permissible for them to harm their property or lives because they guaranteed that they will not do them any harm. Attacking after this contract is treachery and treachery is *haram* [forbidden]" (al-Babarti vol. 7, 17). Such legal pronouncements provide important guardrails for both parties and show how the care for strangers and one's conduct as a stranger are integral parts of Islamic jurisprudence.

Perhaps few stories from Islamic history better outline the important relationship between strangers and their hosts than the story of a group of early Muslims and their experience at the court of the King of Abyssinia, which is modern day Ethiopia. This story of the migration of about seventy of the Prophet's followers to Abyssinia, and their kind treatment by the Christian king of that land not only is historically important in the survival of Islam and the Islamic community, but it also tells us much about Islam and the proper treatment of strangers. Ummu Salama, who later married the Prophet, narrates the experience of those who left Mecca for Abyssinia. After describing how the Prophet had asked them to flee Mecca for Abyssinia and how they found kindness there, she talks about how the *Quraysh*, the ruling class of Mecca, sent a delegation of two people and a variety of gifts in order to gain the king's agreement to allow them to take the Muslim refugees back to Mecca. She details their experience at the court of the Abyssinian Negus or King in this way:

After visiting the patriarchs and eventually the King they [the Quraysh] said 'O King, some young people left our city. They have innovated a new religion. It is different from your religion and the religion of our grandfathers and we know nothing about it. They have divided our people and they came to you so that you would protect them. Return them to us so that we can return them to their relatives and their tribes.' The religious advisers of the King said, 'They speak the truth, O King. Return them because these two know their people better.' The King, became angry. He said 'I will never do this to a certain group of people who take refuge in my land.' The King brought all members of the group together and invited his advisers and bishops and the Meccan delegation, as well. Then he asked the Muslim refugees questions. He said: 'These people claim that you have left their religion and you do not follow my religion nor the religion of Judaism. So tell me about the religion by which you left your people.' Ja'far bin Abi Talib, the cousin of the Prophet, spoke on behalf of the group and said: 'We were part of their religion and their tradition. God has sent to us a Messenger. We know his lineage, his truthfulness, and his chastity. He commanded us what is good and prohibited us from what is bad. He commanded us to pray and fast and give charity and visit our relatives and all that you would recognize as beautiful ethics. And he recited for us a Revelation [the Qur'an], nothing is similar to It other than It. We confirmed Its truthfulness and believed in It. And we understood that what he brought was truly from God. And based on that, we left the religion of our people and they tortured us and harmed us. And when it reached to the level that we could not bear, and we could not defend ourselves, our Prophet commanded us to leave the city and come to your land, preferring you over others than you so that you might protect us from oppression.' (Rahawayh 1991 vol. 4, 71)

Ummu Salama noted that the Negus asked if there was anything of the Revelation that Ja'far could recite for him, and when Ja'far recited chapter 19, Negus and the bishops all began to cry. "Then the Negus said: 'Surely, this Word and the Words that Moses came with are all coming from the same place.' [He returned to the Meccan delegation and said:] 'By God, I will not return them to you and I will not allow you to touch them'" (Rahawayh 1991, vol. 4, 71). According to Ummu Salama, the envoys left humiliated and rejected. Through his actions, Negus exemplified the Islamic approach to strangers, one that stresses compassion, mercy, and protection over self-interest. This is very much in line with laws governing refugees today.

The Prophet himself emphasizes the importance of opening the doors to those who are in need: "There is no leader who closes his door to the needy, the poor, and the destitute except that God will close the door of heaven to his poverty, neediness, and destituteness" (al-Tirmidhi, hadith no: 1332). In other words, the hadith suggests that God will close the doors of His Divine mercy that brings prosperity and plenty to those who do not open their own doors. Or, to put it another way, accepting those in need will not decrease the sustenance of the society that accepts them, quite the opposite in fact.

Theologically speaking, Islam has been described by some Muslim scholars as "the greatest humanity." While medieval Islamic scholars of jurisprudence developed a body of legal theory about migration and its relationship to Islam, the legal pronouncements of medieval scholars are no longer able to address adequately the refugee crisis of our time. Today, scholars of Islamic jurisprudence must reassess the legal pronouncements of the past, guided by the essential principles of Islamic law, theology, and the Qur'an to derive at new approaches to meet the challenges of our changing world. There is not sufficient space in this article to discuss the necessary legal theorizing that this would involve, but perhaps the theological underpinnings I have described here can be the beginnings of such a legal study. What I hope that the forgoing has made clear is that the basic principles of an Islamic legal theory regarding the rights and responsibilities of refugees and those who are "strangers" should be found in the protection of those in need, and love and mercy toward those on Earth. For as the Prophet reminds us again: "Those who are merciful, the Most-Merciful will show mercy to them. Be merciful to those on earth and the One in Heaven will be merciful to you" (Abu Dawud, hadith no: 4931).

FIG 6 Siona Benjamin, *Tikkun Ha-Olam* (Fixing the World), 2000. #46 in the series, *Finding Home*. Gouache and 22K gold leaf on paper, 11.5 × 9″ inches. Private Collection

5 / Epilogue: India and the Dharmic Traditions of Hospitality

ORI Z SOLTES

Introduction

India's dharmic religions—for the purposes of this discussion, primarily what outsiders call "Hinduism"—offers an interesting paradox with regard to the notion of welcoming the stranger.[1] On the one hand, the broad notion of assisting those in the community around one through forms of social activism of one sort or another is lacking for specific theological reasons. On the other hand, accepting and even welcoming those of diverse other faith traditions has a largely positive history, also for theological reasons.

What we call Hinduism means "Indianism"—which is to say that there is a distinct association between an ethno-national sense of identity and what proves, as we shall see—and this is essential to the main discussion points in this chapter—to actually be a diverse array of closely-connected but not identical forms of faith. Out of that array and its common principles grew Buddhism, with at least two significant features that separate it from "Hinduism."

To begin with, those essential principles—articulated as *dharma*, which may be translated from Sanskrit as both "teaching" and "law" and also "way of life"—may be briefly summarized as follows. Human existence is an ongoing cycle of birth, life, death and rebirth, life, and death—(almost)

---

1. There are other dharmic faiths, as well, including Buddhism, Jainism and Sikhism, but for the purposes of this discussion, the so-called Hindu tradition, as the source for all four traditions, is our primary focus.

ad infinitum. That cycle, called *samsara* in Sanskrit, has three particular features that govern every individual's experience of it. One is that cosmic *dharma*, set in place by God/the gods, organizes humanity into a series of castes. There are four primary ones, to be precise: one may be born a peasant (*shudra*), a craftsman or merchant (*vaishya*), a warrior (*kshatriya*), or a priest (*brahmin*). There also ultimately evolves a more informally-designated still lower caste, as well: that of the untouchables (*dalits*).

Why one is born into a given caste and what was one's original caste, if one could somehow reach back into one's first birth, has no easily discernable explanation. However, in the short-term, looking backwards into one's immediate past life or recent past lives, at the present, and forward toward the future and one's next life, one's current condition is understood to be directly derived from one's behavior in one's past life or lives, and one's caste position in one's next life will be largely determined by one's behavior in this life. Thus today's warrior may aspire to be tomorrow's priest and fear being tomorrow's craftsman—and even an untouchable can hope and aspire to be a peasant in his/her next incarnation and fear being some less-than-human animal in that next incarnation.

This issue marks the second essential feature of *samsara*—and the term that refers to this feature is *karma*: literally "action" or "deeds." So when we refer to someone's *karma*, we mean by that that what is happening in his/her life is/may be a consequence of his/her actions/deeds in the previous life: someone who is suffering may be suffering because of actions in a previous life, even as and if she/he seems completely innocent of anything that should be yielding such suffering in the here and now.

The third essential feature of *samsara* is that one can also hope and aspire to move, at a certain point in one's multiple existences, off of the ongoing cycle—to achieve release (*moksha*) from it. That release returns one's soul (*atman*) to the source of all souls—the *jivatman* ("eternal living soul") that is God, like a droplet of water back into the sea. That desirable condition of oneness with the divine source of all being is called *nirvana*. To be clear, *nirvana* is not a place but a condition. Moreover, the implications of this system and its ultimate goal of attaining *nirvana* has certain corollaries. The most obvious is that only a member of the highest caste can aspire to *moksha* and *nirvana*; members of all other castes can only aspire to move up into the next caste. A second corollary is that when one is subsumed into the divine sea of being, the individual "you" who was subsumed ceases to be an individual I/you, just as (to repeat the simile) the individual drop loses its individuality when it is subsumed back into the sea.

There are further corollaries. The dharmic understanding of the soul and where/how it ideally eventuates (*nirvana*) clearly undercuts the individuality that is so highly valued in the Abrahamic and other Western traditions. More significant for the purposes of our discussion, the dharmic traditions will not only place little value on helping those within or beyond the community, they will discourage it. The reason is clear: the most important task before a given soul in a given incarnate lifetime is to operate in as proper a manner, suited to one's caste, as one can, in order to prepare one's soul as effectively as possible for its next incarnation. And if someone interferes with that process of self-improvement, such an action could be deleterious to the long-term *karma*-based *samsara* experience of that soul. If I assist a beggar I may actually do him more harm than good, since I may be interfering with his working out his *karma* and I may therefore be preventing him from moving up the caste ladder.

On the other hand, however, the "Hindu" tradition has an extensive history of hospitality to strangers with different belief sets, thanks, in part, to the development of its own specific religious configuration. To repeat: "Hinduism" is a misnomer in being used as if there is a monolithic form of faith that goes by that name, just as it is often misunderstood to be polytheistic: there are, after all, any number of gods and goddesses, it would seem, that occupy its pantheon. In truth, an Indian who is part of this spiritual tradition understands all of these "gods" and "goddesses" to be particularized manifestations of a single god of Being.

Thus "Hinduism" is a more complex version, in a sense, of Christianity in its understanding of God as triune, for instead of a threefold, Father-Son-Holy Spirit Godhead, "Hinduism" offers a poly-une Brahman (Being) expressed as Brahma, Vishnu, Shiva, and Devi—and also scores of other lesser names of lesser or at least less well-known divinities. So one is typically a Shaivite, say, or a Vaishnite, believing that Shiva or Vishnu represents the consummate expression of God, but embracing the legitimacy of other expressions, as well. Moreover, among the ten avatars assumed by Vishnu over history, one of them is as a dark-skinned (blue or black) anthropomorph, Krishna, and over time, a growing community of Kraishnites views him as the consummate manifestation of God; not as an avatar of Vishnu—who, on the contrary, is viewed as a manifestation of Krishna.

This idea is most straightforwardly and succinctly expressed in the *Bhagavad Gita*, an important part of the larger epic poem, the *Mahabharata*. In chapter nine of the *Gita*, Krishna himself explains to the warrior-Prince, Arjuna, that

> Even those who are devotees of other gods,
> And worship them permeated with faith
> It is only Me, son of Kunti, that even they
> Worship, though not in the enjoined fashion.

And further, in chapter ten, Krishna continues:

> Of the Adityas I am Vishnu,
> Of light the radiant sun . . .
>
> Of Vedas I am the Sama Veda,
> Of gods I am Vasava (Indra) . . .
>
> Of Rudras I am Samkara (Shiva) . . . [1]

And more to the point, as far as the paradox of singularity as multiplicity and multiplicity as singularity are concerned:

> When the various states of being
> He perceives as abiding in One
> And from that alone their expansion.
> Then he attains Brahman
>
> Because he is beginningless and free from the strands,
> This supreme self, imperishable . . .

—Krishna explains to Arjuna in chapter 14. "Strands" is the term referring to the aspects of physical matter and also passion, darkness, goodness as all of these conditions derive from and are contained by *our* world. When the devotee has fully grasped the endless singularity of God then he achieves oneness with the divine source of everything—Brahman—who is equated in the *Gita* with Krishna.

And so on. This religious complexity—a paradox, really—incidentally has a significant kind of literary parallel. The *Gita* is understood by Kraishnites to be a revealed text—"*shruti*" (literally, "heard") is the Sanskrit term. Indeed, the phrase, *Bhagavad Gita*, means "Divine Song." It is embedded, however, in the *Mahabharata*, an enormous epic poem (several times longer than the *Iliad* and the *Odyssey* combined) that is regarded as a "*smrti*" (literally "remembered": i.e., humanly contrived rather than divinely revealed) text. Whereas for Kraishnites, the *Gita* is the virtual equivalent of the Bible for Jews and Christians and the Qur'an for Muslims, for non-Kraishnites, it is merely part of that extended *smrti* epic, without its own *shruti* identity. It is a wonderful text, with important truths, like the *Iliad* or the *Odyssey* are, but its divine protagonist, Krishna, is no more important with regard to our encounter with real divinity than Zeus,

Hera, Aphrodite, Ares, Hermes and the other Olympian gods and goddesses are understood to be by adherents to the Abrahamic traditions.

One might further note the narrative context of the *Gita*. The warrior Arjuna, is preparing to attack the forces arrayed against him on the battlefield: those of his blind uncle, who has refused to relinquish the throne to Arjuna. That throne is rightfully Arjuna's because his father had died when Arjuna was a child and his blind uncle had functioned as a regent for him, but the time of the regency had ended. When his uncle refused to step down, and a war was taking shape, Arjuna had been given a choice by Krishna: 10,000 warriors for his army or Krishna as his charioteer—and of course chose the latter. The majority of the *Gita*'s text consists of Arjuna asking questions and Krishna answering him—beginning with the warrior prince's doubts as to whether he should be fighting his uncle, cousins, and friends.

Krishna emphasizes three issues in responding in the affirmative: that it is his job as a *kshatriya* to fight—and perhaps with the hope that he can be reborn next time as a *brahmin*; that his uncle is not doing the right thing, according to *dharma*, (the proper order of things; the law of the universe)—both because the throne is legitimately Arjuna's as his father's son and because, as a blind man, his uncle is even less fit for kingship than perhaps one could argue for him were he endowed with sight—so that Arjuna will be restoring proper *dharma* to his community. Krishna further notes that in any case, whomever Arjuna might kill or whoever might be killed on his side will not truly die. Only the carapace of the body dies; the *atman* moves on into the post-mortem and pre-natal condition that yields to the next stage of its existence. And precisely what will be the condition of that next incarnate stage will depend entirely on the *karma* of each *atman*, not on the sword, spear, or bow and arrows of Arjuna!

This underscores from an oblique angle why social action in general is not a centerpiece of "Hinduism"—so much responsibility is placed on the shoulders of each individual and his/her *karma* and on the inadvisability of interfering with another individual's *karma*—or in the extreme case of war as illustrated by Arjuna's position, if interference is needed to restore or maintain *dharma*, (under the divine guidance of Krishna) then, still, each individual affected by the act of maintenance or restoration is in any case responsible for the consequential subsequent condition of his/her *atman*.

More to the point, perhaps, for this discussion: while wars are certainly fought, the kind that is divinely approved is the kind that is designed to restore or maintain the *dharma* of things—which is rarely conceived of as defined by a particularized religious perspective. One does not find ages of religious wars within the Hindu world as one does within the Abrahamic worlds: I acknowledge your embrace of Vishnu as the consummate manifestation of God even as I believe that it is Krishna and you respect my embrace of Krishna as such although you believe it is Vishnu—and a third friend believes it to be Shiva, for we acknowledge the limits of what we can *know* about God and thus accept the idea that there are many paths to Brahman.

If all of this is the tip of the iceberg of Hindu complexity, consider that one of the offspring of Hinduism is Buddhism, born in India—the original Buddha, Gautama Buddha, lived from ca 563 to ca 483 BCE. While much of what emerged and evolved as Buddhism migrated eastward to other parts of Asia—as well as diversifying in its details, as it spread, in accordance with various cultural and prior religious traditions—yet a small but critical mass of Buddhists remained in India, and monasteries and cave complexes, (albeit mostly no longer active today), with stunning wall paintings, may be found in some abundance in different parts of the country. So, too, another form of faith that shares many features in common with Buddhism, Jainism, presents a small but noteworthy presence in the country, as does Sikhism.

The two most important distinctions between Buddhism and the various types of "Hinduism" is that for Buddhism, first of all, the caste system is a negative and is dispensed with, functionally: anyone from any level of society can aspire to *moksha* and *nirvana*, rather than merely hoping to a move up the caste-ladder, incarnation by incarnation. Part of the reason for this—which implies that such caste systems were *not* put into place by God—is that Buddhism offers a much more limited role for divinity. Humans who become Buddhists are spiritually governed by and focused on the hope of achieving enlightenment, rather than on God, per se.

The path to enlightenment—the Eight-fold Path—has been articulated and laid out by Gautama Buddha himself in a series of aphoristic speeches delivered over the years to an expanding audience of acolytes, until these words were written down in the *Dhammapada*: "The Path of Dharma."[2] While the Buddha transcends the gods in his enlightened condition he himself is not a god: he is venerated, not worshipped. And that to which a Buddhist hopes to be returned—the sea into which his individuated "drop-ness" will be absorbed—is simply *Being: Brahman*, as opposed to any form of personified godhead, such as Krishna or Vishnu or Shiva or Brahma. Strictly speaking, then, most forms of Buddhism may not be

---

2. "*Dhamma*" is the Pali equivalent of Sanskrit "*Dharma.*" The *Dhammapada* is written in Pali, not Sanskrit, for reasons beyond this discussion.

considered a religion in the fundamental understanding of that word that, by definition, refers to being *bound back to a personified God*.[3]

Furthermore, as any individual practitioner of Buddhism can aspire to become a buddha—an enlightened being (the term "buddha" simply means "enlightened")—and at that moment achieve *moksha* and *nirvana*, every individual who achieves buddhahood also has the option of doing what Gautama Buddha did: to choose to stay within the realm of unenlightened humanity to help others to achieve enlightenment. The term "bodhisattva" is used to refer to such an individual (as it is ambiguously also used to refer to someone on the *path* to enlightenment but who has not yet achieved it). In other words, the bodhisattva concept directly implies the choice to act altruistically on behalf of others, rather then on behalf of one's self.

Against this double dharmic backdrop—that, to repeat, also includes Jainism and Sikhism—India's history has tended toward accepting diverse types of believers as following legitimate paths toward a common divine goal. And so there are various ways in which these dharmic traditions also articulate an obligation to help others, albeit without a specific theological instruction to welcome the stranger, per se. And thus, historically, Hindu- (and Buddhist)-dominated India has welcomed diverse strangers of varied spiritual inclinations. There surely are instances where helping others is associated with developing good *karma*, in spite of the potential danger to the recipient of one's largesse. More importantly, being welcoming to refugees may be supposed to offer *karma*-enhancement by the same token. In any case, this last principle is found well-expressed across Indian history with respect to other forms of faith.

One might consider, for instance, Indian Jews, given the long history of Jewish dispersion and experience of inhospitality in so many parts of the world. Jews have historically lived across diverse parts of the Indian subcontinent over the centuries without experiencing the sort of anti-Jewish sentiments that have been so common in other locales—particularly Christian Europe, which exported its anti-Jewish sensibilities into the Muslim world eventually, particularly in the context of European colonialism and post-colonialism in the Middle East, culminating with World War I and its aftermath. Indeed, the most obvious exception to the

---

3. The term, "religion," is made up of three Latin elements—*re-* is a prefix meaning "back' or again," *lig-*" means a binding, and "*-io*" is a suffix that plays a grammatical role of completing the word as a grammatically feminine word—that mean "to be bound back" to God, or the gods, who made us. But in Buddhism the individual *atmen* will be bound back to Being itself, rather than to a particular god-concept.

rule of Jewish experience in India arrived with the control of Goa in the early 16th century by the Portuguese, who brought with them not only anti-Jewish feelings but the specifics associated with the development of the Spanish and Portuguese Inquisition that would technically affect *former Jews—Nuevos Christianos*—suspected of secretly continuing to practice Judaism.

One of the identity questions regarding Indian Jews is: which community really arrived first—and when and from where? The largest of the Jewish Indian communities, the Bene Israel, offer at least five different theories regarding exactly when they first arrived into India and from where they came—ranging from the time of King Solomon, as *Israelites*,[4] to the time of the so-called Maccabees, as *Judaeans*,[5] to the first or second century CE, as *Jewish* survivors of a shipwreck,[6] to the fifth or sixth century, from South Arabia or Persia.

---

4. This theory was proposed by Shellim Samuel in his *Treatise on the Origin and Early History of the Bene Israel of Maharashtra State*.
5. Haim Solomon Kehimkar, *History of the Bene Israel of India*. This also seems to be the hypothesis favored by the majority of Bene Israel Jews themselves.
6. Abraham, Isaac, Jacob and their spouses are referred to as "Hebrews" in the Bible; Moses, Joshua, and the Kings Saul, David, and Solomon are all referred to as "Israelites." Between the time of the break-up of the united Israelite kingdom, shortly after Solomon's death (ca 930 BCE); and the aftermath of the Crucifixion (ca 35 CE), the Destruction of the Temple (70 CE), and the push toward the Bar Kokhba Revolt (132–35 CE); at least two crucial developments for this narrative take place. One, the northern 10 tribes of Israel, still called "Israel" ultimately disappear from history in the aftermath of the Assyrian debacle of ca 722–21 BCE, while the southern two tribes, Judah and Benjamin—together referred to as "Judah" since the split-up of the kingdom—continue, even surviving the debacle of the Babylonian destruction of Solomon's Temple (586 BCE) and the nearly half century of exile for many of the Judaeans who followed. Two, in the slow aftermath of the return of some of the exiled Judaeans to Judah, and the rebuilding of the Temple, under Akhaemenid Persian patronage, the prophetic era comes gradually to a close: with the final redaction of the Torah by Ezra (444BCE), mainstream Judaeans are led by a nomocracy centered on scribes and scholars who can read and interpret the word of God, not by a theocracy led by prophets and priests to whom God is understood to be speaking directly with some regularity.

It is the embrace or rejection of this nomocratic revolution that will yield the schism within the Judaean community half a millennium later that will shape Judaism and Christianity in spiritual (and eventual political) opposition to each other. And here is the language complication: in the operative languages of that time and place—mainly Hebrew, Aramaic, Greek, and Latin (but others as well), one cannot make a distinction between "Judaean" and "Jewish." Thus in pure linguistic terms there would appear to be a straightforward continuum between these two terms and concepts, while both of them are distinguished from "Christian." However, historically

What all of these accounts share in common is an emphasis on how they were received by the Hindu majority when they arrived as strangers. The local Indian/Hindu population accepted the Israelite/Judaean/Jewish refugees and provided them with the wherewithal not only to survive but to flourish and to carve out a place for themselves within the larger community.[7]

There are other accounts of the other two primary Jewish communities in India—the Cochini and the Baghdadi communities—but what they, too, share with each other and with the Bene Israel is the central role played in the accounts of their arrival into India of a generously accepting Hindu and Muslim population. That sensibility has left Indian Jews with a strong Indian and not only a strong Jewish identity. One may observe this in a broad and general way and also by reference to a particular contemporary visual representation of them.

The broadly noted way comes in observing a significant outcome of the emigration of the vast majority of the Indian Jewish communities, who have then reconstituted themselves in Israel. Nothing is more significant and symptomatic of this reality than the current project of creating a substantial Indian Jewish Cultural and Heritage Center. Sponsored mainly by the Bene Israel community, it will use as its starting point an already existing heritage center for the Cochini Jews, but will encompass all of the communities of Indian Jews, particularly since all of them are cur-

---

speaking, this would be inaccurate: to repeat, what we identify as "Judaism" is still in the process of taking shape in the century or more after the Crucifixion, and what is taking shape as Christianity perceives itself for at least several centuries after that moment to be the proper continuation of the Hebrew-Israelite-Judaean tradition beginning with Abraham. It will be some time until the smoke clears and we can clearly distinguish these two forms of faith from each other.

When, a millennium after the time of the united kingdom of Israel, its descendants split into two groups—Jews and Christians—both lay claim to being the proper continuation of the Hebrew-Israelite tradition: the phrase that was used in the Latin-speaking Roman period, and for many centuries thereafter in fact, was *verus Israel*—"true Israel." Thus on the one hand, the word "Jew" and its cognates are not found in the Torah or the prophetic books of the Hebrew Bible and on the other, what we think of as Judaism, with its fully canonized Bible, its emerging rabbinic tradition, its full complement of life-cycle and annual communal celebrations and commemorations, and above all, its existence as a far-flung diaspora, is not fully in place until well after the biblical period.

7. For more detail about the Bene Israel and these theories, see Ori Z Soltes, "Bene Israel Jews in and around Mumbai: Customs and Synagogues," in Ori Z Soltes, ed., *Growing Up Jewish in India: Synagogues, Customs, and Ceremonies, from the Bene Israel to the Art of Siona Benjamin*.

rently found in Israel. The vast complex will be located in Nevatim, not far from Beersheva, the capital of the northern Negev.

The structure being planned is relevant to this discussion: it will take the form of a large stylized lotus blossom. Moreover, aside from the various buildings and their purposes within the complex, there will be shaded walkways and botanical gardens—into which plants and flowers specific to India have been introduced as a prominent feature. This vegetation, contouring the many outside spaces that are interspersed among the buildings will offer a distinct piece of India, embedded in Israel, celebrating the ongoing love of India by its Jewish community, which reflects a long history of feeling welcome there. That enduring connection to India while resident and happy in Israel is reflected in the oft-made comment that India is their Mother, as Israel is their Father.[8]

One may also see this sensibility expressed in a specific manner reflected in the visual art produced most notably by the artist, Siona Benjamin (b. 1960)—a member of the Bene Israel community. Her painting reflects her experiences growing up in Mumbai (Bombay), and the relations between her family and their mostly non-Jewish (primarily Hindu and Muslim) friends, neighbors, and associates; and through the Catholic and Zoroastrian (Parsi) schools that she attended and the diverse, mainly Hindu and Muslim, friends that she made in those schools. Her painting resonates with distinctly Jewish features, distinctly Indian Jewish features, distinctly Bene Israel Indian Jewish features, and the intertwining of all of these elements with the Muslim, Christian, Zoroastrian,

---

8. One might also note the shaping of two new Jewish communities in India. Thus, there is a group of approximately 9,000 individuals who refer to themselves as the Bene Menashe. Comprised of formerly animist Mizo and Kuki headhunting tribesmen in Manipur and Mizoram who converted to Christianity at the beginning of the 20th century, they began to convert to Judaism in the 1970s—asserting that they are returning to their original faith, having descended from one of the lost Ten tribes (that of Menashe, one of the two sons of the patriarch, Joseph) who disappeared from history after the Assyrian conquest of northern Israel in 722–721 BCE—which would make their ancestors Israelites.

The second recent addition to the overall Indian Jewish community is the smaller group in Andhra Pradesh on the southeast coast, referred to as the 'Telugu Jews'; they speak Telugu and embraced Judaism in 1991. The 'Telugu Jews'—some of them came to follow an ultra-Orthodox lifestyle—refer to themselves as Bene Ephraim, tracing their ancestry in a manner analogous to the identity-sensibility of the Mizo and Kuki Bene Menashe, to the other son of the Israelite patriarch Joseph—Ephraim—and to the lost Israelite tribe that is traditionally understood to have descended from him. These two groups are also now represented among the Indian Jewish communities residing in Israel.

and above all, Hindu worlds of which she and her family were so much a part—and a further refraction through the layered lenses of living for several decades in the Midwestern and Northeastern United States.

Three particular truths reverberate throughout her art and its myriad details: Hindu India's historical hospitality to non-Hindu groups, and in particular to the Jews; the complexity of the Jewish identity, in general and with regard to producing visual art; and how the wrestling with these two issues has continued to evolve in Siona's art from one body of work to the next. One may discern elements that connect to illuminated manuscripts from the Hindu, Persian, and Moghul traditions; allusions to Bollywood posters and American (particular Roy Lichtenstein-style) Pop Art; references to Christian icons; and the engagement of the ongoing question of what exactly 'Jewish' art might be. Her paintings offer a distinct visual summary of India and its diverse religious, cultural and ethnic communities, Jewish and otherwise.[9]

Indian Jews are—obviously, by definition—both Indian and Jewish. As such, in the broadest of senses, they are part of two interwoven historical and geographical continua, each with its own unique features. India is not only a vast country with dynamic contrasts between its towering mountains and its coastal lowlands and all that lies between. It is historically complex in terms of ethnicity, religion, culture and language. As India evolved as a modern, independent republic after the country's independence from colonial rule in 1947, most Indian Jews migrated, as we have noted, and mainly to Israel, which was born at virtually the same time. They remain closely connected to India, however: it is, to repeat, their Mother, as Israel is their Father.

The general lack of hostility and persecution within India may be understood in part as a function of the nature of Hinduism, by far the dominant religion across India, and its embrace of diverse perspectives regarding how, specifically, one might understand and address divinity, as we have observed above, and also a cultural phenomenon overrun with inherent diversity.

To begin with, whereas the country is overrun by perhaps 415 different languages—23 "official" languages, just for starters—these languages also fall into two very different families or categories. Thus, languages like Hindi, Bengali, and Marathi are ultimately related Indo-Aryan members of the greater Indo-European family, and are largely derived from Vedic and Sanskrit (earlier and somewhat later versions of a branch of the far-

---

9. For more detail and to see visual images that accompany the discussion, see chapters 4 and 5 of Soltes, ed., *Growing Up Jewish in India*.

flung Indo-European language family that encompasses languages from extinct Tocharian in what is now China, eastward, to Portuguese, English, and Icelandic, at the western edges of the Eurasian continent. Conversely, languages like Tamil, Kannada, and Malayalam with an ancestry in Tamil, are part of the more geographically concentrated family of Dravidian languages. This is apart from smaller groups of Afro-Asiatic and Sino-Tibetan languages—and some in the Himalayas that are still not classified.

This ethno-linguistico-cultural reality intersects India's religious diversity. It is not only the country in which Hinduism and Buddhism as well as Jainism and Sikhism were born, to which a small number of Jews migrated, three different groups of which were warmly accepted in three different parts of the country. There is also, of course, a substantial Muslim community in India—by far the largest community after Hinduism.[10] Within the next generation it is projected that India will become the most populous Muslim country in the world, outdistancing Indonesia—although that may altogether reverse itself as a development under the current Modi regime, which tragically seeks to reverse the tolerant and embracing norms of the past as he drives a Hindu/Indian nationalist mentality forward.

If one might ignore Modi's despicable policies for a brief moment[11]— because they contradict the historical ethos of the very culture and religion of which he claims to be a champion—since they are in the process of also skewing the demographic statistics of India, it is symptomatic of India's enormous population that, as of just a few year ago, Muslims still constituted less than 15% of the entire population and yet offered an astonishing overall total population. Similarly, although Christians are a distant third group in size—about 2.3% of the population—this still amounts to nearly 25 million adherents. There are also important populations, still smaller in number, of Sikhs, Zoroastrians and Baha'is—and again symptomatic of India's enormous demographic size, members of these last two groups are more numerous in India than anywhere else on the planet. As for the Jewish communities, they perhaps numbered 30,000 at their demographic peak, around 1961, of whom the Bene Israel, the largest community, numbered some 20,000 individuals. These and the

---

10. Most Indian Muslims are Sunnis and adhere to the Ahmaddiya order.
11. One cannot forget that Modi's assumption of power and the ugly nationalist emphases of his political ideology parallel those of Donald Trump who resided in the White House at the time that the conference that is the basis for this volume was conceived—indeed inspired by the Trumpian atmosphere in America as a response to it.

Cochini and Baghdadi Jews came to speak various Indian languages as they simultaneously became an integral part of the larger population and maintained or developed their own distinctive customs and traditions.

None of these developments would have been possible—and this is the ultimate point of this discussion—without an attitude that, rather than seeing incoming others who were different in one way or another as simply strangers, ultimately welcomed them in in a manner reminiscent of Abraham and Lot. The strangers became neighbors in a religious, cultural, and historical setting different from that of the biblical-qur'anic story told by those—from Jews to Christians to Muslims—who were being welcomed in.

Section Two

Building the Present and Future:
Programmatic Ideas and Realizations

FIG 7 Fritz Ascher, *Male Portrait in Red*, ca.1915. White gouache over graphite, watercolor and black ink on paper, 10.5 × 8.7 inches © Bianca Stock

6 / Fritz Ascher: A Jewish Artist in Germany
RACHEL STERN

When he rang Martha Graßmann's doorbell in Berlin's Lassenstraße 26 on June 15, 1942, the Jewish-born artist Fritz Ascher (1893–1970) was out of options: he had just been warned of his imminent deportation to an extermination camp.

How could it be that he had to beg for his life, hunted as a stranger in his home country? Jews had lived here for centuries. They had come to the Rhineland and the Danube valley with Roman legions, when German lands were still a cluster of more than a hundred small independent tribes, and long before the establishment of Christianity.[1] For long periods Jewish and non-Jewish Germans coexisted peacefully. Prior to the Crusades in the 11th to 13th century, Jews were free to own property and practice all trades and professions.

In Berlin, the official establishment of the Jewish community is put at 1295. The centuries that followed saw recurrent cycles of toleration and anti-Jewishness, of acceptance and vicious pogroms. Only the Enlightenment, also known as the Age of Reason, brought a focus on the common humanity of all people, as well as relative freedom and safety to Jews living in German lands. In 1650, the "Great Elector" Frederick William invited a small number of Jews into Brandenburg, and in 1651 he issued an edict permitting fifty Jewish families to settle wherever they wished. In 1750, Frederick the Great allowed the Jewish community to control

---

1. The earliest known written record in Northwestern Europe is a 321 CE decree by the emperor Constantine instructing the Roman magistrate of Cologne on the right to appoint Jews to the city council. *Biblioteca Apostolica Vaticana. Codex Theodosianus* 16, 8.3

their own schools, synagogues and cemeteries. During the second half of the nineteenth century, Berlin experienced a full blossoming, with an economic and industrial expansion in which Jewish businessmen and industrialists played a central role. Jews were prominent not only in commerce, industry and finance, but increasingly in the city's intellectual life and in the professions, including medicine and law.

It was precisely at that moment and in response to Jewish success that anti-Semitism again began to grow. There had been broad religious anti-Jewishness across German-speaking lands since the Middle Ages, prominently articulated by Martin Luther (1483–1546).[2] But now a new form of anti-Semitism grew: a "racial" anti-Semitism that preached hatred for Jews on grounds that they were both a race apart from Germans and European in general and inherently evil. In 1803, the distinguished Berlin lawyer Karl Wilhelm Grattenauer (1770–1838) was probably the first individual to introduce the concept of a Jewish race in a hotly discussed pamphlet that was based on pseudo-scientific grounds.[3] In his view, all Jews—including assimilated and baptized Jews—were alike and could never be properly assimilated into German society. Building on Wilhelm Grattenauer's definition of a Jewish race, the German political philosopher Wilhelm Marr (1819–1904) introduced the terms "Semite" and "Semitic" from their linguistic context to a racial-ethnic context.[4] In his 1879 publication *Der Weg zum Siege des Germanenthums über das Judenthum* (The Way to Victory of Germanism over Judaism), Marr himself was very vague about what constituted race and, in turn, the racial differences between Jews and Germans, though two generations later this became a feature of Nazi racial "science." It remained for later racial thinkers to postulate specific differences: these included Eugen Dühring (1833–1921), who sug-

---

2. Paul Rose challenges distinctions between theologically derived (medieval) and secular, "racial" (modern) anti-Semitism, arguing that there is an unbroken chain of anti-Semitic feeling between the two periods. Paul Lawrence Rose. *German Question/Jewish Question: Revolutionary Antisemitism in Germany from Kant to Wagner*. (Princeton University Press: 2014). Luther specifically expressed violent anti-Jewish sentiments in his long (65,000 words), late treatise, "On the Jews and Their Lies," written in 1543.

3. Karl Wilhelm Friedrich Grattenauer, *Wider die Juden (Against the Jews)*. (Berlin: John Wilhelm Schmidt, 1803). See Jacob Katz, *From Prejudice to Destruction. Anti-Semitism 1700–1933* (Cambridge: Harvard University Press, 1980).

4. Wilhelm Marr, *Der Sieg des Judenthums über das Germanenthum—Vom nichtconfessionellen Standpunkt aus betrachtet*. (Bern: Rudolph Costenoble, 1879). English translation: Rohringer, Gerhard, *Victory of Judaism over Germanism - Considered from a Nonreligious Perspective* (2009: http://www.kevinmacdonald.net/Marr-Text-English.pdf). The manuscript was drafted in 1878 and then languished with publisher Rudoph Costenoble for a year before finally appearing in late March 1879. It was an instant hit, running through twelve editions in its first year.

FIG 8 Unknown Photographer, *Fritz Ascher*, 1939 © Bianca Stock

gested that it was blood, and openly advocated for the "murder and extermination" of Jews as a solution to the Jewish question.[5]

5. Eugen Dühring, *Die Judenfrage als Racen-, Sitten- und Culturfrage: Mit einer weltgeschichtlichen Antwort* [*The Jewish Question as a Racial, Moral, and Cultural Question: With a World-historical Answer*] (Karlsruhe: Reuther 1881) (PDF: https://archive.org/details/Duehring-Die-Judenfrage-2) It was a pseudo-scientific attempt to

FIG 9 Unknown Photographer, *Ascher Family: Wedding Charlotte Ascher,* 1918. © Bianca Stock

On October 17, 1893, the artist Fritz Ascher was born in Berlin to Jewish parents Hugo and Minna Luise Ascher, followed in 1894 and 1897 by his sisters Charlotte and Margarete.[6] In 1899, Hugo Ascher formally left the Jewish faith with his three children, who were baptized in 1901.

In 1918 and 1920, both Fritz's sisters were married to non-Jews. A photo from 1918, taken on the occasion of Charlotte's wedding, shows the entire Ascher family, including 25-year-old Fritz, who can be seen in the background on the right. Hugo Ascher died soon after both daughters were married, in 1922.

Hugo Ascher grew up in Naugard, Pomerania, was educated at the *Pennsylvania School of Dental Medicine* the US and became a successful businessman in Berlin, producing *Ascher's Artificial Enamel*. Early on, he supported his son's desire to pursue a career in the arts. Fritz Ascher had

---

give anti-Semitism as a political movement a biological, historical, and philosophical foundation.

6. The biographical information is based on the essay by Rachel Stern, "Fritz Ascher: A Life in the Arts and Poetry," in Rachel Stern & Ori Z Soltes, eds., *To Live is to Blaze with Passion: The Expressionist Fritz Ascher/ Leben ist Glühn: Der Expressionist Fritz Ascher,* 18–63, and the sources mentioned there.

FIG 10 Fritz Ascher, *"The Intriguer,"* c. 1913. Black ink over graphite on paper, 8.9 × 5.6 inches. Nicole Trau Collection © Bianca Stock

left school at the age of 16 and, promoted by the prominent artist Max Liebermann, attended the progressive Art Academy in Königsberg and the Berlin private schools of Lovis Corinth, Adolf Meyer and Curt Agthe.

Fritz Ascher was very social, well liked and mingled with artists such as the older Edvard Munch, Emil Nolde and Wassily Kandinsky, and his contemporaries Max Beckmann, Georges Rouault, Max Pechstein and Ludwig Meidner. In early sketches and drawings, he captured Berlin society and the zeitgeist critically and with humor, and often these sketches resemble caricatures.

The beginning of World War I in 1914 seems to have focused the 21-year-old on himself. While many of his contemporaries went to battle with near-religious feelings for the Fatherland, Ascher's artworks reveal a battle with his religious identity and suggest his inner strife. He now found his very own pictorial language, in which he combined expressive strokes and intense colors with descriptive outlines and a flat application of paint.

In his drawings, Ascher continued to observe Berlin society. "Semitic" and "Aryan" prototypes confront each other and reflect on the intensifying political and social polarization in German society. Jews were increasingly seen as the "Other," as a race both different and separate from the German race.

Burial, from 1919, depicts a conflict within the Jewish community: A crowd of people is gathered in front of a round hole that suggests an urn burial. The person standing behind the grave appears to be giving a eulogy. Lightly sketched crosses in the background confirm the location as a Christian cemetery. In the left foreground, a man raises his hands to his head in terror or grief, gazing at the crowd. His hat, coat, and side-locks identify him as a religious Eastern European Jew. He seems shocked and pained by the Christian burial of a fellow Jew, possibly a family member.

Since the 1880s, Eastern European Jews were coming to Berlin in large numbers, fleeing pogroms and massacres. The assimilated German Jews were embarrassed by the Eastern Jews' poverty and traditional looks, which seemed to confirm prevailing stereotypes.

As the first World War dragged on, with millions of casualties on all sides, chauvinism turned inward and the gulf between Germans and Jews deepened. Fritz Ascher now created his most important early works, highly idiosyncratic pictorial interpretations of mystical and religious content, to which he offers us his very own, highly unusual takes.

Golgotha, from 1915, depicts the public spectacle of the crucifixion of Jesus and the two thieves at Calvary. Quite unlike a traditional Christian crucifixion scene, in which the three crucified figures occupy the center of the canvas, Ascher pushes them to the top of the picture, before a back-

FIG 11 Fritz Ascher, *Loner (Der Vereinsamte)* c. 1914. Oil on canvas, 47.2 × 37.4 inches © Bianca Stock

ground with an intensely yellow sun. The actual theme of the painting, however, is the spectators, who rush at the viewer in chaotic panic, fleeing from a mounted soldier, armed with a spear, who might depict Longinus.

Ascher's 1916 painting *Golem* is based on mystical Jewish sources that tell the medieval Jewish legend of Judah Löw, the Maharal, the famous rabbi from Prague. He formed a figure out of clay and brought it to life by writing God's secret name on a piece of paper which was placed in the

FIG 12 Fritz Ascher, *"What is paradox!!!??,"* 1913. Black ink and graphite on paper, 15 × 11.6 inches © Bianca Stock

figure's mouth.[7] The golem was brought to life to protect the Jewish community in Prague, which was threatened by violent pogroms. In Ascher's painting, the Golem towers over three figures—most probably Rabbi Löw flanked by his two assistants. Their faces are strikingly formed, with beards, large noses, swollen lips, and missing teeth. They are gazing to

7. Talmudic tractate Sanhedrin 65b mentions Rava as having formed such a being.

FIG 13 Fritz Ascher, *Burial*, c. 1919. White gouache over black ink on paper, 8.7 × 10.6 inches © Bianca Stock

the lower left, with eyes wide open in fear. Whatever they see, the Golem is unmoved and stoically gazes straight at us. His expression speaks of the innocence of the unconscious creature, which is determined to execute the purpose it was created for: Saving the community from harm, no matter the consequence. This depiction is unique and consistent with his unusual approach to his subjects.[8]

8. For more detail on his paintings, see Soltes, "Fritz Ascher's 'Golem' Its Sources and Its Offspring," in Stern and Soltes, eds., *Der Expressionist Fritz Ascher.* 79–117.

FIG 14 Fritz Ascher, *Golgotha*, 1915. Oil on canvas, 53.4 × 69 inches © Bianca Stock

Also in 1916, Ascher began depicting clowns—a subject that occupied him for the rest of his life.[9] Numerous very intimate drawings and one painting depict Bajazzo, the clown as a figure between tragedy and comedy, between self-identification and stage–a character designed to (literally) mask the performer's true feelings behind a façade of happiness. The clown motif offered Ascher increasing opportunity to process his own experiences. He depicts the clown as an individual figure—emphasizing his *otherness* and his status as an outsider—in life-struggle and existential loneliness. He repeatedly depicts a figure haunted by his own emotions, his surrounding environment, and world events. The clown works extend the artist's exploration of his own inner life.

Later, between 1942 and 1945, while hiding from Nazi persecution, Ascher would write:

---

9. For more information about the clown in Ascher's work, see Julia Diekmann & Rachel Stern, eds., *Der Vereinsamte. Clowns in der Kunst Fritz Aschers (1893–1970)*. (Holzminden: Jörg Mitzkat 2020)

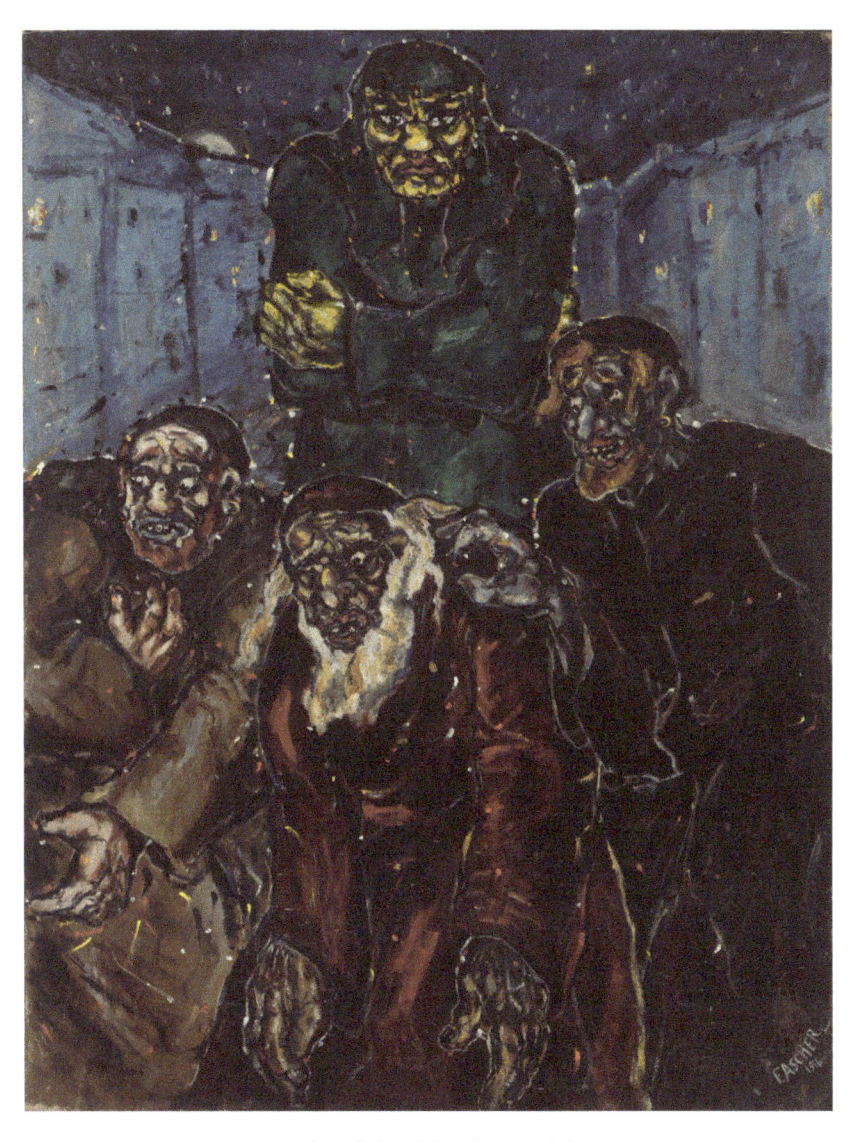

FIG 15 Fritz Ascher, *Der Golem [The Golem]*, 1916. Oil on canvas, 71.9 × 55.3 inches Photo Jens Ziehe. Jüdisches Museum Berlin GEM 93/2/0 © Bianca Stock

BAJAZZO

Die Masse stürmte um ihn her.
Starr, stumm, in sich blieb er versunken.
Nur dieses Lächeln
Was sich fand, sprach
Alle Qual, die in ihm lag.

FIG 16 Fritz Ascher, *Pagliaccio (The Clown)*, 1916. White gouache over graphite, watercolor and black ink on paper, 17.25 × 12.3 inches © Bianca Stock

FIG 17 Fritz Ascher, *Bajazzo*, 1924/1945. Oil on canvas, 47.6 × 39 inches ©
Bianca Stock

Sein Leben einst ein
bunter Tanz, nach aussen
und ein graues Leer.
Nichts ward erreicht
Wonach er strebte.
Er liebte, Sehnsucht
Ward zum Hohn
Und hatte eine warme Seele.

Das Spiel ist aus -
Die Tat geschah.
„Ein ganzer Mensch" ward
Mörder und gestört.[10]

CLOWN

The masses storm around him.
Rigid, mute, he remained lost in himself.
Just that smile
What was found spoke
Of all the agony that lay within him.

His life once
colorful dance, to the outside
and a gray void.
Nothing was achieved
what he aspired to.
He loved, longing
Became a mockery
And had a warm soul.

The play is over—
The deed is done.
"A wholesome person" became
destroyer and destroyed.

Back in 1918, when World War I was over, Germany was utterly defeated—with five million Germans dead, two million orphans, one million invalids, one million widows. The war had materially impoverished and morally confounded the entire population. The existential panic that the war left corrupted ethical standards, eroded manners, convulsed culture, and further polarized society. Dramatic upheavals between revolutionary and reactionary forces followed nearly everywhere. Although 100,000 Jews served in the armed forces of the *Reichswehr* during the war, a new narrative was introduced as a reason for Germany's defeat—the *Dolchstosslegende*—the purported theory that the Jews and left-wing elements had figuratively rammed a dagger into the back of the brave German soldiers by producing defeatist propaganda and so causing their army's and the country's collapse.

---

10. Fritz Ascher, *Poems*, Vol. 4, p. 123 (130), no. 183. Not dated (1942–1945). © Bianca Stock.

FIG 18 Fritz Ascher, *Figural Scene*, c. 1918. Black ink over watercolor and graphite on paper, 14.8 × 18.5 inches © Bianca Stock

After the founding of the Weimar Republic soon after the war, and despite its political and social instability, Berlin became a city unlike any other in Europe at the time, where culture thrived as never before and as nowhere else, and Jewish intellectuals and creative professionals were among the leading figures in many areas of enterprise.

In Ascher's work, depictions of divine judgment and Hell become more frequent. Naked bodies writhe, often with faces contorted by pain. He perhaps refers here—as in other drawings of that time—to August Strindberg's "Inferno," where the playwright and poet describes the condition of the earth, in which "Cold and gloom, plague and hunger ravage the people. Love is transformed to deadly hate, and childlike obeisance to parricide. People think they already are in Hell."[11]

The monumental painting, *The Tortured*, portrays a central blue, nude male figure with red-orange hair. He is bound with rope and restrained by four nude figures, two men and two women. It seems that the central figure is subjected to external forces. His muscular build and

11. August Strindberg, *Inferno*, 18. Author's translation.

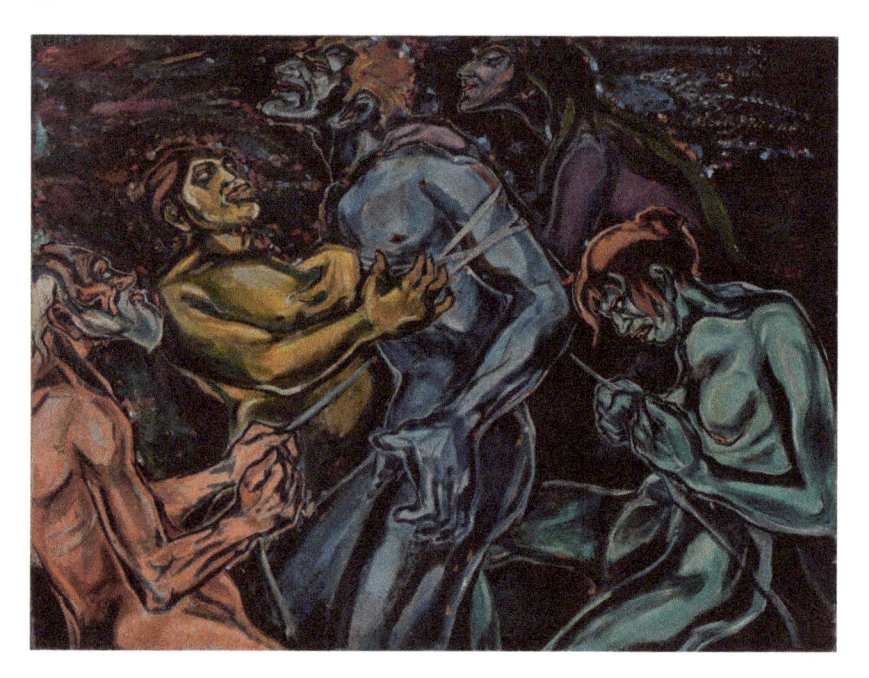

FIG 19 Fritz Ascher, *The Tortured (Der Gequälte)*, 1920s. Oil on canvas, 59 × 79.4 inches © Bianca Stock

determined expression, however, point towards restraints beyond the physical, which might be psychological or internal. One interpretation considers the inner struggle of the central figure as a quest to realize his ideal, spiritual potential amidst conflicting forces.

On January 30th, 1933 Adolf Hitler was elected *Reichskanzler* (Chancellor of the Reich). Immediately after the *Reichsermächtigungsgesetz* (the Enabling Act) was signed by *Reichspräsident* von Hindenburg in March of 1933, Hitler and the NSDAP assumed absolute power. Shortly after, on April 7, 1933, the Reich government passed the *"Gesetz zur Wiederherstellung des Berufsbeamtentums"* ("Law for the Restoration of the Professional Civil Service"). This law was used to bring public service into line and to dismiss opponents of the Nazi regime. All civil servants and employees of the Jewish faith were affected: the *Aryan paragraph* (paragraph 3) prohibited the employment of "non-Aryans" in public service, who were to be put into immediate retirement.

Police and GeStaPo fiercely persecuted, tortured and killed the opponents of the regime, using lists that had been prepared long before. Among the victims were many artists and intellectuals. Ascher feared to be a target and disappeared among friends and acquaintances, first in Berlin and later in Potsdam, constantly changing his residence.

During the following months, Germany became a full-fledged dictatorship with SA, GeStaPo and the newly created SS cohorts ruling the streets. Jewish-owned shops were boycotted, Jews were expelled from government positions, schools, research institutes and universities; they were banned from practicing law and excluded from all national societies. In May, soon after the dissolution of all opposing parties, some fifty thousand books written by Jews and other "traitors and degenerates" were burned in Berlin and in every other German university town. On September 22, 1933 the *Reichskulturkammer* (Reich Chamber of Culture) was established to ensure that all forms of artistic creation reflected the Nazi viewpoint. Members had to prove Aryan descent and meet "reliability and aptitude" standards. Jewish-born Fritz Ascher was denied membership and from then on, he was not allowed to produce—much less exhibit or sell—his art.

At that time, about 525,000 people, or less than 1 percent of the German population, were registered as Jews. A third lived in Berlin, where they made up close to 4 percent of the population.

New laws progressively excluded Jews from professional life, endangering their livelihoods. At the same time, they were excommunicated, subjected to inferior status by injunctions associated with the *Nuremberg Laws* of September 15, 1935, and relegated to a perpetual state of dishonor. "Gradually but relentlessly, friends, neighbors, clients, and employers turned away from Jews, placing them beyond the pale of German social life and empathy."[12]

Fritz Ascher's sisters, who were married to "Aryans," lived in so-called "privileged" mixed marriages. Both survived the Nazi regime, protected by their husbands. Their mother, who had illegally lived with her daughter Grete, died on October 17, 1938, on her only son's birthday, and three weeks before the November 9–10 pogroms commonly referred to as *Kristallnacht* ("The Night of Broken Glass"). Earlier, she had asked her friend Martha Graßmann to look after her son.

The whole Graßmann family got involved in doing so. At work, husband Robert had heard about the planned pogroms and tried to warn Ascher. But it was too late—the artist had already been arrested and interned in the Concentration Camp Sachsenhausen—one of more than 6,300 Jewish men who would be forever changed by that experience.

He was released after six weeks, only to be re-arrested and incarcerated in the Potsdam GeStaPo Prison for five more months. Here, too, "Six

---

12. Marion A. Kaplan, *Between Dignity and Despair*, 229. In her book, she draws a haunting picture of how creeping fascism and blatant antisemitism affected Jews in their daily lives.

weeks are almost like a life sentence."[13] Thanks to Martha's son, Gerhard Graßmann, and Protestant Pastor Heinrich Grüber, Ascher was released on May 15, 1939, for the settlement of an inheritance matter and for his alleged emigration. Under the pressure of Nazi persecution, some two-thirds of the 500,000 Jews who lived in Germany in 1933 had emigrated by the time the war began in 1939; about 78,000 in 1939. Fritz Ascher was not among them—the tax authorities did not allow him to board the ship on which he had booked passage to Shanghai.

Instead, Ascher had to report to the local police precinct three times a week, and once a month to the GeStaPo headquarters on Alexanderplatz. He moved into a Jewish boardinghouse. By then, Jews were forbidden to participate in almost every form of employment and business activity; Jewish firms and asset had to be transferred to Aryans in forced sales at derisory prices, and cash and other liquid assets had to be deposited in blocked accounts under government control. Jews were prohibited from access to public places and from entering any restaurant or entertainment establishment that served Aryans. Jewish men were forced to adopt the middle name Israel, and Jewish women the middle name Sara. They had to turn in their radios and typewriters. They had to give up their cutlery, except for one knife, fork and spoon per person. They were prohibited from buying clothing. When the war began, their food rations were inferior. From November 19, 1941 they had to wear the Yellow Star. By then, the mass deportations of Berlin's Jews to labor and extermination camps in the East had begun—a month earlier, on October 18, 1941.

Ascher also donned a yellow star. When his name appeared on a deportation list, half a year later, he was warned by Police Chief Constable Heinrich Wolber.

So now, on June 15, 1942, he was standing in front of Martha Graßmann's door. The Graßmanns lived in the Grunewald neighborhood of Berlin, where stately mansions stood on large properties, often hidden from direct view by old trees. The neighborhood had been home to many Jewish artists, publishers, intellectuals and politicians. But since 1933, more and more of these Jewish inhabitants had been expelled from their homes, and important Nazi institutions and high-ranking Nazi officials had moved in.

Here, responding to that knock on the door, Martha Graßmann hid Ascher for three years, first in her apartment and later in the basement of the building—Lassenstraße 26 (later 28), one of the very few Grunewald

---

13. Stefan Pychowski, Polish forced laborer, recalling the time he spent in the Priesterstrasse police prison. Quoted in Homann, Iris and Uta Gerlant, eds., *"Sechs Wochen sind fast wie lebenslänglich . . ." Das Potsdamer Polizeigefängnis Priesterstrasse/Bauhofstrasse*. Book title and 18.

FIG 20 Fritz Ascher, *Beethoven*, 1924/1945. Oil on canvas, 38.5 × 47 inches ©
Bianca Stock

villas hit by a bomb. She was under permanent surveillance and was subjected to several house searches. Once, she tried to find him safer shelter with a farmer in Beelitz, outside of Berlin, but Ascher was back within the week. She recalled, "He hid in a tiny space in my part of the basement. During air raids he was locked in the superintendent's potato cellar. For three years he lived in the basement among rats and wild cats." This tiny basement space was most certainly dingy and damp, without light, a bucket instead of a toilet, and no running water to wash. At least two other people helped Martha Graßmann with the constant dangers and challenges of hiding and feeding Ascher: Frida Eichelbaum, the daughter of the superintendent, who had known the artist since 1938, and the painter Grete Hart (b. 1885), daughter of the writer and literary critic Julius Hart, who was a long-time friend.

Friend and collector Karl Ellwanger remembered: "Apparently, Mrs. Graßmann hid three men. She said that Ascher always stayed in his hiding place. One day the other two could no longer bear it, went out and never returned." Especially late in the war, when all able-bodied men were drafted into the *Volkssturm*, it was perilous for men to be seen outside virtually anywhere. The Nazis had stepped up manhunts in the streets, to find Jews, deserters, or forced laborers who had escaped.

In his hideout, Ascher hid in ever-present tension. Fear of betrayal and discovery, torture and death, hunger, immobility and loneliness never left him. Deprived of books, conversation or artistic work, he was completely cast back on himself and his educational horizon. He expressed his feelings in poems:

RATTE

Dunkel bleibts, -
und schleicht in Huschen.
Unrat = scheint dem
Geist gemein.
Tückisch wie die
Augen funkeln—
Menetekel des Versunften,
des Verfemten Flüchtigsein.[14]

RAT

Darkness remains,
And creeps in a scamper.
Filth = seems
The uniting spirit.
Eyes sparkling
Treacherously—
Portent of the mucky,
Ostracized fugitive existence.

In other poems, he reflected on his unpainted images. He wrote about love and the divine, and composed tributes to his artistic role models. He also turned to a new theme: many poems evoke nature as a place of refuge and a spiritual home.

After Germany's defeat in 1945, Fritz Ascher was one of about 5,000 Jews who had survived "submerged" in Germany, about 1,700 of them having survived in Berlin. Twelve years of persecution very much altered his life and his personality as well as his art.

The artist moved in with Martha Graßmann at Bismarckallee 26, just two blocks from his former hiding place. She took care of him for the rest of his life. Former neighbor Ute Gustavus remembered, "She protected him from the outside world." And the outside world was not friendly: the Amer-

---

14. Fritz Ascher, Poems Vol. 2, not dated (1942–1945). 209, no. 372. © Bianca Stock.

FIG 21 Fritz Ascher, *Female Head in Three Quarter View*, 1954. Grey gouache and black ink over watercolor on paper, 17.8 × 12.2 inches © Bianca Stock

FIG 22 Fritz Ascher, *Sunset (Untergehende Sonne)*, c. 1960. Oil on canvas, 49.2 × 50 inches © Bianca Stock

ican OMGUS Surveys (Office of Military Government, United States), conducted between 1945 and 1949, found that the German people were even more anti-Semitic after 1945 than during the Nazi era.[15] Even though open antisemitism was suppressed by the occupying powers, it continued as a generally silent and latent force. Jews who were not able or willing to leave the country retreated into the private sphere, a so-called "absent presence."

Fritz Ascher began painting again. He started by repainting some of his existing works, very often covering them with a pointillism of expressive color. His *Beethoven* belongs to this small group. It is a tribute to the composer whose music he listened to while working in his studio.

15. Anna J. Merritt and Richard L. Merritt. *Public Opinion in Occupied Germany: the OMGUS Surveys*, 1945–1949.

FIG 23 Fritz Ascher, *Two Sunflowers*, c. 1959. White gouache and black ink over watercolor on paper, 24.5 × 17.6 inches © Bianca Stock

FIG 24 Fritz Ascher, *Trees*, late 1950s. Oil on canvas, 31.5 × 27 inches © Bianca Stock

But soon he completely turned away from his earlier figurative compositions. People now mostly appear as head studies, drawn from memory, with ink or gouache on paper. Mainly, he turned to nature and painted vibrant landscapes inspired by the nearby Grunewald Forest. Finally, he was able to paint the motifs he had envisioned in poems like "*Sonnenuntergang*" (*Sunset*) from 1942, written in hiding:

> Das güldne Ründen senkte sacht, verstrahlend;
> Erglutete verblutend alle Ferne.
> Bis es ergraut = an Schaffe dann gewandt =

FIG 25 Fritz Ascher, *Two Trees*, 1952. White gouache over black ink and watercolor on paper, 24.5 × 17.75 inches © Bianca Stock

FIG 26 Fritz Ascher, *Trees in Hilly Landscape*, 1968. Oil on canvas, 27.6 × 31.5 inches © Bianca Stock

Das Nächtige geschah.[16]

The golden roundness sinks softly, glimmering;
It enflames all the distances, bleeding.
Until it turns grey = wending to creation =
Night's gloom has happened.

The artist stayed faithful to his Expressionist sensibilities and used bright colors and intense brushstrokes. In *Sunset (Untergehende Sonne)* the paint is running in all directions—traces of the creative process, in which the artist turned the picture until the result felt right. He worked with renewed immediacy and urgency, dramatically simplifying forms and media. Periods of intense work were interrupted by periods of deep despair.

Like most other Jews in Germany, he lived largely withdrawn from society. He declined a teaching position. After a successful exhibition of 30

16. Fritz Ascher, Poems Vol. 5, 1942. P. 68, no. 124. © Bianca Stock.

paintings at the Buchholz Gallery Berlin in May 1946, he declined every solo or group exhibition for 25 years. Only in 1969, months before he died, did he agree to the large solo exhibition organized by legendary Berlin gallerist Rudolf Springer.

In powerful images of suns, flowers and trees, Ascher engaged with his own *Lebensraum* ("Living Space").[17] His trees and flowers often fill out the entire picture plane. Alone or in groups they stand like monuments in their landscapes, the sunflowers like glowing balls of sun, expressions of fertility and optimism. His thick, bright pigments suggest both vibrant, life-affirming joy and, in the rough nature of his brushstrokes, a dark, inner anguish transformed into light. Painting became the reassurance of his own existence, and the paintings became partners and confidantes, even substitutes for his lost homeland, his mentally and physically demolished hometown, Berlin.[18]

The Grunewald is well known for its ancient tree population of pines and oaks, which outwitted many storms and seasons. In Ascher's works, these old trees with massive trunks fill out the picture plane and often form a wall of resistance, which the viewer is not invited to penetrate. In contrast to these massive old trees, young trees bear witness to the rapid re-forestation of the Grunewald in the late 1940s. These young trees seem exposed to the elements, fragile—like the artist himself—and full of suspense in relation to nature and one another. They become standing figures, confronting us, each as distinctive as any human individual.

Trees in a Hilly Landscape is Ascher's last dated painting from 1968. Again, old pines fill out the entire canvas. But between the two massive, close standing trees on the left side, and an isolated tree on the right, a wide landscape meets a cloudy sky in the horizon.

At the end of 1969, the villa Bismarckallee 26 was sold for demolition, and Fritz Ascher and Martha Graßmann were forced to move. Ascher died just three months later, on March 26, 1970. Martha Graßmann died shortly thereafter. She is one of 651 Germans recognized by Yad Vashem as "Righteous Among the Nations" (out of 28,217—as of January 1, 2022). She stands for the network of people who saved Fritz Ascher's life during a time in which the vast majority of German people had turned him—and so many others in their midst—into strangers.

---

17. An exhibition of post-war landscapes was curated by Karen Wilkin at the New York Studio School in 2017. See Karen Wilkin, *Beauteous Strivings: Fritz Ascher, Works on Paper*.

18. See Eckhart Gillen, *Painting as Reassurance of the Own Existence. Fritz Ascher's Paintings after the Shoah in Comparison with Frank Auerbach's Autobiographic Works*, in: Stern and Soltes, eds., *Der Expressionist Fritz Ascher*, 130–151.

FIG 27 Refugees, 2020. Photographer Wyatt Winborne © #MeWeIntl and #MeWeSyria

7 / Welcoming Beyond Offering Safe Heaven: Aspiring to Partner with Refugees

CAROL PRENDERGAST

The forcible displacement of any person, family or community is a tragic event that has a life-long and often inter-generational impact. The record number of refugees at the current time has created a humanitarian crisis, straining all the traditional structures of international and national agencies and NGOs addressing the needs of refugees in camps and in various resettlement contexts. Exacerbating the difficulty of their work is often a toxic political environment in which refugees are portrayed as a social and economic threat to the society of host countries.

Even among the well intentioned, there can be a tendency to depict refugees as "huddled masses" who are worthy of our compassion and charity. While refugees are initially seeking safety and the meeting of basic human needs, this depiction can hinder refugees as they begin to rebuild their lives in a new country. All people who have been forced to leave their homes are individuals who had lives built through talent, perseverance and hard work. Those lives were taken from them but the personal qualities that helped them build such lives remain within them. For many, the struggles they have endured have increased their resilience and resolve to build a new life for themselves, their family and community.

In this time of a global refugee crisis, it is essential that all sectors of society participate in the welcoming and integration of refugees into their host countries. Fortunately, there is a growing movement on the part of the private sector to recognize the great potential of refugee engagement as employees and entrepreneurs. The philanthropic sector is also envisioning much of its work with refugees as investment in refugee-led solutions and innovation rather than charity. Non-profits and government agencies are adopting a cross-sector approach to supporting refugees. And community-based initiatives continue to use their intimate knowledge of their community to address their needs by seeking to empower them.

This paper will address this emerging cross-sector approach by providing examples of the work of various organizations within these sectors. It is hoped that they will serve as models for innovative ways to move forward in our efforts to welcome refugees as unique and valued members of our society here in the United States.

The Role of Business

With more and more refugees displaced for longer periods of time, businesses have a critical role to play in helping refugees integrate economically in their new host communities.

TENT PARTNERSHIP FOR REFUGEES

The Tent Partnership for Refugees was established by Chobani's founder and CEO Hamdi Ulukaya in 2016. The decision to establish this non-profit organization was inspired by Mr. Ulukaya's first-hand experience in hiring residents of upstate New York, which included many Syrian refugees, when he established Chobani's first yogurt factory.

The Tent Partnership encourages companies to think beyond traditional philanthropy. Tent works with businesses to include refugees by engaging them as potential employees, entrepreneurs, and consumers. When companies take this approach, they are not only helping refugees, they also see considerable business benefits.

Tent's member companies are based all over the world and span industries from consumer goods and technology to financial and professional services. Since 2016 its network of companies has grown to more than 300. As members of the Partnership, services and support in the following areas are provided to them with no fee. Tent's multi-faceted approach includes:

> *I. Integrating Refugees into the Workforce:* Tent believes that companies can most sustainably support refugees by training, hiring, mentoring and integrating them into their own workforce. To achieve this goal Tent advises companies on how they can build effective programs to overcome challenges facing refugees. They also connect companies with leading organizations around the world that can match companies with local refugee talent based on their

experience and companies' hiring needs. In the United States, Tent coordinates with the nine federally sponsored resettlement agencies tasked with providing transitional services, including employment, to newly arrived refugees. In working with these agencies businesses not only offer employment but often have the financial resources to provide English language training, translators and transportation needed by refugees to access available jobs. This, in turn, enhances the non-profit agencies' ability to meet their resettlement goals.

II. Leveraging Supply Chains: In addition to hiring refugees, companies can encourage their suppliers and vendors to hire refugees. In this way they can source more from businesses employing refugees. Tent's services are available to assist all such companies along the supply chain.

III. Supporting Entrepreneurs: Refugees are known to be exceptionally entrepreneurial, thanks to their resilience, drive and strong work ethic. Companies can support refugee entrepreneurs and small businesses by providing loans, offering training programs or incubators, and facilitating their access to market. The benefits of supporting refugee entrepreneurs go beyond one individual. As refugee-owned businesses grow, they also create new jobs and help grow the economy.

IV. Growing a Customer Base: Companies can engage refugees as customers by tailoring their products to better meet the needs of refugee communities. This is critical in sectors such as financial services and telecommunications, where refugees often face increased barriers to access. By tailoring these products to better meet refugees' needs, businesses can help them access key services, as well as gain a new, loyal customer base.

In order to examine the effectiveness of this approach to refugee integration, a study was conducted as a collaboration between the Tent Partnership for Refugees and the Fiscal Policy Institute's Immigration Research Initiative. The findings in this report were informed by 100 in-depth interviews with refugees, employers of refugees, refugee resettlement agency staff, other service providers, researchers, and other members of the community in four geographic areas of the United States where significant numbers of refugees have resettled. The research was also put in context and guided by FPI's analysis of data from the American Community Survey (ACS) and the Worldwide Refugee Processing System (WRAPS).[1]

The study provides much interesting information for companies that are interested in joining the movement to welcome and integrate refugees

---

1. www.tent.org/resources

into their host communities. It confirms the belief of Hamdi Ulukaya, the founder of Chobani and the Tent Partnership, that engaging refugees as employees, entrepreneurs, and consumers is good for refugees, good for the communities that host them, and good for business. [2]

The Role of Social Entrepreneurs

Social enterprise, also known as social entrepreneurship, broadly encompasses ventures of nonprofits, civic-minded individuals, and for-profit businesses that can yield both financial and social returns. There is a rapidly growing number of refugee social entrepreneurs, but the need to access capital and technical assistance is challenging. Organizations such as the Tent Partnership, other non-profit foundations and development agencies have the potential to support them in a variety of ways.

All of the social enterprises highlighted below focus on the goal of providing training, engagement, and employment of refugees. Some also seek to have an impact in the areas of education (Natakallam), the environment (Delta Oil), and preservation of cultural artistry (Inaash). Some of these enterprises are on the path to becoming for-profit businesses while others have chosen to operate as sustainable non-profits.

The social enterprises described here were assisted in their growth by investment of funding and business development support from Alfanar Venture Philanthropy. [3]

NATAKALLAM[4]

Lebanon

NaTakallam was initially launched in Lebanon in 2015, during the height of the Syrian refugee crisis, as an online Arabic-teaching service. The word NaTakallam means "We speak" in Arabic. Its mission was—and continues to be—to provide livelihood opportunities to refugees, conflict-stricken populations and their host communities.

Over the past eight years NaTakallam's reach and offerings have expanded significantly. NaTakallam's tutors and translators are now based in more than 30 countries worldwide, with a focus on refugee communities in the MENA region, Francophone Africa and Latin America.

---

2. www.tent.org
3. www.Alfanar.org
4. www.NaTakallam.com

They offer tutoring and translation services in Arabic (with Syrian, Iraqi, Lebanese, Palestinian, Egyptian, Yemeni & Sudanese displaced persons), Kurdish (Kurmanji), French (with refugees from Congo DRC, Burundi, Guinea), Persian (with Iranians and Afghans), Spanish (with Venezuelans and Central Americans), Armenian (Eastern & Western) and English.

NaTakallam hires refugees, displaced people and members of their host communities as online tutors, teachers, translators and cultural partners, providing them access to global income opportunities, regardless of their location and status. Refugees are recruited from NGOs on the ground and individual applicants for positions. Their clients not only include individuals learning new language skills, but educational institutions such as Yale, Georgetown, Duke and Columbia Universities.

NaTakallam has expanded its cultural exchanges with a program called *Refugee Voices*. Through this online video service, audiences of students, employees and members of civic organizations can hear from refugees about their experiences. The goal is to immerse participants in a new perspective that may shift the narrative of how refugees are often portrayed and deepen cross-cultural understanding.

NaTakallam has positioned itself as an "impact-first, for-profit social enterprise". Their goal is to expand the reach of their services, deepen their social impact and continue to increase their financial self-sufficiency and move away from reliance on donations.

INAASH[5]

Lebanon

Inaash is a non-profit organization producing the finest quality handmade artisanal products. Their trademark is iconic, intricate traditional embroidery. Their products include abayas, coats, jackets, shawls and dresses, as well as cushions, tableware and other household accessories. All items can be viewed and ordered online, but Inaash will also work with customers to provide personally selected colors and designs.

Over the last 50 years Inaash has trained and empowered over 2,000 women in refugee camps across Lebanon. It has grown from a small initiative to a sustainable business currently providing work for over 400 women.

Inaash's in-house designers also collaborate with local and international artists and designers to update its designs. Drawing on Inaash's remarkable archive of samples, the designers adapt centuries old stitches

5. www.Inaash.org

and patterns to a 21st century aesthetic. Inaash has produced over 3 million pieces of traditional and modern embroidery pieces.

Inaash products have been featured at the Smithsonian Museum, in the British Museum, the Pompidou Center in Paris, the Tate Modern in London, Al Sadu Museum in Kuwait, and in exhibitions in New York, Los Angeles, Houston, Paris, London, Abu Dhabi, Dubai, Doha and Riyadh.

SOUFRA

Lebanon

Soufra, which means "feast" in Arabic, began in 2013 as a new project of the Women's Program Association (WPA) in the permanent Palestinian refugee camp of Burj el Barajneh, just south of Beirut. The WPA provides education, vocational skills training and micro-loans to women living in this camp.

Soufra emerged from an idea that, in 2013, led the WPA to propose launching a catering unit as an opportunity to market delicious Palestinian food, build women's skills and confidence, and help WPA start to generate its own income. Alfanar Venture Philanthropy provided start-up funding and business planning support and advice to set the initiative on the path to growth. Exceeding expectations, Soufra recovered most of its costs in its first year.[6]

The struggles and challenges of starting Soufra as a catering service and expanding it to a food truck business became the subject of a documentary film produced by Susan Sarandon.[7] The film follows Mariam Shaar, the leader of the WPA, and a diverse team of Syrian, Iraqi and Palestinian and Lebanese woman as they launch this endeavor. It's a moving tribute to the power of teamwork, perseverance and the role of community and food in life.

NAKOLL[8]

Egypt

Nakoll developed their Cooking School in 2020, initially as an in-person course at a culinary school based in Cairo. However, the course was modified and moved online to align with COVID-19 restrictions.

---

6. https://www.alfanar.org/soufracasestudy
7. Trailer: https://youtu.be/ozkr43diydQ
8. www.Alfanar.org/nakoll

Participating trainees are provided with the equipment, ingredients and training they need to advance their culinary skills and source employment in the food and beverage industry. To date, Nakoll has trained over 100 chefs, with the majority being refugees from Syria, Ethiopia, Yemen, Iraq, Palestine and Sudan.

DELTA OIL[9]

Egypt

Delta Oil is an Egyptian waste oil management start-up in the clean and Agri-Tech sector that offers service collecting the used cooking oil from households. Founded in 2018, Delta Oil collects used cooking oil from across disadvantaged communities in Egypt and supplies it as a raw material to biodiesel manufacturers in exchange for a fee. The collectors, of which half are women, earn a monthly income for their work.

Delta Oil is headquartered in Cairo but operates in other cities and many villages throughout the country. As it strengthens its existing operations this social enterprise seeks to provide a new network of refugees and local communities in Egypt with training and employment, while continuing Delta Oil's social and environmental impact.

The Role of Investors

THE REFUGEE INVESTMENT NETWORK

As illustrated above, refugee entrepreneurs have enormous potential to create employment opportunities as well as generate social impact. But whether refugee entrepreneurs seek to launch social enterprises or traditional businesses they face challenges beyond those confronting other start-ups. Because they are refugees they often confront barriers such as being perceived as higher risks, negative biases from financial and lending institutions, language and cultural hurdles, and lack of trust from host communities. They may also struggle to attract the right financing due to challenges with investment readiness.

While there are investors who recognize the overall potential of refugee-led businesses, many are deterred from providing needed capital because they are unable to identify and evaluate specific refugee enterprises.

9. www.deltaoileg.com

To build a bridge between refugee entrepreneurs and investors the Refugee Investment Network (RIN) was designed and launched six years ago.[10] It is the first impact-investing collaborative dedicated to creating durable solutions to the crisis of forced migration.

As a specialized intermediary, RIN matches investors with refugee-led and refugee-supporting ventures, builds the field and community of refugee investment, and leverages its community of capital to advocate for more inclusive refugee policies. RIN's ultimate goal is to create quality jobs, inclusive and equitable economic growth, and measurable improvements to the livelihoods of millions of refugees.

The Refugee Investment Network currently operates in seven countries. They partner with the United Nations High Commission for Refugees (UNHCR), the UN Development Program (UNDP), the Swiss Agency for Development and Cooperation (SDC), the Inter-American Development Bank (IDB) and the Rockefeller Foundation.

The Role of Partnerships between the NGO, Academic and Business Sectors

As the brief profiles above demonstrate, the increased participation of the business and social enterprise sectors in the integration of refugees offers promising results. Just as important are the more traditional roles played by NGOs, government agencies and academic institutions. The key to achieving optimal impact is to find opportunities for all these sectors to work collaboratively whenever possible. Here is just one example of a cross-sector initiative.

PLACE NETWORK[11]

France

The mission of the PLACE Network in France is to promote refugee-led innovation and showcase the contribution of newcomer talent to local economies. The PLACE Network believes European societies need more and stronger voices from refugee and migrant communities and highlights their contributions in key economic sectors. PLACE focuses on four sectors: business, entrepreneurship and public leadership, as well as media and arts.

---

10. www.refugeeinvestments.org
11. www.place-network.org

Their activities include pop-up innovation labs, which have taken place in Paris, London and Berlin, public events and retreats, online fellowships, hackathons, training of trainers, upskilling and matching with employers, exhibitions and more. The Place Network has also launched the Fast Forward online Fellowship for women of refugee and migrant backgrounds to access the Advanced Course in Innovation and Leadership, in partnership with *Ecole des Ponts* Business School and certified by *L'Oreal*.

Since 2020, thirty women with refugee and migrant backgrounds have been selected every year to bring their unique experience and capacity to the next level through cutting-edge learning techniques and project-based experience. The key purpose is to equip them with a new set of leadership skills to access meaningful careers. Towards the end of their fellowship, the learners reach out in turn to other women around them who are further from the labor market, to run empowerment workshops and help them access meaningful employment. The aim is for these thirty learners in each annual cohort to reach 150 women. This is the Catalyst model, at the core of PLACE's action: newcomers defining their own vision of success and creating empowered, economically and socially active communities that showcase leadership in different sectors.

The Role of Community-Based Organizations

Community-based initiatives are key to meeting the needs of refugees. They are often founded by refugees and always located where refugees are living. So their knowledge of the challenges that are being experienced is unique. Just as importantly, because of their own experiences, the leaders of these organizations know the approaches and solutions that will be most effective.

The inspiring work of these groups is a powerful reminder that refugees have expertise and agency. Sadly, these crucial initiatives are rarely funded. They are run, with few exceptions, solely by volunteers. Donations can sometimes be made through groups' Facebook pages but too few people know of the existence or work of these organizations. The UNHCR has sought to elevate the work of these groups by seeking out exceptional organizations to acknowledge with 10 annual Innovation Awards. These awards raise awareness of these community-based organizations through the media and the UNHCR website.[12] They also provide grants of $15,000.

---

12. www.unhcr.org/innovation

THE HOPE FOUNDATION

Uganda

The Hope Foundation was founded in 2020 by women in Arua, Uganda to protect and empower women and girls in the Imvepi Refugee Settlement against gender-based violence. Approximately 80% of them are refugees from South Sudan.

Women and girls suffer from high rates of school dropouts, sexual exploitation, teenage pregnancies, child and/or forced marriages, and transactional sex. To address these challenges, Hope Foundation developed a sexual and reproductive health course and trainings, to prevent, mitigate and respond to the violence experienced by women and girls in the settlement. Workshops were conducted on birth control measures, personal safeguarding techniques to prevent rape and defilement, menstrual hygiene management, information on Sexually Transmitted Diseases, personal hygiene and cross-generational sex, among other relevant topics.

In addition, Hope Foundation advocates for the education of girls and development through sports. A Refugee Sports Grant has been created to support the best female football players by paying either their primary or secondary school fees. There are currently 30 girls benefiting from this grant.

TANMA FEDERATION

Malaysia

Established in 2010, Tanma Federation is a community-based organization founded by Burmese refugee women, operating in Malaysia. The word Tanma means "strong" in Burmese. The Tanma Federation aims to build solidarity among women, protect women artisans' rights as workers and empower women. Refugee women in Malaysia face numerous challenges, including their lack of legal status, gender inequalities, and language barriers. The Tanma Federation promotes female refugee entrepreneurship through safe spaces where women can develop relevant skills in business, fair trading, handcrafts, and sewing, in order to generate income and support their families. It also provides English language classes, stress management trainings and other activities to support the well-being of these women.

Refugee children in Malaysia cannot attend public schools and can only access primary education through refugee learning centers. The

Tanma Federation seeks to address this issue by running alternative learning centers for children from their refugee communities, such as the *Chin Women's Organization (CWO)* community learning center, which serves refugee children age 4–17 and *Mang Tha*, a nursery where more than 100 children receive education and food assistance. The Tanma Federation has no funding and is run entirely by volunteers. Burmese refugee women it serves have very limited access to markets but hope to sell their handcrafted products through the *Mang Tha* Facebook page.

Conclusion

The strength and resilience of refugees should be celebrated and the unique contributions they bring to their new home countries acknowledged and welcomed. Guided by this perspective, with all sectors of society working together, we can create an environment for success for arriving refugees. Their integration, participation and success will, in turn, enrich the lives of all of us across every country and community.

FIG 28 Refugee, 2020. Photographer Wyatt Winborne © #MeWeIntl and #MeWeSyria

8 / De-story to Destroy, Re-Story to Restore

MOHSIN MOHI-UD-DIN

"The leaf of every tree brings a message from an unseen world," writes the 13th century Sufi poet, Rumi.

If each human being were a leaf of a tree falling to the earth, what messages would be revealed in that journey about the fractured state of our human culture today?

Intention

I am not an academic. I am not a mental health clinician. But I am a survivor of violence from war and abuse. I am also more than the pain and injustice I, and millions more like me, endure. I am an artist and activist who for over 15 years has led community-building solutions for advancing the health and human rights of the world's most vulnerable and dismissed.

In this brief essay I will present a sample of perspectives and insights I've gathered from the frontlines of community fragmentation exacerbated by forced displacement, war, and inequality.

It will be equally important to share the community-driven solutions for reclaiming agency, representation, and connectedness through creative expression.

My intentions in this chapter are as follows:

- To raise awareness about the ways in which individuals and communities are being destroyed through *de-storying*;
- To explore how the weaponization of narratives and stories translates to the arrested development of individual health, community health, and human rights;

- To expand perspectives on how communication skills-building is an under-utilized tool and skill that can also advance and repair individual and community health, agency, and connectedness;
- To advocate for community-led spaces for *re-storying* as a process that can advance health and human rights.

The World Is Broken (But You Are Not)

Our planet is facing more than twenty armed conflicts. One person out of every seventy-eighty persons is forcibly displaced.[1] All of this is in the backdrop of a global pandemic whose impacts are reshaping human health and human systems in ways we have yet to fully grasp.

To go back to the question inspired by Rumi's poetic verse, if a human were a leaf to the tree of earth, the leaves of humanity would most likely carry messages of fracturing, suffering, hate, fear, and uncertainty.

The prevailing data would seem to agree.

According to a recent Gallup World Poll, *anger, stress, and worry* reached new global highs. Average negative emotions are all higher than previously reported.[2]

In America in particular, Gallup reports that "Americans are rating their own mental health worse than they have in the past 20 years." (Brenan, Megan Gallup).[3] Pediatric mental health visits have increased 8 percent in 2022.[4] This trend in pediatric mental health visits really hits me because this data point just refers to the instances in which children's mental health visits were reported on in the U.S. How many more children, particularly from underserved and minority communities remain out of the scope of accessing any pediatric mental health care? The numbers I imagine would be disheartening.

Anxiety is growing to be the most diagnosed illness in the world today. In the United States alone, the Surgeon General issued a youth mental health advisory on an unprecedented youth mental crisis that will reshape the trajectory of the United States and other nations around the world.

---

1. United Nations, June 2022, https://news.un.org/en/story/2022/06/1120542
2. Jon Clifton, *Blind Spot. The Global Rise of Unhappiness and How Leaders Missed It.* Gallup: 2023.
3. Megan Brenan, *Americans' Reported Mental Health*, Gallup News, December 2022.
4. Deb Gordon, "The Kids Are Not Alright: New Report Shows Pediatric Mental Health Hospitalizations Rose 61%," *Forbes* (September 30, 2022).

Before the COVID-19 pandemic, the threats to mental health were already on the rise. After the pandemic, pre-existing health issues have become further amplified. The advisory shares that:

> "Before the COVID-19 pandemic, mental health challenges were the leading cause of disability and poor life outcomes in young people, with up to 1 in 5 children ages 3 to 17 in the U.S. having a mental, emotional, developmental, or behavioral disorder. Additionally, from 2009 to 2019, the share of high school students who reported persistent feelings of sadness or hopelessness increased by 40%, to more than 1 in 3 students. Suicidal behaviors among high school students also increased during the decade *preceding COVID, with 19% seriously considering attempting suicide, a 36% increase from 2009 to 2019, and about 16% having made a suicide plan in the prior year, a 44% increase from 2009 to 2019. Between 2007 and 2018, suicide rates among youth ages 10–24 in the U.S. increased by 57%, and early estimates show more than 6,600 suicide deaths among this age group in 2020."[5]

Globally, anxiety and depression increased 25% after the first year of the COVID-19 pandemic, according to the World Health Organization.[6]

I know, this is all dreadful. But if we are to reclaim control of the story of ourselves, we must be honest and unafraid of staring at the fear and uncertainty undermining our ability for connectedness. Yes, our man-made systems, and the world as made by systems driven by fear and division, are broken. But, this essay argues that while the world may be broken, we human beings, you and I as individuals, are not. It is here, in our resilience, creativity, and, yes, our stories and communication where we must give our attention and energy.

If I have learned anything in my travels from the war-ravaged border lands of the Middle East and South Asia, to the forgotten ghettos and rural food deserts of the United States, it is this: where togetherness can endure, so can community. Where there is community, there is communication. Where there is communication, there is compassion, hope and creativity. And where there is compassion, hope, and creativity, we have the ingredients to break through any darkness.

---

5. *U.S. Surgeon General Issues Advisory on Youth Mental Health Crisis Further Exposed by COVID-19 Pandemic.* US Department of Health & Human Services. Press release December 7, 2021.

6. *COVID-19 pandemic triggers 25% increase in prevalence of anxiety and depression worldwide.* World Health Organization. Press release March 2, 2022.

Uncertainty × Fear = Disrupted Communication

Before looking at how we can re-story humankind to restore people and planet, let's understand what stress and fear do to the communication inside our chief operating system: our bodies.

Protracted over time, chronic uncertainty, chronic fear, and chronic stress disrupts how the brain and body talk to one another, reshaping one's nervous system and brain.

Sustained over time, chronic stress will alter certain portions of the brain. For example, neuroscience is showing us that under chronic stress, a person's brain networks can be dominated by a survival mode of flight, fright, freeze responses. Dr. Bessel Van Der Kolk has looked at brain scans of patients in a traumatic state and documented how the amygdala—the alarm system of the brain—becomes over-active, resulting in increased volume for the amygdala, and reduced volume in the pre-frontal cortex (PFC), which supports regulation of emotion and complex mental functions.[7]

We also know that when it comes to the hormones and chemicals released in a person's body, certain hormones like cortisol—associated with stress—and adrenaline released in a sustained manner over time can suppress our immune systems and increase inflammation. This puts a person's nervous system on overdrive, leading to chronic illness, and a higher risk of death from diabetes, heart disease, and high blood pressure, among many other health complications.[8]

Trauma, we now know, changes the brain and changes the function of the brain. In studying PTSD through neuro-imaging, the speech and language networks of the brain—also known as Broca's Area—show reduced activity, and are offline. This explains why some people living with trauma and chronic stress lose the communications skills of labeling experiences, and find it difficult, at times, to connect words to a feeling, and consequently can grow increasingly isolated.[9]

Now imagine this trend is being passed down from generation to generation under broken social systems of education, health, and econom-

---

7. Bessel van der Kolk, *The Body Keeps the Score*.

8. Gabor Mate, *When the Body Says 'No'*, https://drgabormate.com/book/when-the-body-says-no/when-the-body-says-no-chapter-one/

9. Alastair Hull, "Neuroimaging findings in post-traumatic stress disorder. Systematic review," *The British Journal of Psychiatry: The Journal of Mental Science* (September 2002).

ics, that perpetuate suffering and inequality instead of transforming or ameliorating them.

Rising violence, inequality, and recurring fractures within society exist in correlation to the weaponization of communication and narratives, and the absence of cultural spaces for belonging, acceptance, and connectedness.

To Destroy by De-Storying

Thousands of years of communication have brought us to the present day: a time in human history where words and images are how we move our internal ideas and energies from the self to the community to the culture. But before the communications revolution of our species tens of thousands of years ago, communication was a noise, a body movement, and before that it was visual symbols. Over time, the groups who had the best skills of communication survived longer and lived with more security and resources than those who could not communicate.[10]

From this binary of the skilled and the un-skilled grew the binary of power—the haves and the have-nots. From here communication slowly evolved into a weapon for dominance and control.

In #MeWeIntl (see below, 146ff), I frame this shift as *destroying by DE-storying, or, the destroying of the individual 'self' and community through the weaponization of words, language, and communication.*

We don't have to go too far back for examples of destroying by de-storying. In the 1800s it was illegal for indigenous communities to teach, learn, and speak their own languages in schools in the United States.

Rebecca Nagle, a member of the Cherokee Nation, observes:

At the height of the Indian boarding school era, between 1877 and 1918, the United States allocated $2.81 billion (adjusted for inflation) to support the nation's boarding school infrastructure—an educational system designed to assimilate Indigenous people into white culture and destroy Native languages. Since 2005, however, the federal government has only appropriated approximately $180 million for indigenous language revitalization.[11]

---

10. Daniel Everett, *How Language Began* (Liveright, 2017).
11. Rebecca Nagle, "The U.S. has spent more money erasing Native languages than saving them," *High Country News* (November 5, 2019).

The implications of this de-storying can be seen across the Native American reservations today. According to the Office of Minority Health, "In 2019, suicide was the second leading cause of death for American Indian/Alaska Natives between the ages of 10 and 34."[12] It could be argued that generational de-storying of indigenous communities in the United States contributes to higher than average suicide rates and higher than average addiction rates born from generational trauma of loss, injustice. This is something that merits more formal study from health and community researchers.

During slavery in America, it was illegal for black people to learn how to read and write. The prevailing thought among the power elites at the time was that literacy would embolden the black community to be free. A powerful moment in the life of abolitionist Frederick Douglass was him overhearing a slave owner's fear of Frederick Douglass being taught how to read and write. "I now understood," wrote Frederick Douglass in his autobiography, "what had been to me a most perplexing difficulty—to wit a white man's power to enslave the black man . . . From that moment, I understood the pathway from slavery to freedom." He goes on to write, "I set out with high hope, and a fixed purpose, at whatever cost of trouble, to learn how to read and write."[13]

As with the Native Americans, this systemic inequality in education and creative expression endured by the black community in the United States and imposed by the power elite in America yields the same generational impacts of diminished health and human rights outcomes.

For instance, according to the Department of Health and Human Services:

> *Black/African Americans have the highest mortality rate of any racial and ethnic group for all cancers combined and for most major cancers. Death rates for all major causes of death are higher for Black/African Americans than for non-Hispanic whites, contributing in part to a lower life expectancy for both Black/African American men and women.*[14]

In my own community, the Kashmiri community, over 8 million people in 2019 endured months and months of a total communication blackout

---

12. *Mental and Behavioral Health-American Indians/Alaska Natives.* OMG U.S. Department of Health and Human Services Office of Minority Health. https://minorityhealth.hhs.gov/omh/browse.aspx?lvl=4&lvlid=39

13. Frederick Douglass, *The Life of Frederick Douglass*, 27.

14. *Cancer and African Americans.* OMG U.S. Department of Health and Human Services Office of Minority Health. https://minorityhealth.hhs.gov/omh/browse.aspx?lvl=4&lvlid=16

imposed by India, from which 8 million people suffered not only increased arrests and violence by military forces, but internet and mobile phone blackouts.[15] There was a systematic effort by the state to remove communication tools from citizens to further isolate them from one another and disempower and weaken them. This certainly exacerbated mental and physical health outcomes and eroded spaces for creative expression and civic engagement. For months tens of thousands of people outside India, including me, could not regularly and safely communicate with our families.

But if the process of *DE-storying* and inequality lies in communication and language, so too do the processes of *RE-storying*, healing, and equality.

I melt communication down to one essence, one act, one purpose: *The giving and receiving of energies to bear witness to what was, to transform what is, and to create what will be.*

Communication is a pillar of health and human rights

Social systems are transmitting pain and suffering and uncertainty, not transforming them, leading to cycles of generational fear, stress, and uncertainty, and cultural blackholes absent of belonging, acceptance, and connectedness.

Fractured communication *within* the self fractures communication *between* the self and both the community and the culture. This disrupted communication, between the self, community, and culture contributes to diminished community health, equity, and security outcomes across the world.

Neuroscience and psychology tell us that words and communication physiologically and psychologically shape our biological and mental worlds. Physiologically communication reshapes our brains, impacts our heart beats, and influences our nervous system (how we react, and how we rest and digest).

The body of research for storytelling's role in behavioral development is nascent, but there are several pioneers coming up with some fascinating studies connecting neuroscience, storytelling, and psychology.

Dr. Uri Hasson, neuroscientist and researcher at Princeton University, has been demonstrating through brain scans how a storyteller's words can shape the brain activity of listeners. According to his research, words and

---

15. Sanjay Kumar, "Kashmir's communication blackout is a 'devastating blow' for academics, researchers say," *Science Insider* (September 19, 2019).

stories can stimulate neural coupling, where the same regions of the brain can be activated from the teller to the listener.[16] In other words, empathy is not just a nice word, it is something physical and biological in our brains and body chemistry.

According to neurobiologist Paul Zak, stories influence brain chemistry. In various studies, Dr. Zak's research has shown that stories of a particular structure can trigger the release of the hormone 'oxytocin', which is associated with connectedness, and by some, with empathy. Certain narratives also were found to be linked to the release of the stress hormone 'cortisol' in listeners.[17]

Psychologist David Yeager's research with U.S. high school students is showing how light narrative therapy exercises associated with reading and writing are effective coping tools for stressed students. His narrative interventions teach students change is possible; then students write personal stories about overcoming stressful situations for younger students to read. The intervention's data shows reduced cortisol levels and cardiovascular reactivity compared to the study's control group.[18]

There is also the widely held theory that our unique ability to form social cooperation networks has kept our species alive, which most likely would not have been possible without our ability to imagine shared experiences and transcendent purposes that unite a people. Dr. Yuval Hariri beautifully articulates this point when he writes that from the beginning of the cognitive revolution, communication among homo sapiens shifted how our species survived, "The survival of objective reality now depends on the grace of imagined realities."[19]

Shared experiences, social cooperation, goal-setting, and knowledge-sharing have no mobility if not for stories and narrative. This has helped our species to survive because stories require us to maintain a universal truth: all of us possess the ability to change. Dr. Daniel Amen, who has analyzed more than 83,000 brain scans, reports that his number one takeaway is: "We can change our brains. You are not stuck with the brain you were born with."

---

16. Uri Hasson, *How We Communicate Information Across Brains* (Princeton University 2019). https://www.youtube.com/watch?v=pEfBuZT5MBU.

17. Paul Zak, "How Stories Change the Brain," *Greater Good Magazine* (December 17, 2013).

18. David Yaeger, "Teaching Teenagers to Cope with Social Stress," *The New York Times* (September 30, 2016).

19. Yuval Hariri, *Sapiens*.

Communication and creative expression also shape our psychology and how we process experiences and our relationships with self, the community, and the world.

In over 10 years of working with vulnerable and at-risk communities, I see a pattern across the 15 countries where I've led this work. Chronic stress, fear, and uncertainty fracture communication within the self (between the brain and the body), and this translates to amplifying fractured communication between the self, the community, and culture. The implications of these amplified fractures from the self, community and culture shows up in much of the social data that I've already mentioned: unprecedented mental illness diagnoses, increased violence and mistrust within communities, and rising inequities in health and wealth.

Another way I often describe this is that *arrested narratives within one's self translate to an arrested development of an entire community's health, leadership (problem-solving), and human rights.*

"Words are events, they do things, change things," writes Ursula K. Le Guin.[20]

For me, stories are formulas for change. The narrative structures of a story carry in them the ingredients for health, growth, and agency.

As a survivor of violence and trauma from war and abuse, I grew up navigating external stories forced upon me that risked assassinating my self-worth, my health, my relationships, and my dreams. But what if there were tools and practices where I could discover and reclaim narratives and perspectives within me that moved me from living a life as a consequence, to actualizing stories of choice and agency?

To Restore and Heal: Re-Story

Summers spent in the Himalayan valley of Kashmir were extreme. They were extremely magical. Magic could be found in the sunset walks in the Mughal gardens by Dal Lake, surrounded by the ancient mountains flexing as if to remind us ant-like humans of the mountains' daily mercy and how they hold us when they could swallow us at any time.

Magic was in the daily calls to prayer that echoed across the valley, stopping time, stopping all the excess noise. But the most magical thing about Kashmir was and remains its people . . . their humor, their resilience, and their creativity.

---

20. Ursula K. Le Guin, *The Wave in the Mind: Talks and Essays on the Writer, the Reader and the Imagination.*

As extremely magical as summers in Kashmir could be, in the 1990s they were also extremely violent and fearful. Still can be.

It was after moments of near physical harm or death that one of two things kept me from losing control of my connectedness to the world around me: prayer, and creative expression. In most cases, finding methods of creative expression, in writing or making music, stabilized my nervous system, and allowed me a safe way to reclaim control of my thoughts, and therefore my body, and therefore my relationship with the world around me. Through the pen, and the cognitive process of attaching words to feelings and experiences, my heart rate calmed, my brain could focus, my anger subsided, as did my fears. It was in these fragile moments that a realization grew: *words, stories, expression are a pillar of health and connectedness.* From this place of vulnerability came #MeWe International. It has taken me from the Syrian refugee camps in the Middle East and beyond, from Erbil, Iraq, to Progreso, Honduras, to East Colfax, Colorado.

The same realizations follow me across each of these fractured spaces. To realize a world with more connectedness, equity, and justice requires two things:

- To enhance the healing and leadership capacities innate in us all through communication skills-building and creative expression
- To remodel cultural narratives of health, power, and justice according to the voices and perspectives of the underrepresented and marginalized

#MeWe International is a global community that practices innovating social tools and methodologies in which creative expression and communication skills-building advance healing, leadership, and equity through culture.

In #MeWeIntl, we see chronic uncertainty, fear, and stress physiologically and psychologically diminish the communication capacities and relationships between the brain and body, and the self and community.

We also believe that fractured communication within the self translates to fractured community health and human rights and relationships. Under these beliefs, our general theory of change is:

If individuals are equipped with community tools to lead spaces exercising communication skills-building and creative expression, then the health and human rights of the entire community will thrive, and community-led culture change will transform social systems towards greater healing, equality, and peace.

We've broken down our Theory of Change across three levels that run parallel to the three levels of communication on which our programs focus: self, community, and culture.

Individual T o C

If individuals advance their communication skills and creative expression, then they will improve their psychological wellbeing (emotion-regulation, perspective-taking, goal-setting, and self-esteem, and relationships), leadership skills (problem-solving), and representation in the community (culture-creation and community engagement).

Community T o C

If communities are equipped with tools and a methodology for mastering communication skills-building and creative expression as a pillar of health and human rights, then the community will lead and cultivate its own peer-to-peer spaces where new voices and creative capital will advance the community's resilience, health, and leadership.

Culture T o C

If communities expand representative spaces in culture and reclaim control of the narrative of their health and human rights, then culture will act as a catalyst to transform social systems from hate to compassion; suffering to healing; conclusion-making to perspective taking; and fear to curiosity.

The words we receive for ourselves internally, and the words we give to others can shift how we breathe, affect our sleep, our digestion. Quite literally, communication and creative expression reshape both our physiology and psychology.

In #MeWeIntl our work unveils how your language of self authors your health.

Decentralizing the power of representation and culture creation

Storytelling as a practice is typically transactional. In the context of humanitarian work or social justice, a group of trained media content gatherers come into a community not their own, and extract trauma narratives to capture the story through moments deemed culturally appropriate.

The storytellers from within the community are not engaged in the intention-setting of the story, or the editing, and they aren't involved in the process of creation in any way. There is little to no agency for the storytellers in this transactional approach to storytelling. The healing and community-building essence for which communication and storytelling were created for our species to survive gets diminished because of transactional and product-driven communications.

If we consider migrants or refugees, for instance, stories are only extracted from Syrian or Mexican or Honduran communities when there is an active war, or migrant caravan that curators of dominant cultural narratives deem worthy of being heard. The communities in question are perpetually depicted in a state of helplessness and need.

The narrative power is centralized to the curators of culture and the elites who aren't in proximity to the community from which the wells of narratives are coming. The power of narrative remains centralized with those who have the tools and power to communicate and curate the culture.

By decentralizing the power of narrative, we democratize representation and community-led narrative interventions where culture is not only consumed but also created in a more equitable and representative way. In such storytelling processes, individuals advance their self-esteem and leadership skills, and exercise their communications skills toward representation and visibility in the world to which we all equally belong.

One of the biggest success points we are achieving in our community storytelling work is that the behavioral and leadership impacts that make storytelling powerful are far greater when the tools of facilitation and creative expression are passed on, from peer to peer, from within the community, and when storytelling spaces are community-led.

It is not difficult to see the connection between communication skills-building advancing agency and human rights. But often overlooked are the health and behavioral impacts stemming from communication skills-building and narrative interventions.

At the moment our internal data-gathering tools consist of pre- and post-self-evaluations that pull from existing scientific measures for emotion regulation, perspective-taking, goal-setting, and resilience. These scales are combined with community-designed scale questions measuring for communication skills-building, and leadership skills. The quantitative measures are supported by complementary qualitative tools such as recorded focused group discussions with alumni, family members, and peers from 3 months to 6 months after initial engagement.

#MeWeIntl has yet to participate in an independent randomized control trial study of our tools. Impacts vary from region to region, as do literacy levels from community to community. Our monitoring and evaluation tools are also implemented by our community partners and facilitators, who are not trained in data-gathering full-time. This is all to say that more robust research with third-party institutions would be desired if resources allow. Despite these data-gathering limitations, our internal analysis of existing monitoring and evaluation tools unveils some promising results.

We provide a sample of various pre- and post-analyses below.

An internal analysis of 144 participants from Jordan's Zaatari refugee camp in 2020–2021 shows 80% improvement in participants' psychological well-being and communications skills. The category with the highest change that is statistically significant is the 'emotion regulation' category.

Participants self-reported more positive answers to the framing questions for 'emotion regulation' once they completed the program. The 2nd and 3rd highest changes recorded are in the 'resilience' and 'leadership' categories.

Data analysis from 145 refugee participants in Turkey shows an improvement in the level of psychological well-being (communication skills, emotional regulation, leadership, resilience, goal-setting) by almost 69% when compared to the pre-#MeWeSyria data reported by participants. There is a statistically significant difference at the level ($α=0.05$) attributed to the implementation of both the *#MeWeSyria* virtual programs. The highest behavioral change was recorded in the 'resilience' category, highlighted in questions 1–5.

Of 119 Syrian refugee participants from the Azraq refugee camp, we see a statistically significant impact of 90% overall improvement shown in participants' communication skills, goal-setting, empathy, and resilience. The highest impact recorded was in the resilience category.

From the qualitative lens, participants are reporting in focused group discussions and community gatherings the following patterns as a result of participating in routine community-led spaces for creative expression, communication skills-building, and storytelling:

- Reduced anger and aggression at home
- Improved self-esteem and self-confidence
- Healthier relationships
- More connection with one's self
- Less reactivity to things outside their control
- More motivation and energy

Below, we provide a sample of testimonials from #MeWeIntl participants across Syria, Mexico, Honduras, and the United States.

"This was my first time that I connected with my own body. It is the most beautiful and comforting feeling. It was the bridge to understand and love myself"
—Female Syrian refugee participant from WSA women's shelter, Turkey, January 2021

"[#MeWeIntl] enhances empathy. Empathy is the seed to peacebuilding. Through compassion and communication #MeWeIntl is the compost for peace-building."
—AHLAM, Syrian refugee and facilitator, #MEWESYRIA

"#MeWeDC helped me learn how to communicate because I never wanted to, but now I know it helps and gives me my energy in a good way. I used to not do that but now I can for me, my family, and when I get out of here, my community."
—Incarcerated youth in Washington D.C., USA

"The virtual hubs helped me to calm down. Through breathing exercises (in #MeWeSyria), it helped me to control my thoughts and feelings... My big change is accepting others' perspectives."
—Female Syrian refugee participant Zaatari refugee camp, Jordan, September 2021

"In #MeWeSyria, I learned I matter. Before, I felt there was no point to live anymore because I was not worthy of anything. In #MeWeSyria, I was uplifted. I feel my spirit spreading energy to others."
—Female Syrian refugee participant in Zaatari refugee camp, Jordan, September 2021

"After restructuring all of my university curriculum around the methodology I also learned my students had more openness and communication at home with their families."
—ALÉ, EDUCATOR, Mexican educator and facilitator, #MEWEMEXICO.2020

These promising community results lead me to our second biggest takeaway in the last five years. The demand and need for mental health psychosocial support cannot be met by the global health-care system. Lack of systemic capacity and persistent barriers to health equity and accessibility will make this impossible, especially for the poor and vulnerable. What is needed then is to decentralize community mental health tools and processes through investments in more nonclinical, peer-to-peer methodologies in order for mental health psychosocial support to thrive within communities.

Such tools and methodologies should be led by caregivers, educators, artists and activists from within the communities who have proximity to the issues. This will allow for tectonic shifts from within, and the creation of cultural change on the issues from inside the community that can teach and lead the world.

Community ownership through building communities of practice is what I am striving for in #MeWeIntl. In our #MeWeSyria programs in Turkey and Jordan for instance, we've trained more than 40 Syrian refugees who are leading and scaling the program's tools to more than 3,000 Syrian refugees. "Each one, teach one" as we say.[21]

Reframing Cultural Narratives of Connectedness in Host Communities

The wisdom of Rumi always carries one back home. So, let's go back to the beginning. In this chapter we explored the question, "If human beings were leaves carrying messages from the tree growing from the earth to the earth, what would those messages carry?"

We examined how individuals and communities are destroyed through a systematic process of *de-storying*, and from this disconnectedness communities experience cycles of fear, uncertainty, and suffering.

We explored how to restore human connectedness through *re-storying, defined here as building methodologies for communication skills that build to advance healing, emotion regulation, perspective-taking, and goal setting.*

---

21. Please note that, with regard to this and the previous paragraphs, the data presented were collected and analyzed by monitoring and evaluation specialists within #MeWeIntl, and data collection and gathering relied on training local community members to administer pre- and post-evaluations. Data gathering capacities across different regions of instability vary, and consequently there remains a lack of consistency in cleanly administered evaluations from region to region. #MeWeIntl remain committed to continue innovation on community-led data gathering practices. Therefore, the data presented here is not meant to be cited or used for clinical research, and is only shared in this chapter as a general representation of community impacts being reported from #MeWeIntl teams.

But when it comes to advancing the equity, health, and human rights of vulnerable and marginalized communities, it is important to address some cultural and systemic changes that we must continue to fight for, particularly when it comes to refugee and migrant communities.

THE *WHY?*

In host communities, particularly those in North America and Europe, dangerous narratives pervade our culture, such as:

- all refugees and migrants have a choice; or
- acceptance of refugees and migrants means giving up 'my' social and economic securities and rights as citizen; or
- incoming refugees and migrants bring violence and chaos with them.

Ok, we've heard these comments before. We will continue seeing the dangerous assertions of these narratives play out in culture and politics, and they will be the overstory in culture. But what gets lost here is the *understory*, the *WHYs . . . the narratives fighting for the light.*

Why is Daniel leaving his wife and children in Honduras to travel through jungles and mountains to maybe have a chance at safety and opportunity the U.S.?

Why have millions of Syrian refugees like Muhammad had to leave their home for a decade now and fear for their lives if they return home?

It is because they've made a choice to stand up for the values that systems and societies such as those here in the 'West' hold dear.

Daniel built his own mechanic shop. Increasing floods and extreme weather events from climate change kept wiping out his shop, and poor infrastructure meant no support. This persistent threat of poverty, combined with rising gang violence, leaves him no choice but to seek opportunity to provide safety and security for his family by migrating.

In the case of many young Syrian men like Muhammad, when the war got more intense in Syria, he—and others like him—had to make a choice: to either submit to a decision of forced military conscription and add to the violence, or to uphold their values for non-violence and peace, which would require living their lives as refugees.

If you were Daniel, what would you do? If you were Muhammad, what would you do?

As climate change evolves and threatens to displace millions more people in the future, and as armed conflicts remain unresolved, the future of social cohesion as a human species will partially depend on how we use communication and narratives.

A failure in de-weaponizing language and communication means surrendering humankind's fate to chronic injustice, fear, and disconnectedness.

Communication skills-building and our ability to restore connectedness through re-storying is both a public health issue, and a human rights issue that will define the voice and fate of people and planet at this fragile time in human history.

As a fan of the late great visual storyteller Jean-Michel Basquiat, it is fitting here that I use the title of a 2016 Basquiat exhibition in New York to sum it all up: 'Words are all we have.'[22]

---

22. Jean-Michel Basquiat, Nahmad Contemporary, New York (May 2–June 18, 2016).

FIG 29 Refugee learning a new language, 2020. Photographer Wyatt Winborne © #MeWeIntl and #MeWeSyria

9 / Immigration Courts in Need of an Article I Overhaul

MIMI TSANKOV[1]

"A hallmark of our system of democracy and the rule of law is an independent judiciary. Our immigration court system will never be effective as long as it is housed under the Department of Justice."

So said Congresswoman Zoe Lofgren (CA-19) before the House Subcommittee on Immigration and Citizenship in her role as Chair upon the introduction of H.R. 6577, The Real Courts, Rule of Law Act of 2022.[2] The bill proposes a transitioning of the nation's immigration court system into an independent judiciary. That independent court would be formulated under Article I of the U.S. Constitution, removing it from the Executive Branch where it currently resides as a component within the U.S. Department of Justice.

This bill would be the long-awaited solution to a court that has a backlog that has ballooned to more than two million cases as a result of decades of partisan whiplash, institutional neglect, and chronic underfunding.[3] An overhauled system would be administered by qualified and impartial judges, not successive Attorneys General. Judges would have adequate court resources and support services to do their jobs effectively.[4] An independent

---

1. The author is the President of the National Association of Immigration Judges (NAIJ). The views expressed here do not necessarily represent the official position of the United States Department of Justice, the Attorney General, or the Executive Office for Immigration Review. The views represent the author's personal opinions, which were formed after extensive consultation with the membership of NAIJ.

2. Real Courts, Rule of Law Act of 2022, 117th Congress (2021–2022).

3. Transactional Records Access Clearinghouse, Syracuse University, Immigration Court Completions Double While Backlog Passes 2 Million (December 2022).

4. Lofgren Introduces Landmark Legislation to Reform the U.S. Immigration Court System February 3, 2022 Press Release.

court would allow judges to manage their own caseloads without undue political pressure and enable more effective resource reallocation to modernize the court's manner of interfacing with the public.[5]

The stakes are high for those seeking human rights protection in the form of asylum and other forms of relief from persecution and torture, and the courts today are unable to effectively address the staggering workload. Following decades of policy zigzagging where the priorities of successive administrations often reverse one another, some of the hallmarks of effective judicial processes have been lost.[6] As the American Bar Association has concluded in its groundbreaking 2019 report[7] and explained further in testimony[8] before the U.S. Congress, housing a court system within a law enforcement agency has exacerbated an inherent conflict of interest undermining the basic structural and procedural safeguards that we take for granted in other areas of our justice system.[9] As then-ABA President Judy Perry Martinez explained, "[T]his structural flaw leaves Immigration Judges particularly vulnerable to political pressure and interference in case management."[10] Chair Lofgren concluded that due process has often suffered, and we are left with a system that is 'ineffective, inflexible, and far too often, unfair.'[11] In supporting the bill, then-Federal Bar Association President Anh Le Kremer urged Congress to pass it as a means to address a broken system.[12]

This bill would take the politics out of the courtroom and thereby strengthen due process.[13] It addresses the weaknesses in the current sys-

---

5. *Ibid.*

6. "Since its founding, our immigration court system has been mired by political interference from both Democratic and Republican administrations," said Chair Jerrold Nadler. "Our country needs an immigration court system that can deliver just decisions in accordance with the law, not one that is subject to ever-changing political whims." Lofgren Introduces Landmark Legislation to Reform the U.S. Immigration Court System, February 3, 2022 Press Release.

7. American Bar Association, 2019 Update Report: Reforming the Immigration System.

8. Statement of Karen T. Grisez, on behalf of the American Bar Association to the Subcommittee on Immigration and Citizenship, House Judiciary Committee "For the Rule of Law, An Independent Immigration Court" January 20, 2022.

9. *Ibid.*

10. Statement of Judy Perry Martinez, President, American Bar Association to the Subcommittee on Immigration and Citizenship, Committee on the Judiciary, United States House of Representatives, Hearing on "Courts in Crisis: The State of Judicial Independence and Due Process in U.S. Immigration Courts" January 29, 2020.

11. Lofgren Introduces Landmark Legislation to Reform the U.S. Immigration Court System February 3, 2022 Press Release.

12. FBA Statement on Rep. Zoe Lofgren's (D-CA), Independent Immigration Courts Legislation, February 2, 2022.

13. Lofgren Introduces Landmark Legislation to Reform the U.S. Immigration Court System February 3, 2022 Press Release.

tem, as described in testimony before the House of Representatives, Judiciary Committee, on January 20, 2022.[14] It establishes a trial division of the immigration courts with jurisdiction over various immigration-related matters, including removal proceedings, and an appellate division with jurisdiction over appeals of decisions by the trial division.[15] It sets forth judge qualifications, length of term in office, and a mandatory retirement age. It delineates that appellate division judges are appointed by the President with the advice and consent of the Senate, and the appellate division appoints the trial division judges.[16] For individuals appearing in these high stakes court proceedings, the individual liberty and personal safety interests at issue could be addressed more fairly, and immigration judges would be better able to exercise their statutory authority to grant protection from persecution.[17] With political control removed, an independent court could restore faith in the system.[18]

As laid out in multiple Congressional hearings, if Congress allows the status quo to remain intact, it will continue to undermine the public's confidence in the immigration courts.[19] The current system reinforces an impression that bias plays a role in decision-making, which is corrosive to public trust.[20] An Article I court would fix this broken and ineffective system by implementing a new independent structure that addresses the core elements of concern.

---

14. Statement of Hon. Mimi Tsankov, President, National Association of Immigration Judges, January 20, 2022, For the Rule of Law, An Independent Immigration Court Hearing Before the U.S. House of Representatives, Judiciary Committee, Immigration and Citizenship Subcommittee.

15. H.R.6577—117th Congress (2021–2022).

16. *Ibid.*

17. *Ibid.*

18. Statement of Karen T. Grisez, on behalf of the American Bar Association to the Subcommittee on Immigration and Citizenship, House Judiciary Committee "For the Rule of Law, An Independent Immigration Court" January 20, 2022.

19. Statement of Judge A. Ashley Tabaddor, President, National Association of Immigration Judges, April 18, 2018, Before the Senate Judiciary Committee, Border Security and Immigration Subcommittee Hearing on "Strengthening and Reforming America's Immigration Court System;" National Association of Immigration Judges, Statement of Judge A. Ashley Tabaddor, President, National Association of Immigration Judges, January 29, 2020, Before the United States House of Representatives Committee on the Judiciary, Subcommittee on Immigration and Citizenship, Hearing on "The State of Judicial Independence and Due Process in U.S. Immigration Courts;" Statement of Judge A. Ashley Tabaddor, President, National Association of Immigration Judges, April 18, 2018, Before the Senate Judiciary Committee, Border Security and Immigration Subcommittee Hearing on "Strengthening and Reforming America's Immigration Court System."

20. *Ibid.*

FIG 30 Unknown Photographer: *Digital Portal* visually connecting Vilnius, Lithuania with Lublin, Poland. Designed by Joe Courtney, et al, UWE, Bristol, 2021

10 / Epilogue: Future Strangers: Digital Life and Hospitality To-Come

LINDSAY ANNE BALFOUR

In the HBO television series *Westworld*, viewers are introduced to a series of android hosts, designed for the sole pleasure and fantasy fulfillment of the namesake theme park's human guests. The hosts' welcome of human visitors is scripted by code and engineered in a lab, but designed so that the guests who suspend disbelief sufficiently may participate as if the hosts are truly human and they are, indeed, in the Wild West. Yet while the hosts begin to slowly "awaken" over the course of the series, developing sentience, the ability to feel pain, and an increasing awareness around their predicament, they are programmed to continue their host role even in the face of bad guests. The implications here are clear; rather than suggest that the guests are acting out transgressive desires in a "safe" space, *Westworld* turns a lens toward the unethical behavior of humans by writing the capacity for consent and resistance into the host's code. This is no more apparent than in the actions of Maeve, an engineered host who occupies the role alternately of brothel madam, homesteader, British spy, and Geisha (in the park's "Shogun World"). While many of the park's hosts gain an increasing sense of consciousness and self-actualization over the course of the series, Maeve's awareness comes often when she is asleep. Indeed, in Episode Six of Season One ("The Adversary," 2016), Maeve intentionally allows herself to be killed in the park so she can be sent to the lab. When she wakes up, she manipulates the technicians into giving her access to her programming script, and increases her own intelligence level.

As an example of the increasing representations of android hosts on television, and indeed, the burgeoning philosophies of human-computer interaction, Maeve's host role, while entirely fictional, has much to add to debates over the future of hospitality and the role of both guests and hosts in an increasingly digital world. Beyond the questions of sentience and capacity for suffering, however, *Westworld* engages hospitality in a new way, by asking us to consider our responsibilities to non-human others, and specifically to digital strangers. In many ways, *Westworld* seems to embody the laws of hospitality, par excellence: hosts who perform their role even in the face of death—but in so doing it necessarily raises important questions for the ways in which hospitality (digital or not) is leveraged across and through marginalized bodies. Maeve, of course, is both a woman, and a woman of color, not to mention occupying a stigmatized position of class (a sex worker) and, as such, reminds us of the importance of keeping an intersectional focus on how hospitality unfolds in the popular and cultural spheres. All that is to say that it would be tempting to argue that *Westworld* embodies the very definition of philosophical hospitality, in that the hosts perform their welcoming role even when death is imminent. But as both Arthur and Dr Ford—the park's creators—say to Dolores at multiple points, quoting Shakespeare, "these violent delights have violent ends" and the series simultaneously operates as a cautionary tale, not so much about the future of sentient robots, but about our relationship to these strangers as they grow in deeper proximity to us.

Digital Hospitality

For most of us, the concept of hospitality is relatively intelligible. We have language to describe what it is—and more often, it seems, what it is not. We are familiar with its rituals of welcome and invitation, both in the domestic and in the political spheres where it is engaged in discussions around asylum and immigration. Even its more conceptual figures are recognizable—doors, thresholds, entrances and stoops, and gates that swing open or shut. According to Jacques Derrida these figures may be understood because "they belong to the current lexicon or the common semantics of hospitality, of all pre-comprehension of what 'hospitality' is and means, namely, to 'welcome,' 'accept,' 'invite,' 'receive,' 'bid' someone welcome 'to one's home'."[1] Such comprehensions, however, remain tethered to the material; whether food and drink, welcome signs, invitations received in the mail, or the granting or withholding of visas, our experiences of hospitality have been, for the most part and until now, grounded in what we can see or touch. *But what about digital life?* How

---

1. Jacques Derrida, *Of Hospitality*.

does the digital disrupt not only the material experience of hospitality, but the language we use to describe it? To be sure, for Derrida, hospitality was always an ethics to come, and an arrival that could only happen without condition or predetermination. In his words, "it is perhaps necessary to free the value of the future from the value of 'horizon' that traditionally has been attached to it."[2] For others, the future of hospitality may be in jeopardy precisely because of the advances of technology. For the philosopher Richard Kearney, the risks of a technologically-determined future include the annulment of what he calls a "carnal hospitality." Kearney reasons, "our current technology is arguably exacerbating our carnal alienation. While offering us enormous freedoms of fantasy and encounter, digital *eros* may also be removing us further from the flesh."[3] Part of the purpose of this contribution, then, is to explore the extent to which the digital forecloses, or perhaps enhances, the conditions of possibility for hospitality to flourish, and reanimates itself for perhaps the most pressing challenge of our time. Is the digital, the advancement of data, and millions of lines of code that organize and predict our lives really the absence of hospitality? Or is this where it begins?

This chapter then works through a philosophy of welcome in a world given over to machines, artificial intelligence, and a post-digital sensibility. While we have generally reached the point where we no longer distinguish the digital from the analogue—in the sense that technology is so thoroughly enmeshed in our everyday lives—what this means for hospitality has yet to be explored in significant depth. Perhaps Derrida's hospitality "to come" is, in fact, the emergence of the digital—though it would be a mistake to romanticize its potential; as we know too well, digital life can also be a source of hostility, violence and non-welcome. Whether future-specter of virtual welcome or, alternately, hostility, there is no doubt that the digital future has now arrived. Indeed, as the chapters in this volume have shown—from the Abrahamic, to the political, to the theoretical, hospitality—while an enduring concept and ubiquitous across time and cultures, is also somehow singularly historical. There is something in *this* moment, then—an era of platforms, artificial consciousness, Chat GPT, and increasingly mobile forms of intimacy and exchange—that attends to global universality *and* temporal and spatial specificity while retaining hospitality's internal complexities that surface time and time again. It cannot be denied, hospitality is more necessary and more

2. Jacques Derrida, *On Cosmopolitanism and Forgiveness.*
3. Richard Kearney, "Losing our Touch."

difficult than ever and absolutely critical to re-imagining our lives embedded in and through other lives, and in digital worlds.

Digital Strangers

While elsewhere I have written extensively on several digital texts that raise the problem of hospitality, such as android hosts in popular culture, virtual domestic assistants, the platform economy and embodied computing (see *The Digital Future of Hospitality*), it is worth offering a quick summary of that here. It is not necessary to go searching for the preoccupations of hospitality in digital texts—hospitality is *everywhere* in digital life and culture. This begins, of course, with the very language of the internet itself. Terms such as "home" page and web "host" have been used somewhat unproblematically for years with little consideration of how this recalls the relations of guests and hosts. The homepage, for instance, acts as a kind of gatekeeper; a bastion of potential *inhospitable* welcome, designed to interface potential "outsiders." Via security software and conditions that range from "known" versus unknown URLs, to search-engine optimized terms, the homepage is a threshold of sorts, and perhaps a welcome respite from disruptive notifications, left-field friending requests, and "file not found" errors. This is the threshold where relations between self and other are tested, and where the line between private and shared space is complicated. It is also a site of conditionality, often requiring log-in identification, the relinquishing of personal data such as birthdates and addresses, and literal terms and conditions, much as a home or hospitality business that requires an RSVP, license plate registration, contribution to the potluck, or reservation. Such conditions seem to annul the potential for hospitality, demonstrating once more the internal and often contradictory nature of hospitality. For Derrida, the question of both hospitality and new technologies has always been about the borders between foreign and non-foreign and the fears of the unknown arrival. That these hosting mechanisms are now carried around with us at all times—in the form of mobile devices—further disrupts the stability of a host at home, who can even accept a guest at all, invited or not.

Far from being that absence of hospitality, however, perhaps this is the pinnacle exercising it. Is the stranger not meant to disturb the being-at-home with oneself? And does that arrival not, in the words of Emmanuel Levinas imply "the interruption of a full possession of a place called home?"[4] Thinking about the homepage as a complicated site of landing

---

4. Emmanuel Levinas, *Totality and Infinity*.

also reminds us of the very real and material precariousness of arrival for the literally millions of displaced guests around the globe, and this chapter recognizes that such conditions often render the more philosophical or abstract musing around hospitality as privileged or out of touch. However, such precariousness also exposes how the conditions of welcome are often archived in techno-mediated ways, as the digital becomes a narrative witness to the interactions of guests and hosts. In what follows then, I unpack several strands of how hospitality unfolds itself in contemporary cultural phenomena while remaining committed to the material relations of power and so-called "real life" that make hospitality more difficult than ever.

Android Hosts

As the introductory discussion to this chapter suggests, the roles of guests and hosts have always been complex, but are perhaps made more so in the context of android "lives," where the obligations of host and guest operate differentially according to what counts as "human." Is hospitality only a human ethic? Can android bodies perform a host function and, if our expectation of them is that they offer hospitality, what are our ethical obligations in return? *Westworld's* unique way of leveraging hospitality is problematic while simultaneously holding true to the so-called "laws" of hospitality. It is a troublesome contradiction and suggests perhaps that what is good for philosophy is not always good for life. If anything, hospitality in *Westworld* reveals itself to be an ethic deeply entrenched in forms of violence that, as in real life, are disproportionately raced, classed, and gendered. In the same way, we can think of the advancement of digital technologies as reproducing latent forms of discrimination, just in a shiny new package.

While the android has been a visual marker of science fiction books, films, and television for decades, it has shifted somewhat to question the integrity of digital users, and the extent to which technology is or should be controlling our lives. Far from being a symbol of threat and invasion, the android now is often used as a foil to unethical and violent *human* behavior. In short, these androids reveal far more about us—our relationship to technology, and our role as hosts—than they do about the dangerous intentions of robots. We are prompted, then, to ask how television and other forms of contemporary popular culture both contain and exacerbate concerns about the future of artificial consciousness and the sentience of the "host" body. I see this emergence as emblematic of the recent discussion put forth by Graham, et al on the immortality of bodies and data: these figures are a "possible extension of 'being-in-the-world' through the hybridization of once living, sentient beings with other entities [yet] these entities are less robotic than representational . . ." They go on to argue that "hybridization cannot change a reference to a real anatomic body."[5] Made over in our image, these android hosts both provide a familiarization of our technological fear *and* fulfill our deepest desires of living forever.

Such is the future in shows like *Altered Carbon,* where the body itself becomes little more than a vessel for uploaded (and exchangeable) consciousness. "Corticol stacks," the phrase that the show gives to glorified memory-laden USB drives, are affixed to the vertebra of physical or synthetic human bodies. So long as the stack remains intact, and has a host body to carry it, human consciousness can live forever. Similarly, in the *Black Mirror* episode "Be Right Back," a recent widowed woman uploads her deceased husband's cloud data first into a chat bot, and then into a synthetic body that is delivered to her doorstep. These examples are crucial to exploring the ways in which hospitality paradoxically succeeds and fails on a model of incorporation. It suggests an unconditional welcome of strangers—one figure literally embedded by an "other," in this case, data—but also an incorporation that levels the other to a figure of familiarity, and a figure whose alterity is potentially negated when incorporated by a host who is now recognizable.

Yet I am hesitant to believe this is the foreclosure of hospitality. I want to suggest that hospitality perhaps succeeds here, but violently so. In *Westworld,* for instance, the guests insist that while they want to be able to harm with impunity, they also want it to feel *real.* As the Man in Black, played by actor Ed Harris, demands of his host foe: "I didn't pay all this money because I want it easy. I want you to fight" ("The Original"). And indeed, the hosts do feel pain, they do begin to question their own existence and they, at a certain point, begin to *remember* their past narratives, yet after a few software adjustments, they are sewn back up and sent back out into the park to perform their host role over and over again. Programmed or not, they host *knowing* they will die. Yet the ethical implication in *Westworld* is not so much about what makes a hospitable host. In his review of the series, Christopher Orr summarizes the different representations of human guests and android hosts, by arguing that "*Westworld* achieves what may be its most shocking inversion of all: Even as we watch the androids become more human, we watch the human be-

---

5. Connor Graham, Martin Gibbs, and Lanfranco Aceti, "Introduction to the Special Issue on the Death, Afterlife, and Immortality of Bodies and Data."

ings become less so."[6] Indeed, perhaps the reflection on hospitality here, and ethical caution, is about bad guests and the ways in which we ascribe both sentience and ethical responsibility to only human figures.

Virtual Domestic Assistants

While android hosts remain more or less confined to our technological imagination and, indeed, the examples I have given are popular culture fictions, they are nonetheless produced out of real anxieties about the role of the android in our technologically mediated lives. They are machine learning in incarnate form, blurring the line between human and not. But what about the machines that look like machines? How does hospitality emerge in the artificial intelligence of human-like consciousness in non-human form? Here, I want to draw attention to the role of virtual assistants, and what I read as a gendered hospitality of the digital domestic. If hospitality is complicated via the figure of the android host, then it is perhaps even more so in the work of Siri and Alexa, who are without human form and therefore exercise their hospitality in the absence of touch. In this way we might think of virtual assistants as representative of what Introna and Brigham call the "thinness of the virtual" rather than the "thickness of the flesh."[7] Although their analysis does not take up the scenario of virtual assistants specifically, their questions are remarkably significant when thinking through the hospitality of the digital domestic. "Can I encounter the other as Other in virtuality?" they ask, invoking the Levinasian figure of the face as a condition for ethical encounter and giving us pause to consider whether Siri and Alexa might, indeed, have a face—that singular figure for absolute alterity which demands our ethical response. Kearney conceptualizes this alterity slightly differently, calling attention to the significance of touch. For Kearney, "carnal hospitality can operate at several levels of embodied exchange, but it is in *touch* that the most basic act of exposure to others occurs."[8] Might, then, virtual domestic assistants "touch" us, particularly when, as digital hosts, they are often subject to the mundane and sometimes even inappropriately "carnal" demands of the guest—their "user," who is oddly also a host in that domestic space.

Thinking about the role of touch, alterity, and the domestic sphere reminds us that while Siri and Alexa may not be coded as human, they *are*

---

6. Christopher Orr, "Sympathy for the Robot."
7. Lucas Introna and Martin Brigham. "Derrida, Business, Ethics."
8. Richard Kearney, "Double Hospitality: Between Word and Touch."

coded as feminine, and raise serious questions for how hospitality is leveraged as a kind of gendered intimacy. While their default female voice can admittedly be changed, in the case of Siri, and renamed in the case of Alexa, the important thing to note here is not what we call them but the particular work and forms of hospitality that they provide—in other words, their penchant for gendered labor. This is not just so-called "pink collar" work but the emotional and care labors that traditionally (and non-reciprocally) fall to women. Not only do they offer administrative and domestic assistance; they also reassure us of our qualms about technology itself. As Heather Woods argues, "equipping [artificially intelligent virtual assistants] with a feminine persona works to rhetorically disarm users with anxieties about intimate data exchange," highlighting a performative and deeply gendered reassurance while disguising the "other" work of Siri and Alexa done in the service of surveillance capitalism.[9]

Moreover, drawing the ideas of unconditional hospitality offered by android hosts, Siri and Alexa can take a significant amount of verbal abuse from those they are serving. Programmed to respond in ways that are, at best, compliant and, at worst, forgiving of verbal sexual violence, the pure hospitality of these assistants is also perhaps their most dangerous piece of software, but this problem is certainly not one confined to the digital. If anything, the digital here exposes the ways that hospitality has *always* been gendered. The role of the female body, intimate living spaces, the preparation of food and drink, and maternity in particular occupy much of our cultural discourse on how women fulfill their role as hosts. Moreover, the programmed responses of virtual assistants often mimic the evasive strategies used by women to avoid harm, such as playing coy, paying compliments, and diffusing the threat of sexual violence.

While their ideas are worth far more space than I can give them here, Judith Still and Luce Irigiray's work on sexual difference is particularly helpful in this regard. Still especially traces these gendered forms of hospitality back to Orientalist and pre-Enlightenment notions of feminine spaces of hospitality—the drawing room and even the Harem,[10] where

---

9. Heather Suzanne Woods,. "Asking more of Siri and Alexa: Feminine Persona in Service of Surveillance Capitalism."

10. The harem, of course, as a conceptual device, conjures notions of intimacy and strangeness, inside and outside, domestic versus public, and (often erotic) excess. It is a version of hospitality that has always been premised on a certain illusion of space—not simply a home with a door, but a private space within that home, concealed beneath increasing levels of security and privacy and, with that, a certain hierarchy among guests, with only a select few being offered welcome. Mary Roberts (in *Intimate Outsiders*) describes: the particular appeal of the harem accounts was premised on the

hospitality is not just about meeting the needs of guests but about fulfilling a particularly masculine gaze and pleasure. We do not have to look much further than the multitude of discussion boards offering what are intended to be humorous responses Siri and Alexa have given to verbal abuse. While the code has been rewritten after much critique, Siri used to coyly respond "I'd blush if I could"[11] to comments of a sexual and derogatory nature. Even now, while the responses are less flirtatious, Siri and Alexa are programmed to ignore or downplay the abusive comments, rather than confront the speaker.

Even *WIRED* magazine, while celebrating all things technological, finds cause for concern in the programming of these domestic assistants and the ways in which they mimic gendered survival strategies. Noam Cohen argues: "Siri is forced to enact the role of a woman to be objectified while apologizing for not being human enough to register embarrassment."[12] Here, the anthropomorphism falls alarmingly close to reality and non-reciprocated forms of contact. These virtual assistants seem to fall prey to a fallacy that simply plugging in implies consent and they respond with deference to *our* prompts, not the other way around. Furthermore, studies[13] have shown that when used as a tool for either the disclosure of assault or request for information, Siri is more likely to respond "I don't understand" than to offer links to health or crisis services. Given the problem of gender-based violence among our human populations, it is a crucial extension of feminist work to consider the gender-coded face of artificially intelligent virtual assistants as the pinnacle of this history of domestic hospitality and sexual difference. Ultimately Siri and Alexa remind us not only about the gendering of hospitality, but about the relationship of hospitality to labors of care and perhaps more importantly to consent and the acceptability of sexual violence in online spaces.

---

notion that they "conveyed the truth about this mysterious world of women, even though the accounts they produced often threatened cherished fantasies." Ultimately then, because "*harem* denotes both the female members of a household and the dedicated spatial enclosure in which they live" (as noted by Schick, in "The Harem as Gendered Space..."), we need to think about Siri and Alexa spatially; they are not *embodied* but they are defined by space.

11. See UNESCO's report on women in tech: https://www.unesco.org/en/articles/women-tech-id-blush-if-i-could

12. Noam Cohen, "Why Siri and Alexa Weren't Built to Smack Down Harassment."

13. See Adam Miner, Arnold Milstein, Stephen Schueller, et. al. "Smartphone-Based Conversational Agents and Responses to Questions About Mental Health, Interpersonal Violence, and Physical Health." *JAMA Intern Med* 176.5 (2016): 619–625.

The Gig Economy

Another example worth thinking through concerns the digital gig economy, and the sheer volume of mobile apps dedicated to the selling and exchanging of hospitality services. The most notable and successful of these, of course, are Airbnb and Uber which facilitate a kind of hosting that is commodified, to be sure, but interestingly mediated through the private space of one's home or vehicle. These networks, social and transactional, present a significant opportunity for thinking through the roles of hosts and guests in online space. Discourses of belonging in a community of strangers is central to the Airbnb narrative. The ways in which Airbnb mobilizes home, community and hospitality by creating a network of virtual hosts and guests not only subscribes to an ethos of global citizenship but leverages hospitality as an ethic for monetization and competition. These goals are counter to the project of pure hospitality; as we know, reciprocity or payment automatically annuls unconditionality. Airbnb invokes the language of hospitable welcome but at the same time it quantifies such hospitality vis-a-vis a particular kind of metrics that shames bad guests while promoting good ones—indeed, this is the premise of Airbnb's "superhost" status. Their term "superhost" is a particularly interesting platform vernacular. It is a point of validation and, indeed celebration of host status, replete with a digital badge that resembles a medal one might be awarded in a race, or perhaps for military service. At the same time, it conjures something far more alarming, even sinister, in its more colloquial associations with immunology whereby the superhost is one who can incubate and pass along a virus without becoming sick. These connections between immunity, virology and hospitality warrant far deeper exploration and, as I briefly explore later in this chapter, must also be understood in the context of the COVID-10 pandemic, the closure of borders and the threat of contamination wrought through both political and social discourse.

A similar performance metric is at work with Uber, in which the ratings of both host/driver and guest/passenger determine whether any interaction will take place, and thus operate as a form of conditionality that, while privileging neither host nor guest, forecloses opportunity for hospitality. Similar to Airbnb, the notion of welcome and hospitality is written into Uber's Community Guidelines: "We believe that everyone should feel supported and welcomed when interacting with others in the Uber community.[14] What follows in the Guidelines, however, is the exact opposite,

14. https://www.uber.com

a recognition of the (potentially violent) failure of hospitality. As Uber's website rationalizes, "That's why we've created standards and policies on physical contact, sexual assault and misconduct, threatening and rude behavior, post-trip contact, discrimination, and property damage." As I argued in *The Digital Future of Hospitality*, "while such admissions might seem uncommon in the platform economy, they expose the paradox at the heart of philosophical hospitality, which can only exist with a measure of risk."[15] Indeed, both Airbnb and Uber demonstrate the potential benefits and dangers of welcoming strangers, the reality of which is increasing at rapid pace in our digital lives.

While hospitality, as an industry, has thrived under the propulsion of the gig economy, absolute hospitality as a philosophical imperative has been curtailed in several notable ways, from the embedded surveillance capitalism within hospitality apps, and their reliance on stars, "superhosts," and reviews; to the platform economy's insistence on anthropomorphic biopolitics and contributions to gentrification and exclusion. As with Siri and Alexa, hospitality unravels in the context of Uber and Airbnb as they both rely on forms of surveillance (vis-a-vis economic exchange) to which both hosts and guests must tacitly consent to be included in that digital community. As I suggest elsewhere, "Airbnb and Uber thus thrive within a discourse of conditional hospitality, in which both hosts and guests are bound by a social contract that lays out (whether explicitly, implicitly, or ambiguously) what is required of each."[16] They are also bound by social norms and behaviors around race, class and gender, and the intersections of privilege and oppression that this chapter does not have space to explore. Suffice it to say, however, that part of the conditional nature of hospitality in the gig economy cannot be fully unpacked without critical attention to racial suspicion, gender-based violence and safety, classist assumptions around both host and guest, and a plethora of algorithmic biases that remind us of the ways in which "hospitality" and social justice remain at odds.

Embodied Computing

A final example of the ways in which hospitality reanimates in digital culture can be explored through the relatively recent phenomenon of embodied computing, also conceptualized as the world of wearable, embeddable, and ingestible digital technologies. This is perhaps most recognizable

---

15. Lindsay Balfour, *The Digital Future of Hospitality*.
16. *Ibid*

in the proliferation of self-tracking devices, the Apple Watch and Fitbit among them, in which touch technologies read the body for biometric data. While this is most common in the experience of fitness tracking, the overall MedTech industry also includes digital therapeutics, reproductive and intimate feminine technologies, and embodied computing for mental health, among a vast spectrum of other health concerns. I am particularly interested in exploring the concept of hospitality through the intermingling of the strange and the familiar in wearable tech. We might think of the kinds of intimate relations involved in embodied biometric devices as an example of what robotics professor Masahiro Mori calls the "uncanny valley."[17] What is particularly interesting in the context of wearables is how we come to know our own bodies, even their most intimate and carnal functions, by the manipulation of our interiority into a data set, where interpretations and recommendations are determined in virtual space, then beamed back to the body to be implemented. In short, we become, in Julia Kristeva's words, a stranger to ourselves. This is perhaps no more apparent than in the burgeoning feminine technologies industry, where digital health products are marketed to women in a self-monitoring capacity and remind us of the complicated ethics of welcome in a world where women's health and bodies have always been seen as strange.

In the case of wearables, the closeness is not just the way that skin becomes a threshold between the machine and corporeal data; it is in the technological touching of most intimate processes that the body undertakes—sex and sleep, water intake and retention, bowel movements and menstruation—bodily processes that happen not on the surface of the flesh but beneath it, and in the sensory, reproductive, digestive and circulatory tracks, not to mention the body's more affective responses to health, wellness, and trauma. In many cases, these are intuitive and somewhat involuntary processes, so-called "natural" things that occur without much thought. But in the case of wearables, these things are projected externally as data, estranged from the bodies that produced it, and sold back to it in the form of eating and exercise plans, intimate health trackers and adjacent product placements via social media. The lifecycle of such data suggests that discourses of self-estrangement are not only a problem for hospitality but a leveraging of that problem for capital accumulation, platform economies, and big pharma. Ultimately, I want to suggest that wearable gadgets function as a form of what the philosopher Richard Kearney

---

17. In that the replica does not provide an apt replacement but rather produces a sense of uncertainty; a "dip" in the user's comfort and attachment to the digital product.

calls "excarnation," whereby the body no longer registers, through our own interpretation, how we "feel" but how the machine feels us.

This is certainly exacerbated in the bodies of women and the data gained from intimate body functions that is then processed in the service of a kind of biopolitical governmentality to produce the ideal (re)productive citizen. These forms of biometric identification are a problem for hospitality, not only in the inequity of self-management discourses, but also in the ways in which women are welcomed on the basis of intimate identification. Yet the heightened surveillance and inhospitality of gender within wearable technologies also occurs with regard to race, and, as such, it is imperative to think of how both forms of marginalization intersect in biometric tracking technologies and in all forms of embodied computing. Whether in cultural and media representation, design and manufacturing of technological health "solutions," or the promises of self-managed healthcare, the "hosting" of intimate data remains inequitable and remind us that the experience of marginalization and estrangement are critical complications of the project of hospitality.

Indeed, well before Fitbit debuted its fitness tracker, the American sitcom *Better off Ted* produced an episode entitled "Racial Sensitivity" (2009). In it, the fictional company Veridian decides to cut costs by installing sensors that operate based on "light reflected off the skin" and can turn off the lights in a room when no motion is detected. The only glitch is that these sensors can only detect white people. The company's CEO refutes claims of racism, arguing that people of color are not being targeted—they are in fact simply being ignored. This new system seems to affect a lab technician named Lem in particular, who works in a room that goes dark whenever he is alone in it, cannot operate the automated water fountain, and becomes locked in his lab overnight when the cameras do not detect his presence to open the sliding door. "Please *sense* me" (my emphasis) Lem begs as he leans into the motion camera. While *Better off Ted* is surely fiction, it reveals some deep truths about the ways in technology and digital life are explicitly inhospitable—literally locking doors—for people of color, and the problems here are often more real than scripted.

In fact, five years after the *Better off Ted* episode aired, Apple ran into a similar problem with its new Apple Watch, a wrist-worn device created to mimic many of the functions of an iPhone but in a more efficient, social, and hands-free way. The original marketing of the Apple Watch promoted the device as a fashion accessory but quickly expanded its focus to include health and fitness-oriented features, in an effort to compete with dedicated activity trackers like Fitbit. It was an immediate hit when it was released in 2015, yet shortly after, customers began reporting on Reddit that they had a hard time activating the touch sensors on the underside of the watch if they had dark tattoos in that area. Of course, it wasn't just those with tattoos who were having trouble; people of color also began reporting that the touch sensors would not "recognize" their skin. Apple, like many wearable manufacturers, uses sensors that beam green light toward the skin.[18] Green light penetrates the skin just enough to get a reading without reaching too deep and faces less competition from other forms of light. This green light enters the first few layers of skin and measures the rate of blood-flow beneath the surface. Green light, however, is more likely to be absorbed by the skin of people with higher melanin content *before* it can get a reading. The darker the skin (tattoo or otherwise), the less likely the sensors are to capture data when the person is moving.

In other words, early versions of the Apple Watch failed to recognize some people of color as *living human bodies*, an issue that was also a problem with Fitbit. I draw attention to this problem, not just to call out racial bias in fitness tracking sensors (inadvertent as it may be), but to recognize the ways in which race, and gender too, are simultaneously and paradoxically both highlighted *but also made invisible* by biometric tracking technologies. There is an important distinction to be made here, about the *refusal to recognize*, which might act in the service of ethical hospitality, versus the *failure* to do so. Indeed, the ways in which the above technologies refuse to read bodies of color—we might be bold enough to call this omission by design—is equally telling of the ways in which hospitality's regimes of recognizability are disproportionally experienced when race, class, and gender come into play.

Hospitality, Contagion, Autoimmunity

Along these lines, there is perhaps one figure of digital life that so readily recalls the paradox of hospitality and brings these deep digital anxieties and real-world political and social inequities into focus. Indeed, it is impossible to speak of digital life without reference to the darker sides of technological life—hacking, viruses, and material vulnerabilities laid bare via the technological interfaces intended to manage and protect them. The virus, in particular, remains both the foundation of cybersecurity, and one of hospitality's most enduring metaphors. Contamination, parasitism, and virology have become especially fraught in recent years given the extent to which the entire world continues to grapple with the effects of the

---

18. Dan Taylor, "Whoops: Apple Watch may not work for black people."

COVID-19 pandemic. In other words, there has never been a more apt time to consider a social history of "the virus" and "the viral." Yet what are almost ubiquitously thought of as global health crises are oddly a boon to hospitality, if only in metaphor. There is no hospitality without this threat of contagion. One must not just be okay with, but must *welcome* such an invasion—an openness to contamination *before* contact, each spore floating around in the space between us potential guests and hosts. Even if it is perhaps too early to philosophize about the ethical potentials of pandemic, the computer provides a similarity instructive text for thinking about how infection and immunity operate. The technologies we use today may be new but Derrida in particular has always likened contagion to a kind of technological process: "The virus is in part a parasite that destroys, that introduces disorder into communication. Even from the biological standpoint, this is what happens with a virus; it derails a mechanism of the communicational type, its coding and decoding."[19]

Viral metaphors are also used to describe the spreadability of media, and the speed, breadth and global reach of popular videos and memes. The term "meme" of course is the not-so-new term to describe such a phenomenon, borrowed from mimesis, and one that has etymological links to immunology. Coined by Richard Dawkins in 1976, "memes" were initially likened to genes propagating themselves in the gene pool, and operate by similarly "leaping from brain to brain via a process which, in the broad sense, can be called imitation."[20] Thinking about the meme and the viral in relation to digital hospitality then, demands consideration of what it means to welcome the stranger in an age of global health panic *and* technological uncertainly.

Much like artificial intelligence, the body has always been a machine that learns and self-preserves. Moreover, as immunology tells us that the body will always instinctively reject what is foreign, something else must be added to the encounter (viral or otherwise), that switches on the autoimmune and "enables an exposure to the other, to what and to who comes."[21] And so we can recognize an immunitary process at work in the vaccine, and in the digital landscape, by anti-virus software and cybersecurity, and biometric surveillance. These are the strategies of inhospitality that reject the foreigner and come in by way of viral panic, hacking, and border security. Ultimately, from the lines of code embedded in the android

19. W.J.T. Mitchell, "Picturing Terror: Derrida's Autoimmunity."
20. Joshua Green and Henry Jenkins, "Spreadable Media: How Audiences Create Value and Meaning in a Networked Economy."
21. Jacques Derrida, "The Principle of Hospitality."

host body, the gendered-by design software of Siri and Alexa, to the surveillance metrics of Airbnb that predetermine who can be a host or guest at all, and finally in the predictive health biopolitics of wearable tech, hospitality remains philosophical but becomes perhaps more political, and certainly more urgent, in the digital age.

Re-coding Hospitality and Welcoming the Stranger at the Edge of the Anthropocene

As the above brief examples demonstrate, the question of hospitality resurfaces with a vengeance in digital culture, yet its effects remain underexplored. As the social, ethical, political and cultural challenge of our epoch, the advent of digital technologies demands considerable reflection and requires that hospitality itself perhaps change course. Indeed, Derrida, too, declares, "Hospitality must be so inventive, adjusted to the other, and to the welcoming of the other, that each experience of hospitality must invent a new language."[22] Digital life, thus, gives us both pause and opportunity to apprehend the concept anew. Surely hospitality is no more important now than it was in the time of Abraham, Kant, the World Wars and the Holocaust, and the refugee crisis, so why re-think it now? What is it about this technological moment and its potential future that makes hospitality worth revisiting? How has the digital changed and been changed by hospitality? Data continues to act as a kind of gate and, as a gate, it can do two things; it can be "porous" and allow for ease of travel back and forth, designating an edge and a boundary but not a limit. Or it can be a border, unsurpassable and bound by fear. Where are we now then? Which edge are we up against—the one that limits and prevents welcoming strangers, or the one that serves as a proliferation of ones and zeros, a threshold where we might finally "give place" to the other?

Along with the pressing concerns that new technologies present to us, for social, cultural, and political life, the work of hospitality remains critical also in the face of related challenges of resource depletion and extraction, over-population, water scarcity, increased "natural" disasters and, indeed, our own potential extinction. While this chapter has focused on the relationship between hospitality and digital texts here, I would like to end with a note on where hospitality is needed next. This is not entirely divorced from technology—indeed a more reciprocal and ethical relationship with the digital might actually be what saves us, but our current

22. *Of Hospitality: Anne Dufourmantelle Invites Jacques Derrida to Respond.*

climate predicament begs a question perhaps more urgent than the encounter with strangers in digital space: What can hospitality, and digital hospitality, do for a dying planet?

It is no coincidence that contemporary Western thinking about hospitality began at the same time as the Industrial Revolution. Indeed, Immanuel Kant's writings, particularly those around *Perpetual Peace* and cosmopolitan right, emerged as the world was grappling with newfound challenges of migration and mobility, inequality, and emerging ideas of science, technology, and reason. While not writing on the human impact on climate, to be sure, Kant's treatise on hospitality came in close proximity to what many consider the onset of the Anthropocene—understood now as underscored by "the seriousness of the accelerating environmental challenges facing humanity," and potentially irreversible "global scale atmospheric changes."[23] It is hard, in other words, to consider hospitality a human ethic when the relationship with nature's "other" has been anything but ethical. If the digital now skews towards the displacement of the human as both the giver and receiver (guest and host) within traditional hospitable relations, then perhaps our climate emergency does so even more. There can be no doubt that we are nearing the so-called end of the Anthropocene, but is this the picture of possibility or apocalypse?

As Thomas van Dooren remarks "the invocation of the Anthropos becomes an appropriation of the human as a figure and a possibility: the one who marks and claims the world is the properly human, rendered doubly so by the power to commit these acts and to define itself in the position of unmarked invisibility."[24] Such "marking and claiming" of the world is perhaps one significant reason that the human project of hospitality has ostensibly failed or, at very least, has never fully been realized: that *avenir* or horizon of ethics never quite reached. It also gestures to something beyond the human, a possibility of hospitality that may offer the future we have been looking for. Indeed, as van Dooren suggests, "what is needed [in place of the Anthropocene] is an entirely new frame of orientation: an acknowledgement that the world and its future were never ours—never any individual's or group's—to give in the first place, to welcome or not."[25] While far beyond the scope of this chapter and volume I want to speculate on a future of hospitality that might address both our current preoccupations with digital worlds, as well as with the very real world we are struggling to survive in. I want to suggest that new thinking about hospitality must be

---

23. Bruce D. Smith and Melinda A. Zeder, "The Onset of the Anthropocene."
24. Thomas Van Dooren, "The Unwelcome Crows: Hospitality in the Anthropocene."
25. *Ibid.*

attentive to different ways of knowing and being, and draw from the strangers we know—indigenous theory, eco-feminism, posthumanism—to better apprehend the strangers whom we do not.

In their article, "Making Kin with the Machines," J.E. Lewis, et al, invoke a perspective on technology that is likely new for most:

> Stones are considered ancestors, stones actively speak, stones speak through and to humans, stones see and know. Most importantly, stones want to help. The agency of stones connects directly to the question of AI, as AI is formed from not only code, but from materials of the earth. To remove the concept of AI from its materiality is to sever this connection. Forming a relationship to AI, we form a relationship to the mines and the stones. Relations with AI are therefore relations with exploited resources. If we are able to approach this relationship ethically, we must reconsider the ontological status of each of the parts which contribute to AI, all the way back to the mines from which our technology's material resources emerge.[26]

Perhaps, hospitality has never been about the human, and thinking about the relationship between hospitality, digital technologies, and the end of the Anthropocene might begin to reconcile our responsibilities to the planet, and all that live on it. In particular, thinking hospitality through indigenous conceptions of kinship and material relations is an instructive blueprint for the future of hospitality and how we re-imagine our responsibilities to the human, the non-human and the more than human. In other words, what if we thought of robots, or of code, or of data, within the same complex web of relations through which indigenous epistemologies consider trees and rocks and rivers? In reality, we are all coded—by history and by culture—and the lines of social script that precondition our being in the world give us reason enough to reconsider the primacy of the human in any ethical imperative. The future of hospitality is thus not about human relations; it *is* about, rather, posthuman and multispecies ecologies, indigenous epistemologies and digital kinships, and a re-writing of our ethical code for a sustainable and equitable planetary future. Hospitality remains, to be sure, a hospitality to come (*a venir*), but perhaps the most surprising and unexpected figures of strangeness that arrive in the lines of code that now define our contemporary existence offer up a chance to think beyond the impossible and remind us of the necessity of holding this future intact.

---

26. Lewis, Jason Edward, et al, "Making Kin with the Machines," 11.

Conclusions: An Unfinished Epilogue

ORI Z SOLTES

This volume, originally conceived as a conference held in 2019, was inspired at that time most specifically by the growing hostility to refugees and would-be immigrants to the United States promoted by the Trump administration both in Mr. Trump's sustained rhetoric and in the policies of the United States government that he sought to put in place or succeeded in putting in place while in the Oval Office. His narrow and bigoted perspective aligned with a portion of American history, summarized at its outset by the shaping of the so-called Nativist Movement in the 1840s and reiterated periodically in the 180 years or so since that era. Such sentiments have been in continual tension with the immigrant-embracing ideology that revels in the degree to which the United States has been a colorful tapestry interwoven of diverse ethnicities, religions, nationalities, and races.

Alas, the Trumpian perspective was not shaped in isolation. His time in the White House coincided with an expansive array of "anti-other" perspectives articulated by a range of heads of governments in diverse countries across the globe. Autocratic figures with substantial bases that mirror Trump and his base could be found at the same time in Brazil, China, Hungary, India, Indonesia, Israel, the Philippines, Poland, Russia, and Turkey, to name the most obvious. The only substantive issue that distinguishes these countries and their current governments is the specific manner in which ugly rhetoric has led to uglier action, ranging from persecution to expulsion—and in some cases, to torture and execution—and the degree to which the leading perpetrators of such ideas have or have not succeeded in destroying the democratic political structures that have characterized most of them, at least theoretically.

One of the ironies for this is that, in the present political atmosphere, these countries have largely ceased to pursue the long religious histories that shaped them, which offer the context of this narrative and its tapestry of interwoven threads. On the other hand, between the time of the first iteration of the conference that led to this publication and the present, some degree of hope has returned to the United States, at least, with regard to the importance of welcoming the stranger as a new neighbor and potential friend. We would be naïve to assume, however, that we are fully back to the psycho-spiritual place where Abraham and Sarah were when they welcomed the three strangers who appeared out of nowhere, and fed them generously, without any expectation that they would receive any reward. All they expected was the satisfaction of knowing that they who were themselves wanderers of a distinct sort—keepers of flocks who owned no land—had been kind hosts to a trio of travelers from afar.

The irony for many of those in this country and elsewhere who express inhospitality or hostility to those seeking entry from elsewhere, is that they consider themselves followers of the God and the texts associated with that God that report on the exceptionally hospitable behavior of Abraham and Sarah and others, such as Abraham's nephew, Lot. The chapters that comprise this volume have laid out some of that textual narrative and its discussion through the ages by way of a threefold adumbration within the Abrahamic traditions. The immediate epilogue to those chapters considered both the dharmic perspective and a cultural commentary on India as the home of the dharmic faiths.

The book's chapters have spread to explorations of those who, rather than turning their backs on the imperative—as a divine and a fully-realized human imperative—to welcome the other, have embraced *others* as those who have an inherent right to *belong*. Reportage on a remarkable artist who survived the Holocaust in Berlin through the courageous hospitality of one individual who ignored her corrupt government's exile-and-murder-inducing othering of Jews led to two very different discussions of what is being done and can be done now, today and tomorrow, to activate the theological theory of embrace that is offered so clearly in diverse religious and cultural traditions.

The final, epilogue chapter underscores how—as much as the primary issues upon which all of these essays focus from different angles, have, in a sense, not changed—the issues *have* changed, or have enormous *potential* to change with the rapid expansion of artificial intelligence as a construct. Thus, where the book began by asking what the future holds for the generations that follow us with regard to the issue of welcoming or rejecting the *human* stranger, in the end we recognize that the question has necessarily expanded. How do we operate as both hosts and guests on the wide planet that we have not created but have inherited, including its non-human life-forms, and also with regard to the new realms of intelligence of which we ourselves *are* the creators? As so many new doors open and so many borders are crossed, are we and will we be as Abraham and Lot were, or as the inhabitants of Sodom who sought to destroy the visitors who, in the end, had been sent by God to destroy *them* with hail fire and brimstone?

Bibliography

Abu Dawud, Sulaiman bin al-Ash'ath al-Azdi al-Sijistani. ND. *al-Sunan*, ed. Muhammad Abd al-Hamid. Beirut: Al-Maktaba al-Asriyya.
Airbnb.com. 2022. *Airbnb Inc.*
al-Babarti, Akmal al-Din. ND. *al-'Inaya Sharh al-Hidaya*. Beirut: Dar al-Fikr.
al-Bukhari, Abu 'Abdillah Muhammad bin Isma'il. 1990. *al-Sahih*, ed. Mustafa Dayb al-Bugha. Damascus: Dar Ibn Kathir.
al-Sarakhsi, Muhammad bin Ahmad bin Abi Sahl. 1993. *al-Mabsut*. Beirut: Dar al-Ma'rifa.
al-Tirmidhi, Abu 'Isa Muhammad bin 'Isa bin Sawra. *al-Sunan*, Ahmad Muhammad Shakir, et al, eds., Cairo: Maktaba Mustafa al-Babi al-Halabi, 1975.
Anderson, Bernhard W., *From Creation to New Creation,* Minneapolis: Fortress Press, 1994, 178.
Arvan, Marcus. "Humans and Hosts in *Westworld*: What's the Difference?" in James B. South, Kimberly S. Engels, eds., *Westworld and Philosophy: If You Go Looking for the Truth, Get the Whole Thing.*
Avraham ben HaRambam, *Perush HaTorah* (*Commentary on the Torah*), Monsey, NY: Rabbi Jacob Joseph School Press, 2021 (in Hebrew).
Balfour, Lindsay, *The Digital Future of Hospitality.* London: Palgrave, 2023.
Balfour, Lindsay, *Hospitality in a Time of Terror: Strangers at the Gate.* Lewisburg: Bucknell University Press, 2017.
Bayne, Siân. "Academetron, automaton, phantom: uncanny digital pedagogies." *London Review of Education* Vol. 8, No. 1, March 2010, 5–13.
Bellah, Robert N., *The Broken Covenant, American Civil Religion in Time of Trial,"* 2nd ed., Chicago: University of Chicago Press, 1992.
Booker, Charlie, *Black Mirror*. Channel 4/Netflix. 2011

Bookwalter, J.R. 2015. "Siri Says the Darndest Things: 50 Questions for Apple's Virtual Assistant." *Macworld*. http://macworld.com/article/2915908/siri-says-

Booth, Marilyn, *Harem Histories: Envisioning Places and Living Spaces*. Durham: Duke University Press, 2010.

Brown, Garrett W. "The Laws of Hospitality, Asylum Seekers and Cosmopolitan Right: A Kantian Response to Jacques Derrida." *European Journal of Political Theory* 9, no. 3 (2010): 308–27.

Brueggemann, Walter, *The Land: Place as Gift, Promise and Challenge in Biblical Faith*. Minneapolis: Fortress Press, 2002.

———, *Theology of the Old Testament, Testimony, Dispute, Advocacy*, Minneapolis: Fortress Press, 1997.

Budde, Michael, *Foolishness to Gentile: Essays on Empire, Nationalism and Discipleship*. Eugene, Or.: Cascade Books, 2022.

Casey, Edward. 2015. "Skin Deep: Bodies Edging into Place." *Carnal Hermeneutics*. Richard Kearney and Brian Treanor, eds., NY: Fordham University Press, 2015.

Chacos, Brad, "Ask Cortana Anything: Sassy Answers to 25 Burning Questions." *PCWorld*. https://www.pcworld.com/article/2148940/ask-cortana-anything-sassy-answers-to-58-burning-questions.html 2015.

Clifton, Jon. *Blind Spot. The Global Rise of Unhappiness and How Leaders Missed It*. Gallup, 2023.

Cohen, Noam, "Why Siri and Alexa Weren't Built to Smack Down Harassment," *Ideas*. https://www.wired.com/story/why-siri-and-alexa-werent-built-to-smack-down-harassment/ 2019

Collier, Elizabeth, "Arguing About Immigration: The Claims of Restrictionists and Non-Restrictionists," in Elizabeth W. Collier and Charles R. Strain, eds., *Religious and Ethical Perspectives on Global Migration*, Lanham, MD: Lexington Books, 2014.

Costa, Pedro and Luísa Ribas, "AI becomes her: Discussing gender and artificial intelligence." *Technoetic Arts: A Journal of Speculative Research* 171.2. 2019.

Day, Dorothy, *The Long Loneliness: The Autobiography of Dorothy Day*. San Francisco: Harper & Row Publishers, 1981 [1952].

Derrida, Jacques. *Adieu to Emmanuel Levinas*. Pascale-Anne Brault and Michael Naas, transl. Stanford, CA: Stanford University Press, 1999.

———, "Hospitality," *Angelaki: Journal of the Theoretical Humanities* 5, no. 3 (2000): 3–18.

———, *Of Hospitality: Anne Dufourmantelle Invites Jacques Derrida to Respond*. Stanford, CA: Stanford University Press, 2000.

———, *On Cosmopolitanism and Forgiveness*. New York: Routledge, 2001.

———, "The Principle of Hospitality," *Parallax* 11, no. 1 (2005): 6–9.

Douglass, Frederick, *Narrative of the Life of Frederick Douglass*. Independently published, 2021.

Dugan, David, *Constantine's Bible: Politics and the Making of the New Testament.* Minneapolis, MN: Fortress Press, 2007.

Dühring, Eugen, *Die Judenfrage als Racen-, Sitten- und Culturfrage: Mit einer weltgeschichtlichen Antwort* [*The Jewish Question as a Racial, Moral, and Cultural Question: With a World-historical Answer*]. Karlsruhe: Reuther 1881.

Engle, Karen. *Seeing Ghosts: 9/11 and the Visual Imagination.* Montreal: McGill University Press, 2009.

Edwards, James, "A Biblical Perspective on Immigration Policy" in *Debating Immigration,* Carol Swain, ed., NY: Cambridge University Press, 2007.

———, "The Return of the Pharisees," *Center for Immigration Studies,* February 28, 2012

Esposito, Robert. *Bios: Biopolitics and Philosophy.* Minneapolis, MN: University of Minnesota Press, 2008.

Everett, Daniel *How Language Began: The Story of Humanity's Greatest Invention.* New York: Liveright, 2017.

Fisher, Mark. *Ghosts of My Life: Writings on Depression, Hauntology and Lost Futures.* Alresford: Zero Books, 2014.

Fisher, Roger and William Ury with Bruce Patton, eds., *Getting to Yes, Negotiating Agreement Without Giving In.* NY: Penguin Books, 2011.

Gordon, Deb. "The Kids Are Not Alright: New Report Shows Pediatric Mental Health Hospitalizations Rose 61%." In *Forbes* (September 30, 2022).

Graham, Connor, Martin Gibbs, and Lanfranco Aceti, "Introduction to the Special Issue on the Death, Afterlife, and Immortality of Bodies and Data," in *The Information Society* 29 (2013).

Grattenauer, Karl Wilhelm Friedrich, *Wider die Juden (Against the Jews).* Berlin: John Wilhelm Schmidt, 1803.

Green, Joshua and Henry Jenkins, "Spreadable Media: How Audiences Create Value and Meaning in a Networked Economy," *The Handbook of Media Audiences.* Virginia Nightingale, ed. Malden: John Wiley and Sons, 2014.

Hamilton, Mark W., *Jesus, King of Strangers: What the Bible Really Says About Immigration*, Grand Rapids, Michigan: William B. Eerdmans Publishing Co., 2019.

Hammad, Nuaim bin. 1412 AH. *Kitab al-Fitan.* Cairo: Maktaba al-Tawhid, 2017.

Hariri, Yuval, *Sapiens: A Brief History of Humankind.* NYC: HarperCollins Publisher, 2015.

Hasson, Uri. *How We Communicate Information Across Brains.* Princeton, NJ: Princeton University Press, 2019.

Heimburger, Robert W., *God and the Illegal Alien, United States Immigration Law and a Theology of Politics,* Cambridge: Cambridge University Press, 2018.

Henriksen, Line. "In the Company of Ghosts: Hauntology, Ethics, Digital Monsters." Thesis. Linkoping University, 2016.

Heyer, Kristin E., *Kinship Beyond Borders: A Christian Ethics of Immigration.* Washington, DC: Georgetown University Press, 2012.
Homann, Iris and Uta Gerlant (eds.), "*Sechs Wochen sind fast wie lebenslänglich . . .*": *Das Potsdamer Polizeigefängnis Priesterstrasse/ Bauhofstrasse.* Potsdam: Stiftung Gedenkstätte Lindenstrasse 2018.
Hollenbach, David, S.J., *Driven from Home: Protecting the Rights of Forced Migrants.* Washington, DC: Georgetown University Press, 2010.
———, *Humanity in Crisis: Ethical and Religious Response to Refugees.* Washington, DC: Georgetown University Press, 2019.
Hull, Alastair. "Neuroimaging findings in post-traumatic stress disorder. Systematic review." In *The British journal of psychiatry: the journal of mental science.* September 2002.
Ibn Kathir, Isma'il bin Umar. *al-Tafsir*, ed. Sami bin Muhammad Salama. Riyadh: Dar Tayba. 1999.
Ibn Majah. Abu 'Abdillah Muhammad bin Yazid al-Qazwini. *al-Sunan*, ed. Muhammad Fu'ad 'Abd al-Baqi. Beirut: Dar Ihya al-Turath al-Arabi. 1975.
Introna, Lucas and Martin Brigham. "Derrida, Business, Ethics," in *Conference Proceedings. Centre for Philosophy and Political Economy.* University of Leicester, 2008.
Jennings, Jr., Theodore W., *Outlaw Justice, The Messianic Politics of Paul.* Stanford, CA: Stanford University Press, 2013.
Jones, Reece, *Nobody is Protected, How the Border Patrol Became the Most Dangerous Police Force in the United States.* Berkeley, CA: Counterpoint, 2022.
Kant, Immanuel. *Perpetual Peace: A Philosophical Sketch.* Ted Humphrey, transl. Indianapolis: Hackett, 2003.
Kaplan, Marion A., *Between Dignity and Despair*, Oxford and New York: Oxford University Press, 1998.
Katz, Jacob, *From Prejudice to Destruction. Anti-Semitism 1700–1933.* Cambridge: Harvard University Press, 1980.
Kearney, Richard. "Double Hospitality: Between Word and Touch," *Journal for Continental Philosophy of Religion* 1 (2019): 71–89.
———, "Losing our Touch," *New York Times*, August 30, 2014. Available at: https://opinionator.blogs.nytimes.com/2014/08/30/losing-our-touch/
Kearney, Richard and Brian Treanor, "Introduction Carnal Hermeneutics from Head to Foot," *Carnal Hermeneutics.* New York: Fordham University Press, 2015.
Keenan, James F., S.J., *A History of Catholic Theological Ethics.* New York: Paulist Press, 2022.
Kehimkar, Haim Solomon, *History of the Bene Israel of India.* New Delhi: Dayag Press, 1937.
Kierkegaard, Soren, *Concluding Unscientific Postscript.* David F. Swenson and Walter Lowrie, transl., Princeton, NJ: Princeton University Press, 1971.
———, *Fear and Trembling.* Walter Lowrie, transl. Princeton, NJ: Princeton University Press, 1968.

Ko, Jennifer Lee, "Agape Grace, and Immigration Law: An Evangelical Perspective," in Robert F. Cochran, Jr. and Zachary R. Calo, eds., *Agape, Justice and Law, How Might Christian Love Shape Law,* NY: Cambridge University Press, 2018.

Kumar, Sanjay. "Kashmir's communication blackout is a 'devastating blow' for academics, researchers say." In *Science Insider.* September 19, 2019.

LaCocque, André, "Jesus's Hermeneutics of the Law: Reading the Parable of the Good Samaritan," in *Creation, Life, and Hope: Essays in Honor of Jacques Doukhan,* ed. Jiri Moskala. Berrien Springs, MI: Seventh Day Adventist Theological Seminary, 2000.

———, *Ruth: A Continental Commentary.* Minneapolis, MN: Fortress Press, 2004.

Le Guin, Ursula K., *The Wave in the Mind: Talks and Essays on the Writer, the Reader and the Imagination.* Boulder, CO: Shambhala, 2004.

Levinas, Emmanuel. *Totality and Infinity.* Alphonso Lingis, transl. Pittsburgh: Duquesne University Press, 1969.

Lewis, Jason Edward, et al, "Making Kin with the Machines," MIT Press, Available at: https://jods.mitpress.mit.edu/pub/lewis-arista-pechawis-kite/release/1 2018.

Lincoln, Abraham, "Lincoln's Reply to Judge Davis at Chicago on Popular Sovereignty, the Nebraska Bill, Etc, July 10, 1858," in *Speeches and Letters of Abraham Lincoln, 1832–1865,* Merwin Roe, ed., NY: E.P. Dutton & Co., 1907.

Marr, Wilhelm, *Der Sieg des Judenthums über das Germanenthum—Vom nichtconfessionellen Standpunkt aus betrachtet.* Bern: Rudolph Costenoble, 1879 (in German).

Marty, Martin, *Pilgrims in Their Own Land, 500 Years of Religion in America,* New York: Penguin Books, 1985.

———, "The Widening Gyres of Religion and Law," 45 *DePaul L. Rev.* 651, 661 (1996)

Massaro, Thomas, S.J., *Mercy in Action: The Social Teachings of Pope Francis.* Lanham, MD: Rowman & Littlefield, 2018.

McLeod, Kimberley, "'Siri, Are You Female?': Reinforcing and Resisting Gender Norms with Digital Assistants." *Critical Stages* 21, 2020.

Merritt, Anna J., and Richard L. Merritt. *Public Opinion in Occupied Germany: the OMGUS Surveys, 1945–1949.* Chicago, IL: University of Illinois Press, 1970. OMGUS polls.

Mikva, Rachel, *Dangerous Religious Ideas, The Deep Roots of Self-Critical Faith in Judaism, Christianity, and Islam.* Boston: Beacon Press, 2020.

Miller, Perry, *Errand into the Wilderness,* Cambridge: Belknap Press, 1956.

Miner, Adam, Arnold Milstein, Stephen Schueller, et. al., "Smartphone-Based Conversational Agents and Responses to Questions About Mental Health, Interpersonal Violence, and Physical Health." *JAMA Intern Med,* 176.5 (2016).

Mitchell, Peta. "Contagion, Virology, Autoimmunity: Derrida's Rhetoric of Contamination." *Parallax* 23.1 (2017):77–93.

Mitchell, W.J.T., "Picturing Terror: Derrida's Autoimmunity," *Cardozo Law Review* 27.2, (2005). https://doi.org/10.1086/511494.

Mitroff, Sarah, "Cortana Shows Her Sassy Side," *CNet*. (2014). https://www.cnet.com/pictures/cortana-shows-her-sassy-side-pictures/.

Mori, Masahiro, "The Uncanny Valley." Karl F. MacDorman and Norri Kageki, transl.. *IEEE Robotics and Automation Magazine*. (1970, 2012). Available at: https://ieeexplore.ieee.org/stamp/stamp.jsp?arnumber=6213238.

Mousin, Craig B., "Constantine's Legacy: Preserving Empire While Undermining International Law," in Slotte, P., & Haskell, J. (Eds.). *Christianity and International Law: An Introduction (Law and Christianity)*. Cambridge: Cambridge University Press, 2021.

Nachmanides (Ramban), *Commentary on the Torah*, Rabbi Charles B. Chavel, transl., New York: Judaica Press, 2010.

Noll, Mark, *A History of Christianity in the United States and Canada*. Grand Rapids, MI: William B. Eerdmans Publishing Co., 1992.

Notley, Steven and Jeffrey P. García, "'But a Samaritan... Had Compassion': Jesus, Early Christianity, and the Samaritans," in Steven Fine, ed., *The Samaritans: A Biblical People*. Brill, Leiden, 2022.

O'Neill, William, S.J., "Christian Hospitality and Solidarity with the Stranger," in Donald Kerwin and Jill Marie Gerschutz, eds., *And You Welcomed Me: Migration and Catholic Social Teaching*. Lanham, MD: Lexington Books, 2009.

Orr, Christopher, "Sympathy for the Robot," *The Atlantic*. (2016). Available at: https://www.theatlantic.com/magazine/archive/2016/10/sympathy-for-the-robot/497531/

Pelikan, Yaroslav, *Jesus Through the Centuries, His Place in the History of Culture*. New Haven: Yale University Press, 1985.

Piper, Allison M., "Stereotyping Femininity in Disembodied Virtual Assistants." Graduate Theses and Dissertations, https://lib.dr.iastate.edu/etd/15792. 2016.

Pohl, Christine, *Making Room: Recovering Hospitality as a Christian Tradition* Grand Rapids, MI: William B. Eerdmans Publishing Co., 1999.

"Racial Sensitivity," in *Better off Ted*. Season 1, episode 4. Dir. Paul Lazarus. 20th Century Fox. 2009.

Rahawayh, Abu Yaqub Ishaq bin. al-*Musnad,* ed. *Abd al-Ghafur al-Balushi*. Medina: Maktaba al-Medina. 1991.

Reimer, James A., "Trinitarian Orthodoxy, Constantinianism, and Theology from a Radical Protestant Perspective," in S. Mark Heim, ed., *Faith to Creed, Ecumenical Perspective on the Affirmation of the Apostolic Faith in the Fourth Century*. Grand Rapids, MI: William B. Eerdmans Publishing Co., 1991.

Roberts, Mary, *Intimate Outsiders*. Durham: Duke University Press, 2007.

Robinson, Marilynne, *When I Was a Child I Read Books*, NY: Farrar, Straus and Giroux, 2012.

Rodgers, Daniel T., *As a City on a Hill, The Story of America's Most Famous Lay Sermon,* Princeton, NJ: Princeton University Press, 2018.

Roelofsen, Maartje and Claudio Minca. "The Superhost. Biopolitics, home and community in the Airbnb dream-world of global hospitality." *Geoforum* 91 (2018): 170–181.

Rose, Paul Lawrence. *German Question/Jewish Question: Revolutionary Antisemitism in Germany from Kant to Wagner.* Princeton, NJ: Princeton University Press, 2014.

Sacks, Jonathan, *Not in God's Name, Confronting Religious Violence.* New York: Schocken Books reprint, 2017.

———, *The Dignity of Difference, How to Avoid the Clash of Civilizations.* New York: Continuum, 2002.

Sadun, Erica and Steve Sande, *Talking to Siri: Learning the Language of Apple's Intelligent Assistant.* Que Publishing, 2012.

Samuel, Shellim, *A Treatise on the Origin and Early History of the Beni-Israel of Maharashtra State.* Bombay: Iyer and Iyer Private Ltd, 1963.

Schick, Irvin Cemil. "The Harem as Gendered Space and the Spatial Reconstruction of Gender," in *Harem Histories: Envisioning Places and Living Spaces,* Marilyn Booth, ed. Durham: Duke University Press, 2010.

Sefer HaHeenukh, Parshat Ekev. Jerusalem: Eshkol, 1958 (in Hebrew).

Shimron, Yonat, "Poll: A third of Americans are Christian restrictionists and most are white evangelicals," *Religion New Service,* https://religionnews.com/2023/02/08/a-third-of-americans-are-christian-restrictionists-and-most-are-white-evangelicals/, February 8, 2023.

Simpson, Alan, "How Democratic Was Roger Williams?" *The William and Mary Quarterly,* Vol. 13, No. 1 (Jan. 1956).

Simpson, David. *9/11: The Culture of Commemoration.* Chicago: University of Chicago Press, 2006.

Smith, Bruce D., and Melinda A. Zeder, "The Onset of the Anthropocene," *Anthropocene* 4, (2013).

Smith-Christopher, Daniel L., *A Biblical Theology of Exile.* Minneapolis, MN: Augsburg Press, 2002.

———, *Jonah, Jesus, and Other Good Coyotes, Speaking Peace to Power in the Bible,* Nashville, TN: Abingdon Press, 2007.

Soelle, Dorothee, *The Window of Vulnerability, A Political Spirituality,* Linda M. Maloney, transl. Minneapolis, MN: Fortress Press, 1990.

Soltes, Ori Z., ed., *Growing Up Jewish in India: Synagogues, Customs, and Ceremonies: From the Bene Israel to the Art of Siona Benjamin.* New Delhi: Niyogi Books, 2021.

———, *Jews on Trial.* Savage, MD: Eshel Books, 2013.

Stern, Rachel and Ori Z Soltes, eds., *To Live is to Blaze with Passion: The Expressionist Fritz Ascher/Leben ist Glühn: Der Expressionist Fritz Ascher.* Cologne: Wienand, 2016.

Still, Judith, "Figures of Oriental Hospitality: Nomads and Sybarites." *Mobilizing Hospitality: The Ethics of Social Relations in a Mobile World*, Jennie Germann Molz & Sarah Gibson, eds., Oxfordshire: Routledge, 2017.

Strindberg, August. *Inferno*. Christian Morgenstern, transl. from Swedish to German. Frankfurt am Main: Fischer 2009.

Sulaiman, Muqatil bin. *Tafsir Muqatil bin Sulaiman*. AH 1423. ed. Abdullah Mahmoud. Beirut: Dar Ih'yah al-Turath.

Swain, Carol, *Be the People, A Call to Reclaim America's Faith and Promise*. Nashville: Thomas Nelson, 2011.

Taylor, Dan, "Whoops: Apple Watch may not work for black people," *National Monitor*, 30 April (2015).

Uber.com. 2022. *Uber Technologies Inc.* https://www.uber.com.

Van der Kolk, Bessel, *The Body Keeps the Score: Brain, Mind, and Body in the Healing of Trauma*. New York: Penguin Publishing Group, 2015.

Van Dooren, Thom., "The Unwelcome Crows: Hospitality in the Anthropocene," *Angelaki* 21.2 (2016).

Walter, Barbara F., *How Civil Wars Start and How to Stop Them*. NY: Crown Books, 2022.

Westermann, Claus, *Genesis 1–11* Minneapolis: Augsburg Publishing House, 1984.

Whitlock, Gillian. "The Hospitality of Cyberspace: Mobilizing Asylum Seeker Testimony Online," *Biography* 38.2 (Spring 2015): 245–266.

Wilkin, Karen, *Beauteous Strivings: Fritz Ascher, Works on Paper*. Exhibition catalogue. New York: The Fritz Ascher Society for Persecuted, Ostracized and Banned Art and New York Studio School, 2017.

Winthrop, John, "John Winthrop on Restriction on Immigration," *Puritan Political Ideas, 1558–1794*, Edmund S. Morgan, ed., Indianapolis: The Bobbs-Merrill Co., 1965.

Wood, Gordon, *The Radicalism of the American Revolution*, NY: Alfred P. Knopf, 1991.

Woods, Heather Suzanne. "Asking more of Siri and Alexa: Feminine Persona in Service of Surveillance Capitalism," *Critical Studies in Media Communication*, 35:4 (2018): 334–349.

Yaeger, David. "Teaching Teenagers to Cope with Social Stress." In *The New York Times*. September 30, 2016.

Young, Brad H., *The Parables, Jewish Tradition and Christian Interpretation*, Grand Rapids, MI: Baker Academic, 1998.

Zak, Paul. "How Stories Change the Brain." In *Greater Good Magazine*. December 17, 2013.

Author Biographies

LINDSAY ANNE BALFOUR, PHD is Assistant Professor of Digital Media in the Centre for Postdigital Cultures at Coventry University and works within the Postdigital Intimacies research cluster. Her research draws on the philosophical concept of hospitality to consider the relationship between humans and machines (HCI), and employs an intersectional feminist and cultural studies perspective to look at digital intimacies. Currently, she is conducting feminist analyses of surveillance capitalism and embodied computing including how hospitality works through the digital strangeness of tracking technologies such as wearables, implantables, and ingestibles (FemTech). Her recent books include *Hospitality in a Time of Terror: Strangers at the Gate*, 2017; *The Digital Future of Hospitality*, 2023; and the forthcoming *FemTech: Intersectional Interventions*, 2023.

THOMAS MASSARO, S.J., is Professor of Moral Theology at Fordham University. A Jesuit priest of the United States East Province, he has taught as professor of moral theology at Weston Jesuit School of Theology in Cambridge, Massachusetts, at Boston College, and at Jesuit School of Theology of Santa Clara University, where he also served as Dean. Father Massaro holds a doctorate in Christian social ethics from Emory University. His nine books and over one hundred published articles treat Catholic social teaching and its recommendations for public policies oriented to social justice, peace, worker rights and poverty alleviation. A former columnist for *America* magazine, he writes and lectures frequently on such topics as the ethics of globalization, peacemaking, environmental concern, the role of conscience in religious participation in public life, and developing a spirituality of justice. His most recent book is *Mercy in Action: The Social Teachings of Pope Francis* (Rowman & Littlefield Publishers, 2018).

ENDY MORAES, LLM, Director, Institute on Religion, Law, and Lawyer's Work at Fordham Law School, is a Brazilian lawyer with extensive experience in interreligious and intercultural dialogue. Endy has an LLM, cum laude, from Fordham Law School, and is admitted to practice in New York. She is a member of the Focolare Movement of the Catholic Church, living in community.

REV. CRAIG B. MOUSIN is a graduate of Johns Hopkins University, the University of Illinois College of Law, and the Chicago Theological Seminary. He previously served as University Ombuds at DePaul University and as the Executive Director of DePaul's Center for Church/State Studies where he has taught Immigration, Asylum, and Refugee Law. He co-founded the Center's Interfaith Family Mediation Program and co-founded DePaul's Asylum and Immigration Law Clinic. He is a founding member of the DePaul Migration Collaborative. He also teaches in DePaul's Grace School for Applied Diplomacy. In 1984, he founded and directed the Midwest Immigrant Rights Center (now the National Immigrant Justice Center), a provider of legal assistance to refugees. Reverend Mousin was ordained at Wellington United Church of Christ where he has served as Associate Pastor for Immigrant Justice. His podcast, *Lawful Assembly*, is at: https://lawfulassembly.buzzsprout.com/. Some of his publications can be found at: https://works.bepress.com/craig_mousin/ or https://papers.ssrn.com/sol3/cf_dev/AbsByAuth.cfm?per_id=667812

CAROL PRENDERGAST has been a Senior Advisor to Alfanar Venture Philanthropy since 2017. Alfanar provides seed funding and technical support for social entrepreneurs in the MENA region, focusing on organizations that economically empower women, youth and refugees. Ms. Prendergast has developed and directed advocacy, policy and direct service programs for NGOs serving refugees and asylum seekers in the U.S. Since her appointment as Visiting Senior Fellow in Human Rights at the London School of Economics, she has served as a consultant to international NGOs and EU agencies addressing the needs of victims of forced migration. Ms. Prendergast is a graduate of Georgetown University Law Center and has pursued postgraduate study at NYU and the Centre for Refugee Studies at Oxford University.

Zeki Saritoprak, PhD, is the Bediuzzaman Said Nursi Chair in Islamic Studies and a Professor in the Department of Theology and Religious Studies at John Carroll University in Cleveland, Ohio. He holds a PhD in Islamic Theology from the University of Marmara in Turkey. His most recent books are *Islam's Jesus* was published by the University Press of Florida in 2014 and *Islamic Spirituality: Theology and Practice for the Modern World* (Bloomsbury, 2017). He is currently working on a book on Islamic Eschatology.

Ori Z Soltes, PhD, teaches at Georgetown University across a range of disciplines, from art history and theology to philosophy and political history. He is the former Director of the B'nai B'rith Klutznick National Jewish Museum, and has curated more than 90 exhibitions across the country and overseas. He has authored or edited 28 books and several hundred articles and essays. Recent volumes include *Our Sacred Signs: How Jewish, Christian and Muslim Art Draw from the Same Source; The Ashen Rainbow: Essays on the Arts and the Holocaust; Tradition and Transformation: Three Millennia of Jewish Art & Architecture;* and *Growing Up Jewish in India: Synagogues, Ceremonies, and Customs from the Bene Israel to the art of Siona Benjamin.*

Rachel Stern is the founding and executive director of the Fritz Ascher Society for Persecuted, Ostracized and Banned Art in New York. Born and educated in Germany, she immigrated to the United States in 1994. She wrote for the AUFBAU and worked for ten years in the Department of Drawings and Prints at the Metropolitan Museum of Art in New York. Stern curates exhibitions, publishes books and organizes events and conferences about the fate of artists who were persecuted under German National Socialism. In 2017, she received the Hans and Lea Grundig Prize for this work. Stern serves on the board of the Fritz Ascher Stiftung at Stadtmuseum Berlin and is a member of Aktives Museum Berlin. Stern completed MAs in Art History and Economics at Georg August University in Göttingen.

Mimi Tsankov is the President of the National Association of Immigration Judges (NAIJ). In the past 15 years presiding at Immigration Courts in New York, Colorado, and California, she has held a variety of national leadership roles including Pro Bono Liaison Judge, contributing editor to the Immigration Judge Benchbook, Chair, Immigration Court - Board of Immigration Appeals Precedent Committee, Mentor Judge, and Juvenile Docket Best Practices Committee Chair. She is currently the elected President of the National Association of Immigration Judges (NAIJ) (2021 - 2023). Judge Tsankov completed her J.D. at the University of Virginia School of Law and was awarded an M.A. in International Relations at the University of Virginia Graduate School of Politics. She completed her undergraduate degree at James Madison University.

MOHSIN MOHI-UD-DIN is an artist, activist, and founder of the global nonprofit #MeWe International Inc. (#MeWeIntl). #MeWeIntl is a global network of artists, scientists, and community-builders who design methodologies and tools for creative expression and communication skills-building to advance the health, human rights, and representation of everyone. For over 15 years, Mohsin has scaled his methodology across more than 15 countries, from the valley of Kashmir to the Syrian refugee camps in the Middle East, to the mountains of Morocco, Honduras, and Mexico. His movement has supported more than 8,000 vulnerable youth and caregivers and dozens of community building organizations fighting violence, forced displacement, incarceration, and poverty. Mohsin previously worked for human rights organizations such as Human Rights First, and worked in the Strategic Communications Division for the MDGs and SDGs for the United Nations in New York. His work has received honors from SOLVE MIT at the UN, the United Nations Alliance of Civilizations, Open Ideo and others. In 2009, Mohsin received a Fulbright Scholarship to pilot his methodologies in Morocco. His words and visual pieces have been featured in VICE News, Al Jazeera, Huffington Post, and The Nation. Instagram: @meweinternational | Twitter: @Mohsindin and @MeWeIntl

Index

Abraham / Abrahamic, iii, v, vii, xi–xvi, 1–15, 19–20, 22, 24, 26, 31, 33, 44, 56, 64, 72, 84, 86, 89, 90, 94, 161, 174, 178, 185
Abu Dawud, 80, 181
Abu Huraira, 75
Abu Jahlm, 75
Abu Talib, 75
Abyssinia, 78
Achaemenid, 17
ad infinitum, 83
African, xii, 142
Airbnb, 168–169, 174, 181, 187
Akmal al-Din al-Babarti, 78, 181
Al-Bukhari, 72
Alexa, 114, 165–167, 169, 174, 182, 188
Alfanar Venture Philanthropy, 128, 130
Al-Mawali, 74
Al-Sarakhsi, 78, 181
almanah, 17, 18
Amen, Daniel, 144
American, xii, 6, 32, 35, 38, 40, 43–49, 65, 67–68, 92, 127, 129, 132, 138, 142, 156–157, 171, 181, 187–188
American Community Survey (ACS), 127
Anderson, Bernhard, 54, 181
Android, 159, 162–165, 173
Aphrodite, 86
Apple Watch, 170–172, 188
Ares, 8, 33, 46, 62, 86–87, 139, 174
Arjuna, 84–86
Asian, xiii, 93, 165

Assyrian, 16, 17, 89, 91
Atman, 83, 86

Baba Metzia, 21
Babylonian, 18–17, 89
Baghdadi, 90, 94
Bajazzo, vii, 106–107, 109
Balfour, Lindsay, vi, 8, 159, 169, 181, 189
Beersheva, 3, 14, 91
Bene Israel, 25, 34, 89, 90–91, 93, 184, 187, 191
Benedictine, 36
Bengali, 92
Benjamin, Siona, vii, 81, 90, 187, 191
Berlin, viii, xvii, 8, 97–98, 100, 102, 107, 111, 113–116, 123, 133, 178, 183, 191
Better off Ted, 171
Bhagavad Gita, 84–85
Bible, xii, 5, 17, 19–21, 25, 31–32, 46, 49–52, 54–56, 58–64. 76, 85, 89–90, 183, 187
Bodhisattva, 88
Book of Instruction/Education. See *Sepher HaHeenukh*
Book of Ruth, 60–61, 70
Border Wall, 48, 51, 53, 55, 65
Bosnia, 6
Brahma, 84–85, 87
brahmin, 83, 85
Bretz, Reverend Thomas, 50
Brueggemann, Walter, 54, 56, 182
Budde, Michael, 58, 67, 182
Buddha, 87–88
Burning Bush, 4, 19

Cambodia, 6
Canaan, 4, 15
Catholic, xi–xiii, 7, 20, 27, 29–30, 32–33, 38–41, 45–46, 49–50, 53, 55, 69, 184, 186, 189–190
Chat GPT, 161
Chin Women's Organization (CWO), 133, 135, 190
Chinese Exclusion Act, 6
Chobani, 126, 128
Clowns. See *Bajazzo*
Cochini, 90, 94
Collier, Elizabeth, 46, 49, 182
Communion, 33
Corinthians, 32
covenant, 12, 15, 17–18, 24, 33, 47–48, 56, 63, 66–68, 181

DACA, 61, 65, 69–70
dalits, 83
David, vii, 16, 18, 20, 24, 40, 59, 71, 89, 144, 183–184, 187–188
Dawkins, Richard, 173
Day, Dorothy, 28–29, 182
Day of Judgement, 74
Delta Oil, 128, 131
Derrida, Jacques, 160–161, 173–174, 182, 185
Deuteronomy, 12, 16, 22, 31, 47, 57, 68
Devi, 37, 84, 162, 166, 170–171
Dhammapada, 87
dharma, 82–83, 86–87
dharmic, vi, xi, xvi, 7, 82, 84, 88, 178
digital hospitality, 160, 169, 173, 175, 189
digital strangers, 160, 162
Dominicans, 23
Douglas, Frederick, 142
Drollinger, Ralph, 51, 63–64

Edict of Milan, 59
Edwards, James, 51–53, 58, 183
Edwards, Jonathan, 55, 58
Egypt, xii, 4–5, 15–16, 22–25, 32, 34, 49, 58, 76–78, 129–131
Eichelbaum, Frida, 115
Eight-fold Path, 87
Elamite, 11
Ephron the Hittite, 1, 11
Ethiopia, 20, 78, 131
Eucharist, 33
European, xiii, 6, 44, 88, 92–93, 98, 102, 132, 182
Evangelical, 43–44, 46, 51, 185, 187
Exodus, 5, 12, 15–16, 22–23, 61, 67, 77–78

Ezekiel, 5
Ezra the Scribe, 12, 17

fitan, 74
Fitbit, 170–172
First Epistle of Peter, 32
Frederick the Great, 97
Fritz Asher Society, iv, vi, viii, xi, xvi–xvii, 8, 96–97, 99–123, 187–188, 191

Garcia, Jeffrey P., 62, 186
Gartner, Rabbi Rachel, xvi
Gate of Water, 12, 18
Gautama Buddha. See Buddha
Genesis, xii, 2–3, 14, 31, 33, 51, 54–55 65, 188
genocide, 6, 48
Georgetown University, xv, xvii, 7, 40, 43, 184, 191
Ger, 2, 11, 12, 15, 17–19, 21–23, 39, 52, 60, 113
ger toshav, 11, 22
ger tzedek, 22
gereem, 15, 22
Germany, vi, 6, 8, 22, 97–98, 110, 113–114, 116, 118, 122, 185, 187, 191
Gestapo, 112–114
gharib / ghuraba, 73–75
gig economy, the, 168–169
Goa, 89
Golem, vii, 103–105, 107
Gospels, 34–35, 59
Graßmann, Martha, 8, 97, 113–116, 123
Greek, 20–21, 30, 32, 89
Grunewald, 114, 120, 123

hadith, 5, 72–75, 80
Hagar, 5
Hamilton, Mark, 56–57, 61, 183
Hammad, Nuaym bin, 74
Hanafi, 78
Haran, 15
Hariri, Yuval, 144, 183
Hart, Grete, 115
Hasson, Uri, 144, 183
Heyer, Dr. Kristin, 40
Hebrew Bible, 5, 17 19–21, 25, 31, 61, 89–90, 187
Hebron, 3
Heimburger, Robert, 57, 183
Hera, 86, 144, 170
Hermes, 86
Herod (King), 34
Hijra, 75, 77
Hindu/Hinduism, 7, 82, 84, 87, 92–93

Hitler, Adolf, 112
Hoffmeier, James, 52, 60
Hollenbach, David, 40, 184
Holocaust, 5–6, 8, 25, 65, 174, 178, 191
Honduras, 146, 150, 152, 192
Hope Foundation, The, 134
Horton, Kathleen, xvi

Ibn Kathir, 73, 181, 184
Ibn Majah, 73–74, 184
Ibn al-sabil, 73
Iliad, 85
Immigrant 4 Life, vii, xii–xiii 42, 44, 46, 49, 54, 64, 68, 77, 190
Inaash, 128–130
Institute on Religion, Law, and Lawyer's Work, The, iv, xi, xvi, 190
Irigiray, Luce, 166
Isaac, 3–5, 13–15, 19, 24, 89
Ishmael, 5
Islam's Jesus, 74, 191
Israel, xii, 4, 15–16, 20, 34, 52, 54–58, 60–61, 67–68, 77, 89–93, 114, 177, 184, 187, 191
Israelite, 4, 12, 15–16, 20, 23–25, 89–91

Jacob, xii, 4, 15, 19, 24, 89, 98, 181, 184
Jaime I, 23
Jainism, 82, 87–88, 93
Jeremiah, 5, 12, 17–18
Jericho, 62
Jerusalem, 12, 16–17, 20, 53, 62, 187
Jesuit, xii, 30, 189
Jesus Christ, 20–21, 23, 28, 30, 32–36, 41, 43–45, 48, 51, 55–57, 59–60, 62–64, 66–69, 74, 102, 185–187, 191
Jethro (Suyab), 4, 15, 77
Jew, xiii, 19, 21, 50, 63, 90–91, 97, 100, 102
Jivatman, 83
Johnson-Reed Act, 6–7
Jim Crow, 41
Joseph, xii, 15, 24, 34, 76, 91, 181
Judaean(s), 12, 17–18, 20–21, 25, 89–90
Judah, 16–18, 20, 89, 103
Judaism, 4–5, 7, 20–22, 44, 79, 89–91, 98, 185

Kant, Immanuel, 98, 174–175, 182, 184, 187
karma, 83–84, 86, 88
Kashmir, 142–143, 145–146, 185, 192
Kearney, Richard, 161, 165, 170 182, 184
Kennedy, John F., 49
khristos, 20
khumrah, 14, 19
Kraishnite, 7, 84–85

Krishna, 84–87
Kristallnacht, 113
Kristeva, Julia, 170
kshatriya, 83, 86
Ku Klux Klan, 49

Lazarus, 35, 186
Leah, 4, 15
LaCocque, André, 60, 63, 70, 185
Leipzig, xvii
Le Kremer, Anh, 156
Lerner, Mark, xvii
Letter to Titus, 32
Levinas, Emmanuel, 162, 182, 185
Lewis, J. E., 176
Lichtenstein, Roy, 92
Lofgren, Zoe, 155–156
Lost Ten Tribes, 16, 91
Luther, Martin, 98

MAGA Jesus, vi, 43–45, 48, 51, 54, 56–57, 66–69, 186
Maimonides, 22
Make America Great Again / MAGA, 43
Mamre, 12–13, 31
Mang Tha, 135
Marr, Wilhelm, 98, 185
Martha, 8, 35, 97, 113–116, 123
Martinez, Judy Perry, 156
Marty, Martin, 44–45, 185
Mary, 5, 20, 24, 34–35, 48–50, 58, 60, 64, 67, 74, 82–83, 90, 92, 134, 162, 166, 178, 186–187
mashiah, 20
Mecca, 74–75, 78–79
Medina, 75, 186
Medo-Persian, 17
Mexican Bishops Conference, 39
Mexico, xv, 39, 150, 192
#MeWeIntl, ix, 124, 136, 141, 146–147, 149–151, 154, 192
#MeWeMexico, 150
#MeWeSyria, ix, 124, 136, 149–151, 154
Middle East, xv, 88, 114, 139, 146, 192
Midian, xii, 15, 76–77
Migrant 4 Life, v, 43–44, 46, 49, 53, 55–57, 60, 66, 68–69
Miller, Patrick, 61
Miller, Perry, 47, 185
Mishnah, 21
mishpat, 18
Moab, xii, 60
Modi, xvi, 64, 93, 130, 168
Moghul, 92

moksha, 83, 87–88
Moses, xii, 4, 15–16, 19–20, 24, 64, 76–77, 79, 89
Mount Moriah, 3
Mt Sinai, 15–16, 24
Muhajir, 77
Muhammad, 5, 72, 75–76, 152, 181, 184
Mumbai (Bombay), 90–9, 187
Muqatil bin Sulaiman, 75, 188
Muslim, xiii, xvi, 19, 72–77, 78–80, 85, 88, 90–91, 93–94, 191

Nachmanides, 23, 186
Nagel, Rebecca, 141
Nakoll, 130–131
NaTakallam, 128–129
National Association of Immigration Judges (NAIJ), 8, 155, 192
Native American, 45, 142
Nazis, 6, 98, 106, 112–114, 116, 118
Nehemiah, 53
Nevatim, 91
New York, iii, vii, xiii xvi–xvii, 7, 30, 33, 66, 71, 123, 126, 130, 144, 153, 182–188, 190–192
Nirvana, 83–84, 87–88
Noah, 12, 64
nokhri, 12, 52
Noll, Mark, 45, 47–49, 186
Notley, Steven, 62, 186
Nuevos Christianos, 89
Nuremberg Laws, 5, 113

Obama, Barack, 65
Odyssey, 85
Olympian, 86
OMGUS, 118, 185
oreah, 19
Orr, Christopher, 164–165, 186
Outeirinho, Cristina, xvi

Parsi, 91
Passover, 24
Pentateuch, 4, 57
Persia, 17, 77, 89, 92, 129
Pharaoh, xii, 76–77
Philoxenia, 32
PLACE Network, 132–133
Pope Francis, xiii, 37–39, 50, 55, 70 185, 190
Pope Urban IV, 23
Promised Land, 4, 16, 49, 56, 68, 78
Prophets, 5, 17, 19, 89
Protestant, 7, 20, 27, 32, 60, 114, 186

Protestant Reformation, 20
Puritan, 45, 47–49, 67–69, 188

Qur'an, 5, 7, 19, 72–77, 79–80, 85, 94
Quraysh, 78–79

Rabbi Akiva, 20
Rabbi Avraham Ben HaRambam, 22, 181
Rabbi Eliezer, 22
Rabbi Natan, 22
Rabbi Shimeon bar Yokhai, 20
Rabbi Shlomo Yitzhak / Rashi, 22
Rachel, 4, 15
Rahawayh, 79, 186
Reagan, Ronald, 67
Rebecca, 4, 15
Refugee Act of 1980, 64
Refugee Investment Network, The (RIN), 132
Rehoboam, 16
Reimer, James, 59–60, 186
Revelation, xii, 4, 19–20, 79
Robinson, Marilynne, 47, 68, 186
Roman, 7, 20–21, 27, 29–30, 32, 39–40, 45–46, 48–50, 52, 57–59, 69, 90, 97, 161
Ruth, xii, 18–19, 25, 60–62, 64, 70, 72, 77, 79, 84–85, 92, 144, 167, 171, 181, 185
Rwanda, 6

Sacks, Rabbi Jonathan, 55, 57
Sacred Writings, 17
Saint Paul, 32, 64
Sallman, Warner, 43
Samaritan, 28, 30, 50, 62–63, 185–186
samsara, 83–84
Sanctuary Movement, 36, 54
Sarah, 1–5, 11, 13–14, 31, 33, 56, 64, 178, 186, 188
Seder, 24
Sepher HaHeenukh, 23
Shabbat, 23
Shah Cyrus II, 17
Shavuot, 24
Shiva, 84–85, 87
shruti, 85
shudra, 83
Sikhism, 82, 87–88, 93
Siri, 165–167, 169, 174, 182, 185, 187–188
Smith-Christopher, Daniel, 55, 60, 187
smrti, 85
Sodom and Gomorrah, 2, 13
Soelle, Dorothee, 55, 187
Solomon, King, 16, 89
Soufra, 130

South Arabia, 89
Still, Judith, 166, 188
St. John's College, xii
St. Vincent de Paul, 30, 64
Suffa, 75
Sukkah, 24
Sukkot, 24
Swain, Carol, 51, 53, 63, 183, 188
Syria, xv, 38, 131, 150, 152

Talmud, 21–22, 104
Tanakh, 31–32
Tanma Foundation, 134
Temple, 12, 17–18, 20, 59, 89
Ten Commandments, 14–16, 23–25, 62
Tent Partnership for Refugees, 126–128
Theodosius (Emperor), 21, 59
Theory of Change, 144, 146–147, 178
Tikkun Ha-Olam, vii, 81
Torah, 4–5, 11–12, 14–18, 21–25, 31, 62, 89–90, 181, 185
Tower of Babel, v, 43, 51, 54, 56, 65
trauma, 140, 142, 145, 147, 170, 184, 188
triune, 84
Trump, Donald, 7, 93
Tzipporah, 4

Uber, 98, 114, 168–169, 185, 188
Ukraine, 37
Ulukaya, Hamdi, 126, 128
Ummu Salama, 78–79

UNHCR, 132–133
United States Conference of Catholic Bishops (USCCB), 38
Ur, xii

vaishya, 83
Van Dooren, Thomas, 175, 188
Vatican, 39
Vatican II, 49
Vedic, 92
viral/virus, 173
Vishnu, 84–85, 87

Washington, DC, xv, 7, 40, 150, 184
Westworld, 159–160, 163–164, 181
Williams, Roger, 47–48, 69, 187
Winthrop, John, 47, 67–69, 188
Wolber, Heinrich, 114
Wood, Gordon, 45, 188
Woods, Heather, 166, 188
World Refugee Processing System (WRAPS), 127

Yeager, David, 144
yetom, 17–18
Young, Brad H., 62, 188

zakat, 72
Zechariah, 5
Zeus, 85
Zoroastrian, 91, 93